CW01574385

The PARADIGM of GOLF

PALMETTO
PUBLISHING
Charleston, SC
www.PalmettoPublishing.com

Copyright © 2024 by Gregory M. Skovira

All rights reserved

No portion of this book may be reproduced, stored in a retrieval system, or transmitted in any form by any means–electronic, mechanical, photocopy, recording, or other–except for brief quotations in printed reviews, without prior permission of the author.

Hardcover ISBN: 9798822951419
Paperback ISBN: 9798822951426
eBook ISBN: 9798822951433

The PARADIGM of GOLF

UNLOCKING THE SECRETS

WRITTEN AND ILLUSTRATED BY

GREGORY M. SKOVIRA

Dedication

To my incredible mother, Theresa, who at ninety-five years young is a true inspiration to everyone she touches including her eight children and their spouses, her 28 grandchildren and 38 great grandchildren. She is an exemplar of the aphorism

"It's not how old you grow, it's how you grow old."

And to my wife, Joan, who is my lifelong partner, the love of my life, my girlfriend, my best friend.

Acknowledgments

Special thanks to the Seabrook Island Golf Club, the instructors and the many wonderful people I have met there while spending countless hours practicing, studying and learning.

Preface

I am not crazy; my reality is just different from yours.

—Lewis Carroll, author

The game of golf has been around since the fifteenth century. Except for recent technological advances in equipment, little has changed, including the paradigm for teaching and learning how to swing a golf club properly. For centuries, the game has relied on the time-honored approach of imitating and repeating with little, if any, emphasis on understanding the motions required to swing a golf club. As a result, most mere mortals never come close to reaching their full potential with their golf game.

I am a relative newcomer to the game of golf, having both the advantage and disadvantage of picking up the game relatively late in my life, as I have passed the midcentury mark. I spent the first ten years trying to learn to hit a golf ball by following the accepted paradigms of the game, which revolve around imitation (learning how) and repetition (practice). I took countless lessons, read numerous books and magazines, watched YouTube videos ad nauseum, and practiced, practiced, practiced. In the end, like so many others before me, my investment of time and money in the game yielded diminishing results.

The world is awash with golf books that deal with just about every aspect of the game of golf. Many of the books written by golf professionals do a good job of explaining how to swing a golf club but not why. Other books have been written about the physics of golf, which can be interesting but often of little practical value when learning to swing a golf club. I returned to what I knew: the fundamentals of the golf swing and specifically the mechanics (aka the kinematics) of the swing. What I found was both fascinating and wonderfully useful. This book is my attempt to share that knowledge with the reader. And I believe that knowledge will forever change the way you view and play the game of golf.

With the knowledge I gained from studying the kinematics of the golf swing, my understanding of the golf swing and my ability to strike the golf ball correctly have improved by leaps and bounds. I wish that I had this book, this knowledge, and this understanding when I started to learn the game. If you teach golf, I hope that the knowledge in these pages helps you become a better teacher.

If you are an experienced golfer, I hope that you find this book insightful and can use the knowledge to further improve your golf swing. If you are new to the game of golf, I hope that you find the knowledge contained herein useful in making your new journey easier.

You can't fault someone for not knowing what they don't know, but you can fault them for not wanting to learn something new.

—Anonymous

Gregory Skovira

Table of Contents

Table of Contents

CHAPTER 1

Introduction

Golf is a bit like life: the journey is perhaps more important than the destination.

> **The person who follows the crowd will usually go no further than the crowd. The person who walks alone is likely to find himself in places no one has ever seen before.**
>
> —Albert Einstein

This book is about golf or, more precisely, the golf *swing*. In full disclosure, it was written by a mechanical engineer who also loves golf. As a result, it's different from other golf books. Those books—some good, some not so good—were mostly written through the lens of the golf professional's eyes. *This book* was written through the eyes of an engineer who wanted to better understand the mechanics of the golf swing.

Golf, as viewed through a professional golfer's eyes, can provide insights into *how* to swing a golf club—and that's important. But golf viewed through an engineer's eyes provides amazing insight into the *whys* of the golf swing—the yin and yang. And the *why* is vital if you want to improve your game.

In this opening chapter, I provide a little background to the rest of the book. I hope you'll find it both relevant and entertaining. This book contains gems of knowledge I certainly could have used when I first started learning the game.

Though you might be tempted to jump to the next chapter, I'd encourage you to continue reading; you'll gain perspective that will prove valuable in the journey ahead.

If you don't know where you've come from, you don't know where you're going.

—Maya Angelou

How It Began

Over a decade ago, with my kids nearly through college and me looking down the pike at retirement, I decided to learn to play golf. I was a relative latecomer but not afraid to make a serious effort at learning the game.

I started with the traditional approach. I enrolled in group and private lessons from the local professionals, read every book and magazine I could get my hands on, and practiced, practiced, practiced.

Initially, all the hard work paid off. Over time, I went from frequently mishitting—and sometimes just plain missing—the ball to being able to swing the club and make contact. My scores went from 200 to 150 to 110. And after years of due diligence and hard work—aka practice—I could break one hundred on a good day.

But the progress came to a grinding halt. Regardless of the effort, regardless of the hours of practice, regardless of the lessons, my handicap barely budged. I had plateaued.

Sound familiar?

Since the path I was on was no longer working, I decided to shake things up. That meant I had to find a different path.

Two roads diverged in a yellow wood,
And sorry I could not travel both
And be one traveler, long I stood
And looked down one as far as I could
To where it bent in the undergrowth.
Then took the other, as just as fair,
And having perhaps the better claim,
Because it was grassy and wanted wear;
Though as for that the passing there
Had worn them really about the same,
And both that morning equally lay
In leaves no step had trodden black.
Oh, I kept the first for another day!
Yet knowing how way leads on to way,
I doubted if I should ever come back.
I shall be telling this with a sigh
Somewhere ages and ages hence:
Two roads diverged in a wood, and I—
I took the one less traveled by,
And that has made all the difference.

—Robert Frost

Finding a Different Path

So I'd been down the one road, but it could only take me so far. After years of taking the traditional approach, my game had stalled regardless of how hard I tried. If I wanted to get ahead, I'd have to back up and try a different approach.

He who has a why to live for can bear almost any how.

—Friedrich Nietzsche

Engineers are taught to solve problems.

To solve a problem, you need to understand what the problem is. One reason my game hadn't improved was because I didn't understand the *why* of the golf swing. Many good instructors and books explain the *how* and *what* of the golf swing but seldom the why. Though important, the how *without the why* didn't provide the proper foundation for me to improve.

So I returned to fundamentals.

I studied the golf swing from a basic mechanical viewpoint. And in my studies, the light bulb came on. I share more of what I learned on my journey later, but for now, I'll get straight to the point and explain *why* my golf swing didn't improve.

The golf swing is not a swing.

Take a second to let that sink in.

As I've mentioned, I've read many instructional books on golf. I've watched videos and paid for many lessons. The emphasis in all of these has been on the golf swing. But to really understand how to properly execute a golf *swing*, you need to start thinking in terms of rotation.

You don't *swing* a golf club. You *rotate* it.

Before I continue, I'll share a short story.

When you were born, among the first things you did in life after breathing was wave your arms and put your hands in your mouth. As you grew and developed, your brain and arms became best friends. They went everywhere together and did everything together. You used your arms for many things: waving, eating, drinking, driving, playing, and just about everything else. In the meantime, your shoulders—even though closer to your brain than your arms—seemed to go relatively unnoticed.

Until one day, you took up the sport of golf.

Thanks for noticing me.

—Eeyore

Here's where the story gets interesting. Since your brain and arms had developed such a close friendship, your arms decided to continue doing what they'd always done—almost everything. And why not? Everyone was telling you to swing the club, and the arms did what the brain heard. In the meantime, the poor old shoulders continued to go unnoticed.

But here's the conundrum: to properly hit a golf ball, your brain should not let your arms *swing* the club. Rather, your brain should instruct your shoulders to *rotate* the club.

Revelation #1

The golf swing is not a swing but rather a rotation, and to be more precise, it's the combination of two rotations—the primary rotation and the secondary rotation—which are tied together using tertiary motion.

It may come as a surprise to you to learn the deltoids—your shoulders—are among the largest muscle groups in the upper body. The hands and arms are used in golf to connect the club to the shoulders. The rotation of the shoulders and arms holding a club traces a semicircle around the body. The rotation of the shoulders around the body is referred to as the **primary rotation**.

As your shoulders—connected to the club by the arms—rotate the club back, the straight leading arm (the left arm for right-handed golfers and right arm for left-handed golfers) should rotate the clubhead around an axis that runs through the left arm. The rotation of the leading arm holding a club traces a semicircle around the straight leading arm. Going forward, this will be referred to as the **secondary rotation**.

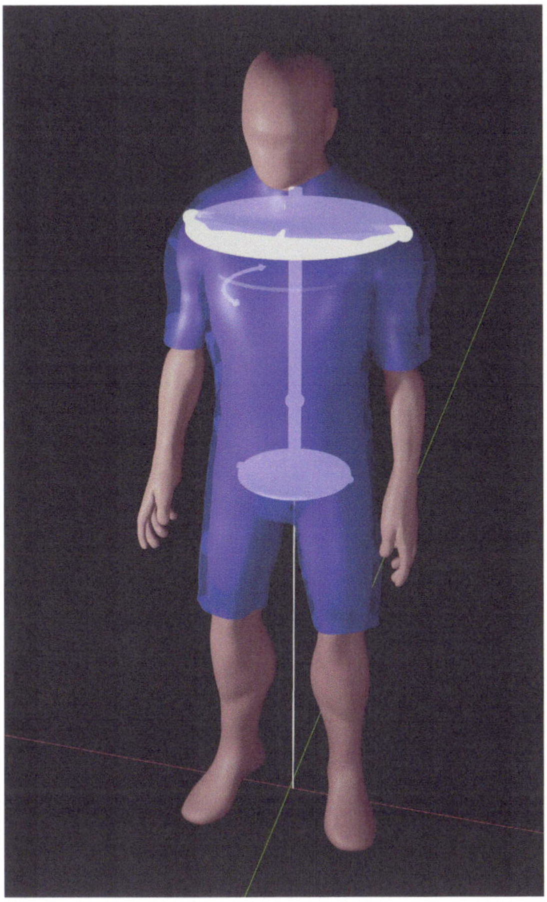

Figure 1: Primary Rotation

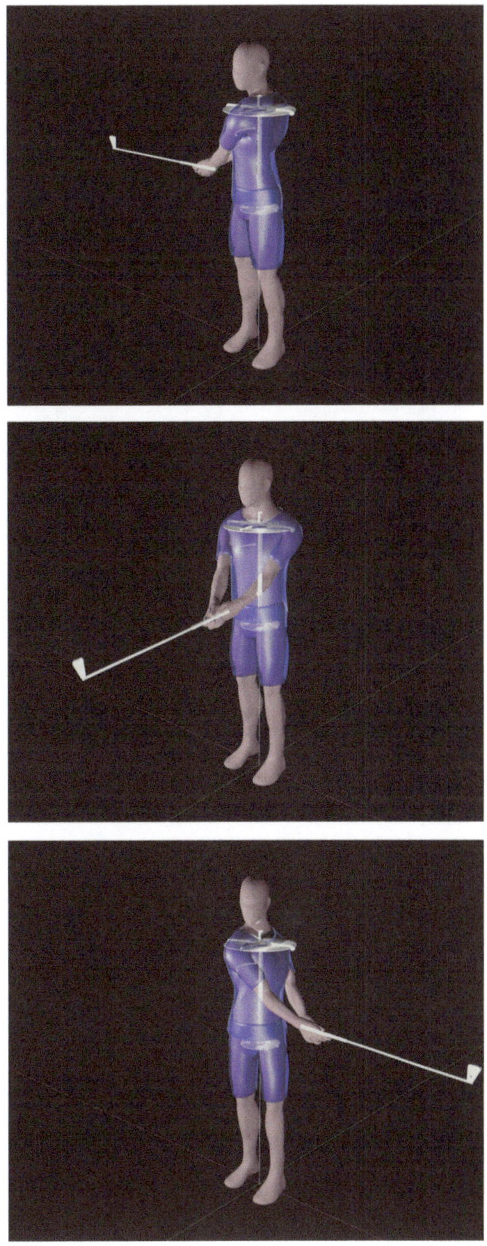

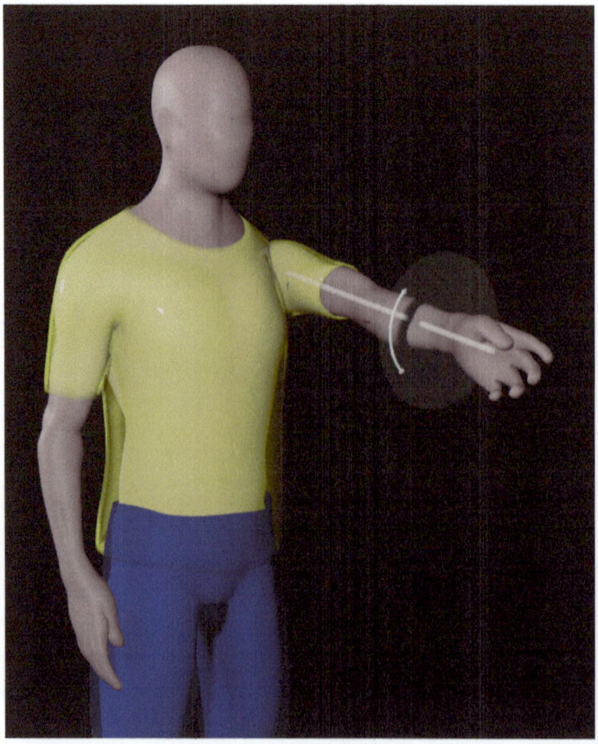

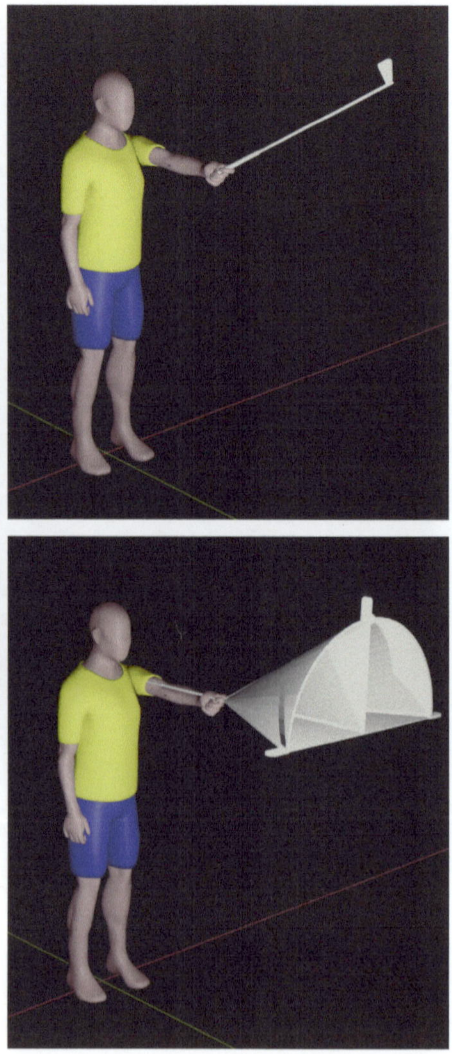

Figure 3: Secondary Rotation

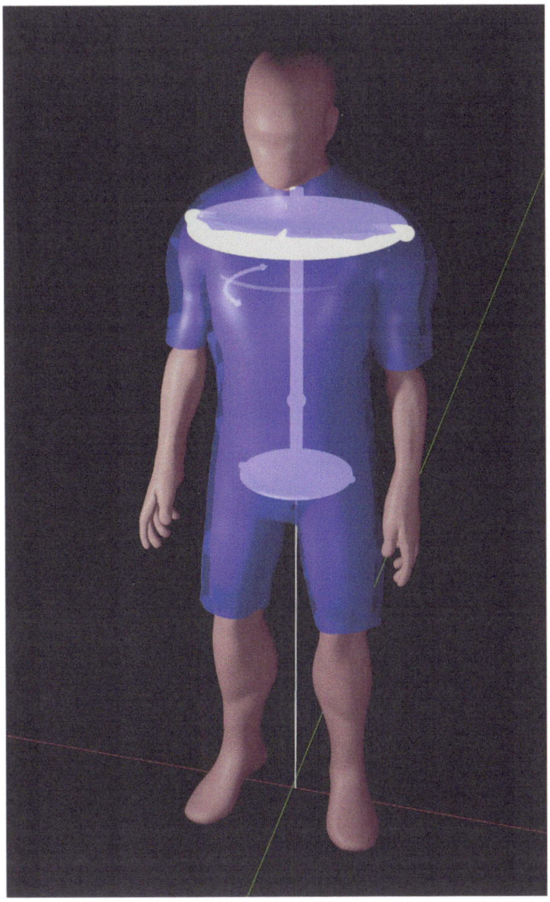

Figure 1: Primary Rotation

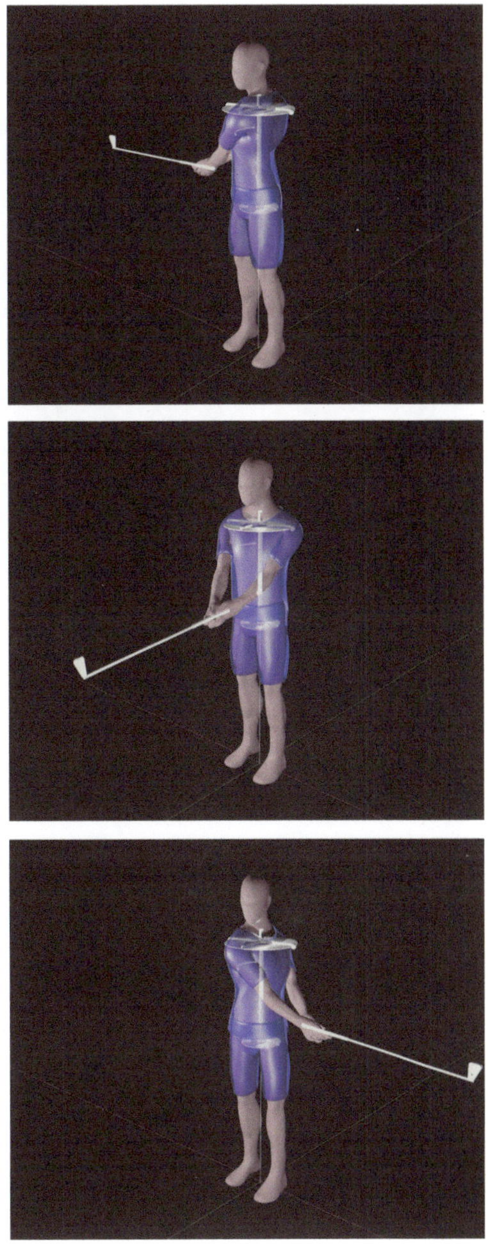

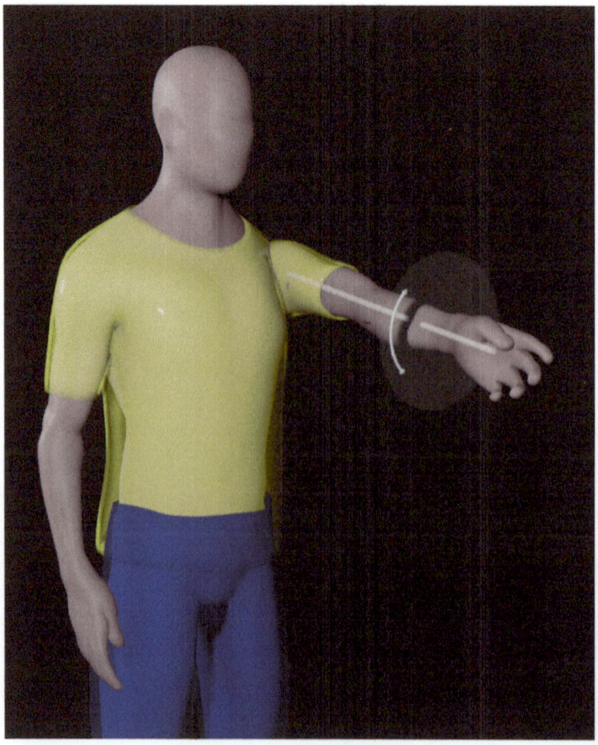

Figure 3: Secondary Rotation

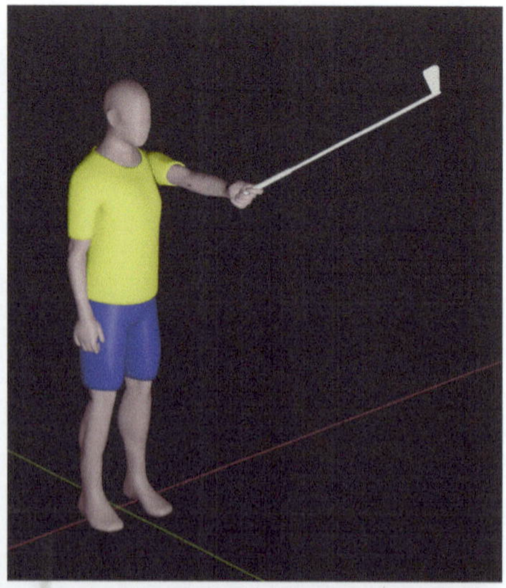

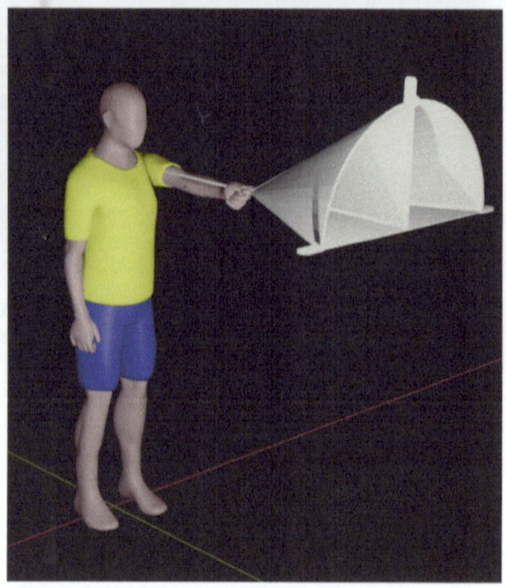

You must execute these rotations together in a coordinated motion. This is done by shortening the distance between the wrists and the right shoulder while bending the right arm and elbow against the side of your body and during the backswing, which we'll refer to as the **tertiary motion**.

I know there's a lot packed into these last few paragraphs, but here's a quick recap. The golf swing is not a swing but rather a rotation, and to be more precise, it's the combination of two rotations—the primary rotation and the secondary rotation, which are tied together using tertiary motion.

This simple revelation has completely changed my entire understanding of how to swing a club properly.

To keep things simple, I'll use the term "swing" often in this book, but you now know the secret. What it really means is the *rotation* of the club.

The Secret: Kinematics

After studying the golf swing for many years, I realized that the geometry and the physics of properly hitting a golf ball require a precise, defined combination of movements that rely on the rotation of the club. With this new knowledge, my understanding of the golf swing and my ability to strike the ball correctly have improved immeasurably.

That's because the conventional teaching methods emphasize how to swing the club. But remember that close friendship between your brain and your arms? Teaching golf based on the swing only reenforces that relationship.

By realizing that rotation is key, you see the emphasis is *not* on swinging the arms but rather on the shoulders and the geometry of the motion—the kinematics.

> *Noun: kinematics—the branch of mechanics concerned with the motion of objects without reference to the forces which cause the motion. The features or properties of motion in an object.*
>
> —*Oxford Languages*

The change in emphasis to rotation changes almost everything, and the focus becomes the shoulders and not the arms.

The task of learning to hit the ball is no longer relegated to trial and error and being taught the *whats* of the game. Instead, the task of learning can be put into a succinct series of steps that includes both the *what* and, more importantly, the *why*.

Building a good, repeatable golf swing must start with basics, which must be developed one step at a time. Understanding these steps is critical to effective development and practice.

Please indulge me once more for another short story.

You go to the range for a lesson because you can't seem to hit the ball properly, and the only consistent thing you can do is slice the ball. After you have a few swings at the ball, the instructor tells you to move the ball further back in your stance, strengthen your grip, and keep your elbow tucked. All good advice (maybe).

You do these things and hit a couple of good balls. Lesson over, and $100 well spent (maybe). You practice what the instructor told you to do and then head out to the course. After eighteen excruciating holes, you head back to the clubhouse to drown your frustrations with a cold beer.

What went wrong? (Hint: it wasn't the cold beer.)

The instructor told you what to do, and you did it. But you may not have understood why you did what you did. Each piece of advice taken alone was not necessarily wrong, but that advice without any context could be misdirected. If the slice was a result of an incorrect spine tilt (axis of rotation), the recommendations could be doing more harm than good. In the end, all the additional practice could be reinforcing bad habits to correct other bad habits instead of addressing the root issue.

Blind faith can be a dangerous thing.

A man with a fading vision walked to the wise man.
Oh, wise man, I am going to be blind soon, what should I do?
Wise man: Cross the road.

The blind man hurriedly left the room and crossed the road. Nothing happened. Assuming it to be a ritual, he kept crossing road after road. It went on for days, and nothing was happening, so he increased the intensity of his efforts and started crossing more roads.

He heard a voice one day while crossing one of the roads.

How is your vision?

No improvement, sir, I still can't see properly. Despite crossing many roads, I see no improvement in my vision.

Wise man: Did you go to see the doctor, located just opposite side of my house, across the road?

Which doctor? You never mentioned doctors.

Wise man: You left in a hurry and never asked. Some questions need to be fully understood before grasping the logic of the answer. You were so convinced with the ritual that you kept following it, and after a while, it became an addiction. You could have come back and asked, but you were unsure and petrified of starting a new ritual—what if? The new ritual will bring more difficulties. So you got stuck with the old and nonworking ritual.

But I can't see properly, so maybe I wasn't able to see the clinic.

No, it's not about looking at things. It's about looking out for things. Even if you had vision, you would have still missed it because mentally you were not ready to go to the doctor. You were looking for a miracle to happen and your mind assumed that crossing the road ritual is the key that will eventually unlock that miracle.

Remember, the miracle is nothing but a fruit of our labor, and loss in vision is not only related to loss of eyesight. You will find many people who can see properly but are still blind to the failure of their own efforts.

Not only that, people notice what you are doing. Believing in some miracle, they also change, and then they change other people. That's how one man's lack of vision becomes the cause of blindness to the entire group.

—Shahenshah Hafeez Khan

As a mechanical engineer, I've recognized the importance of understanding kinematics and the geometry of the golf swing. Kinematics is the branch of mechanics concerned with the motion of objects without reference to the dynamic forces that cause the motion.

Revelation #2

If you don't get the kinematics of the golf swing right, the physics of the golf swing don't really matter.

The physics (dynamic forces) of the swing are well studied and are important. Some of the physics of the golf swing will be touched on in this book, but the real focus here will be on the study of geometry of motion. I promise the discussion will be simple and understandable.

Applying the Concept of Kinematics

The golf swing can be divided into a set of kinematic motions, and each motion has a geometry associated with it. As you'll see in the following chapters, these specific motions, when combined, form the golf swing.

Figure 5: Applying Kinetics

The goal of this book is to provide you with knowledge, and with that knowledge comes an understanding of the geometry of the motions. You'll understand the how and the why of the golf swing—truly the yin and the yang of golf.

If you give a man a fish, he will be hungry tomorrow, but if you teach him how to fish, you feed him for a lifetime.

—Lao Tzu, Chinese philosopher

A Final Thought

The golf swing is a combination of synchronized motions, and these motions can be described in geometric terms. There are fundamental mechanics that govern every person's swing regardless of age, build, or ability. Each part of the swing has specific anatomical relationships that are geometrically correct; for example, how your body parts (shoulders, wrists, arms, legs, elbows, etc.) are positioned matters. If there's a flaw in one (or more) of the geometric relationships, there will most certainly be issues with the swing. Correcting these flaws in geometry goes a long way to correcting flaws in the golf swing that present themselves as slices, hooks, and a loss of power.

Now comes the conundrum.

There are many excellent golfers out there, even some professionals, who can strike a ball well despite having flaws in the geometry of the swing. But rather than correct a flaw, what they've done is introduce another flaw to compensate for the initial flaw.

Professionals can often get away with this because of their innate athleticism, but mostly because they're willing and able to practice every day for hours and hours. We mere mortals (most of the rest of the world) can't afford to do that.

Rather than correcting a swing flaw by compensating with another swing flaw and then spending countless hours practicing to program the body to repeat two (or more) flaws, it makes more sense to just eliminate the original flaw.

Please indulge me in one last story in this chapter.

You go to the club to get fitted for new clubs because you're not happy with how you hit the ball. Someone watches your swing and may get some data with a swing monitor. Sure enough, your numbers show what is obvious to you. You have a wicked hook. The solution is a new set of clubs that allows you to adjust the fade or draw of the clubhead to correct the flight path of the ball.

You have now likely tried to correct a fundamental kinematic swing flaw by introducing an altered club. You'll now spend countless hours practicing to perfect two (or more) flaws. Sound familiar?

In the end, with countless hours of practice, it might even work. But the more likely outcome is that you won't get the consistent golf swing you're looking for.

The traditional approach to learning golf has been based on the IR method: imitate and repeat. Someone shows you what to do, and you repeat that motion until you can do it. That is a very ineffective way to learn to golf. This book focuses on explaining the mechanics of the swing so there is a better understanding of the motions needed to properly swing a golf club, i.e., understand and repeat.

I wish that I had this book, this knowledge, and this understanding when I first started to learn the game. With this book, I could have properly channeled the countless hours of practice required to train the mind and the body to properly hit a golf ball.

All of us seem to know what we know.
Some of us seem to know what we don't know!
The rest of us seem to know that we don't know what we don't know!

—Anonymous

Now, with this book, you have the tools to properly hit a golf ball.

Takeaways:

So what did we learn in Chapter 1?

1. Much of golf instruction is focused on the *how* of the golf swing, but little is taught about the *why*. This book looks at both the *what* and the *why*.
2. There are fundamental mechanics that govern every person's swing regardless of age, build, or ability. Understanding the kinematics—the motions—of the golf swing can dramatically improve a golfer's ability to understand how to hit a golf ball properly.
3. Golf has traditionally been taught by the IR method: imitation and repetition. This book focuses on the UR method, which relies more on understanding and repetition.
4. This book provides a step-by-step approach to learning and practicing through exercises how to correctly strike the ball.

CHAPTER 2

The Model (PST Golf)

A mind that is stretched by a new experience can never go back to its old dimensions.

—Oliver Wendell Holmes Jr.

The golf swing has traditionally been viewed as a combination of athleticism, art, and black magic. When viewed through the eyes of an engineer, however, the golf swing can be modeled into a sequence of purely geometric motions. It's not magic—it's geometry!

The traditional swing model has relied on the concept of the double (or triple) pendulum. Many serious swing-model researchers have written their own programs using this model. This would be perfect if golfers lived only on the pages of a two-dimensional book. The use of the word "swing" when describing golf only reinforces the traditional model, which has numerous shortcomings.

The golf swing is very much a three-dimensional event and requires a more appropriate three-dimensional model. The first step in creating such a model starts with recognizing that the golf swing is more about rotation and that the term "swing" is just a common colloquialism.

Rotation is the basis of the PST model presented in this book, which recognizes that the golf swing is not actually a swing but rather a rotation and, to be more precise, the combination of two rotations—primary rotation and secondary rotation, which are tied together using tertiary motion.

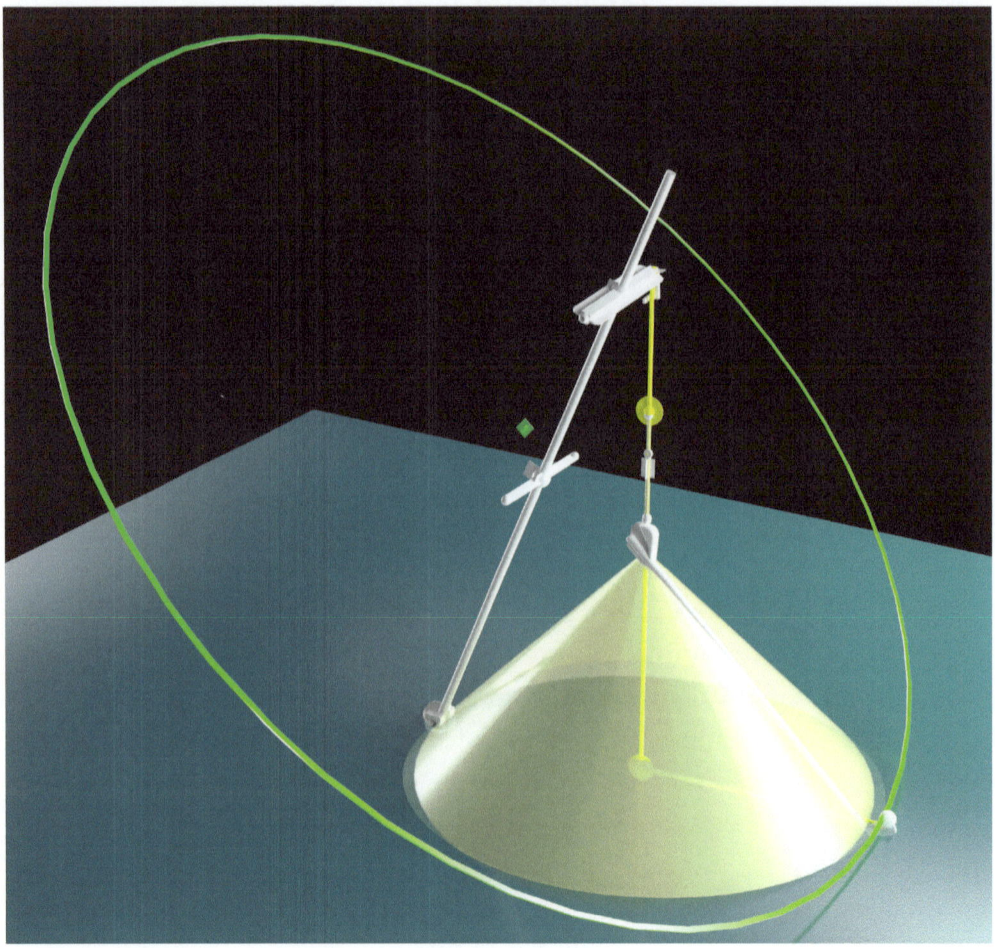

Figure 6: The Model

The model is a three-dimensional representation of the golf swing and breaks the swing into the three distinct motions: primary rotation, secondary rotation, and tertiary motion. With a three-dimensional model, the golf swing can be more accurately represented and understood. The acronym PST refers to the **p**rimary rotation, **s**econdary rotation and **t**ertiary motion that are the basis for the model. The model is a simple and yet groundbreaking way to understand the golf swing without a lot of complicated mechanics or physics.

PST golf is a new way of learning golf based on understanding (i.e., the UR method: understand and repeat). You are taught both the *what* and the *why*, then you repeat the motion until you can do it. It is a step-by-step approach to learn the proper way to swing a golf club and a much more effective way to learn.

So let's get started!

The Vitruvian Man and Golf

Italian polymath and skilled anatomist Leonardo da Vinci drew *The Vitruvian Man*—also known as *The Proportions of the Human Body According to Vitruvius*—in 1942. Vitruvius was a Roman architect from the first century BC. The piece depicts a nude male standing within a square and a circle.

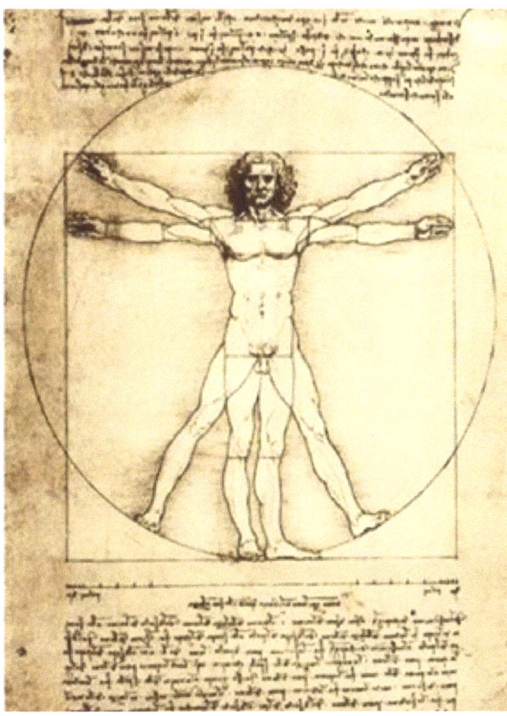

Figure 7: The Vitruvian Man

Leonardo was fascinated by the human form, and *Vitruvian Man* was a way for him to explore the symmetry and proportion of the human body as well as its mechanics. Based on his observations of the European people of his day, Leonardo believed that arm span was equal to height in a perfectly proportioned body. He believed the workings of the human body to be an analogy for the workings of the universe.[1]

So what does that have to do with golf? Valid question.

For our purposes, the universe is the game of golf—and more specifically, the motions needed to properly *hit* a golf ball. To understand these motions, you must understand the geometry of the human body as it relates to the golf swing.

Geometry and Physics in Motion

Hitting a golf ball correctly involves a basic understanding of both geometry and physics. The physics of the swing is meaningless if the geometry of the swing is incorrect. That's why the first part of this book focuses on geometry—it's the simplest part. Physics can get complicated, but it's important if you want to better your game. However, physics doesn't matter if you don't get the geometry right.

No two people have the same physical body dimensions, and therefore, we all swing a golf club slightly differently. That said, there are certain elements of the swing that are the same for everyone.

The following is just enough of a primer of the basic geometry of the golf swing to provide a solid understanding of *why* we do *what* we do when we hit a golf ball and how the model helps to explain it.

Before we dive into the specifics, though, let's look at some basic definitions.

Kinematics

As we discussed previously, kinematics is often described as a geometry of motion. More specifically, it is the branch of physics and a subdivision of classical mechanics concerned with the *geometrically* possible motion of a body, or system of bodies, without consideration of the forces involved.[2] To understand

[1] "Why do you see this man everywhere?" ScienceABC (October 19, 2023), https://www.scienceabc.com/social-science/the-vitruvian-man-leonardo-da-vinci.html

[2] Encyclopædia Britannica, inc. (n.d.). "Kinematics." *Encyclopædia Britannica*. https://www.britannica.com/science/kinematics

the model for the golf swing, let's start with some simple geometry—more specifically, a point, a line, or a plane as it applies to the golf swing.

Origin

The origin is a point on the ground between your feet when you're standing straight up in a vertical position.

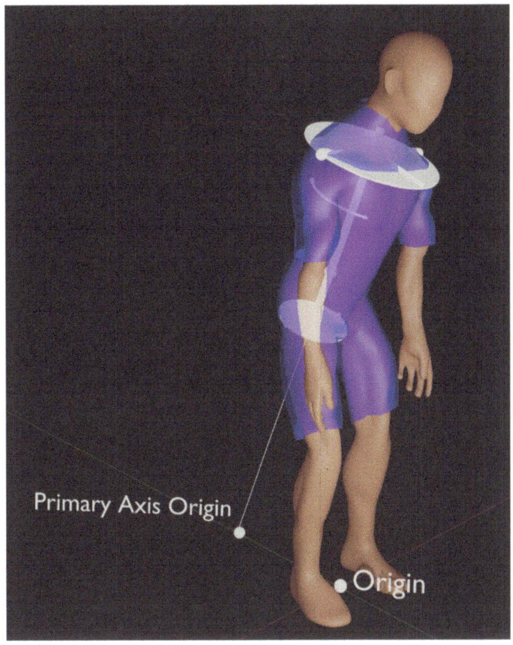

Figure 8: Reference Origins

Primary Axis Origin

The primary axis origin is the point on the ground that intersects the primary axis. When you're standing straight up, the primary axis origin is the same as the neutral origin, which is a point on the ground between your feet. However, at setup when you are inclined, the primary axis origin is about twenty-two inches behind the golfer's neutral origin but still on the midplane.

Axis of Rotation

The axis of rotation is a straight line around which an object (or objects) rotates.

In the approach presented in this book, there are two axes that are important in the golf swing: the primary axis (the anchor for the primary rotation) and the secondary axis (the anchor for the secondary rotation).

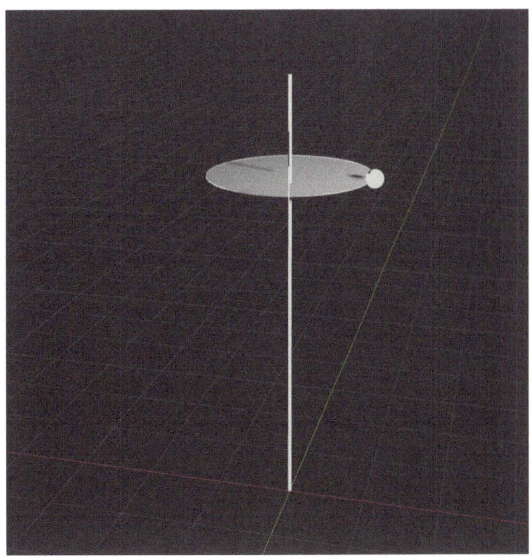

Figure 9: Axis of Rotation

Primary Axis of Rotation

The primary axis of rotation is the line through the center of the body and is perpendicular to the shoulder plane. When you're standing straight, it doesn't matter, because the axis of rotation is through the entire body. But when you tilt your body, the axis of rotation also tilts as it follows the axis though the upper body (the torso). More on this in Chapter 4.

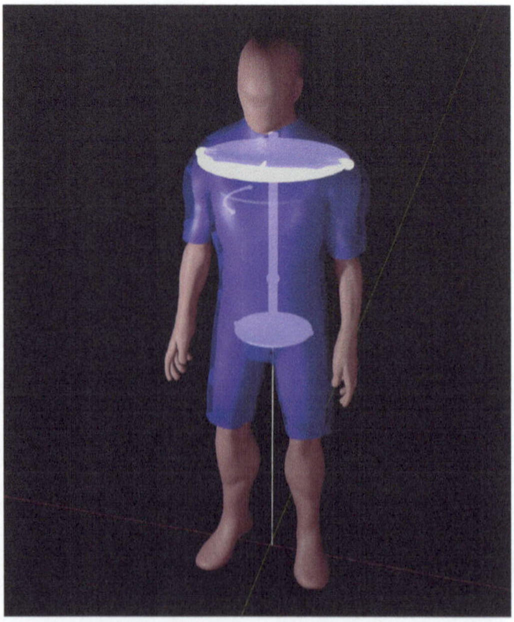

Figure 10: Primary Axis of Rotation

Secondary Axis of Rotation

The secondary axis of rotation is a line through your straight leading arm (SLA) on the backswing (left arm for right-handed golfers) and the rotation of the straight right arm on the follow-through.

In the golf world, this is commonly referred to as "wrist rotation," but the wrist is a hinged joint and does not actually rotate. The entire arm rotates, including the wrist and hand and the club.

More on this in Chapter 5.

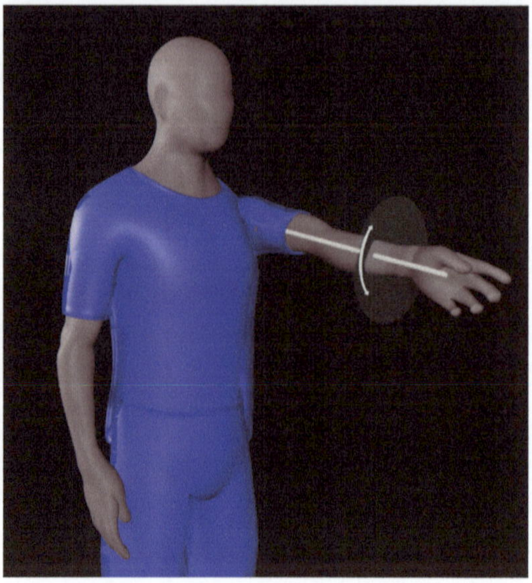

Figure 11: Secondary Axis of Rotation

Three-Dimensional Coordinate System

So let's get just a little bit geeky and look at how to represent three-dimensional space. A Cartesian coordinate system for a three-dimensional space consists of an ordered triplet of lines (the axes) that go through a common point (the origin) and are pairwise perpendicular. The origin is the orientation for each axis, and there is a single unit of length for all three axes.[3]

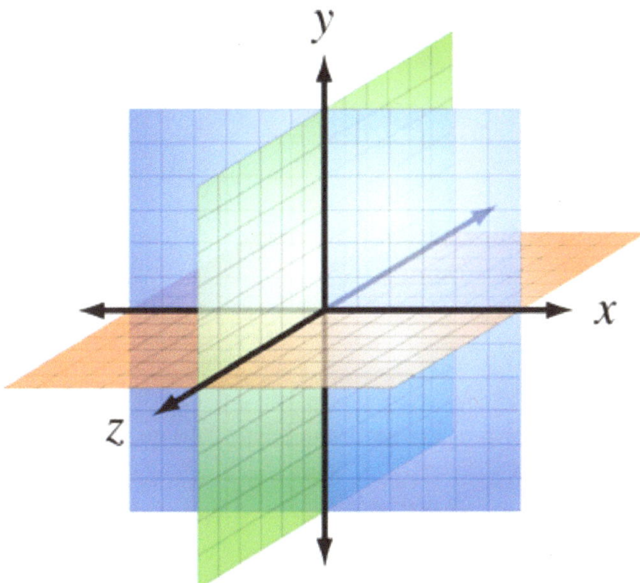

Figure 12: Cartesian Coordinate System

In geometry, a plane is a flat surface of two dimensions. It extends endlessly and has no thickness. You can think of a piece of paper or the surface of a wall as a part of a geometric plane. There are three planes (flat surfaces) of particular interest in this book and to the game of golf: the floor plane, the midplane, and the cross plane.

---

[3] Wikimedia Foundation, "Cartesian coordinate system." Wikipedia (June 15, 2024), https://en.wikipedia.org/wiki/Cartesian_coordinate_system

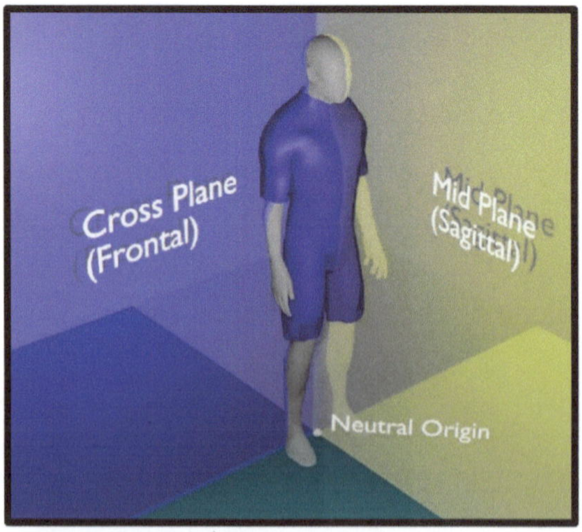

Figure 13: Floor Plane/Midplane/Cross Plane

Floor Plane (Bottom Plane)

The floor plane is the flat surface that we stand on. It is the main reference plane for measuring just about everything.

Midplane (Sagittal Plane)

The sagittal plane divides the body into the left and right sections. We'll refer to this plane as the midplane. This is the plane perpendicular to the ground that runs through the origin and separates your left side from your right side (i.e., perpendicular to the target line).

Cross Plane (Frontal Plane)

The frontal plane divides the body into the front and back sections. We'll refer to this plane as the cross plane. This is the plane perpendicular to the ground that runs through the origin and separates your front half from your back half (i.e., parallel to the target line).

In addition to the floor plane, the cross plane, and the midplane, there are a couple of other planes that are of particular interest in this book and to the game of golf: the base plane, the shoulder plane, and the swing plane.

Base Plane

The base plane is a flat surface that is created by the head of the golf club as it is rotated around the primary axis of rotation. When you are standing vertically, it is parallel to the ground and about knee level. It is the base for the swing path of the clubhead when you are only using shoulder rotation.

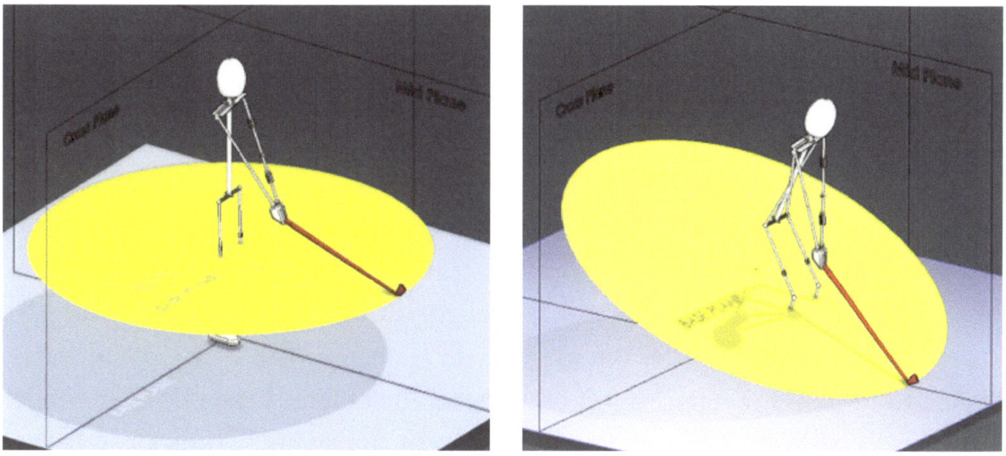

Figure 14: Base Plane

When you tilt the primary axis at address position (i.e., the inclined world), the base plane also tilts the same amount. The base plane then intersects the ground where the golf club meets the ball and extends at an angle perpendicular to the primary axis of rotation and is parallel to shoulder plane, described below.

Shoulder Plane (Top Plane)

The shoulder plane is the flat surface defined by the rotation of the shoulders around the center of the body (primary axis). When you are standing vertically, it is parallel to the ground and at shoulder level. It is an important reference point for the swing path, as you will see.

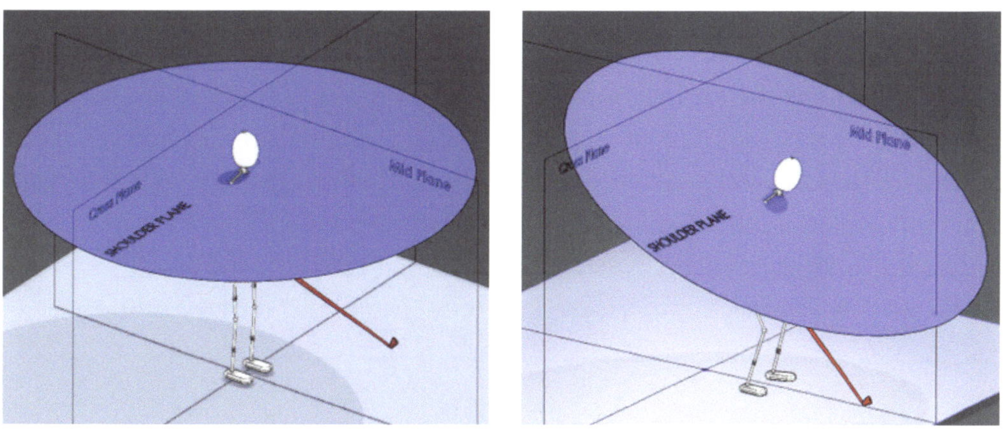

Figure 15: Shoulder Plane

When you tilt the primary axis at address position (i.e., the inclined world), the shoulder plane also tilts the same amount. The shoulder plane extends at an angle perpendicular to the primary axis of rotation and is parallel to the base plane, described above.

Swing Plane

The swing plane is a flat surface that is created by the head of the golf club as it is rotated around the primary axis of rotation when using *both* primary rotation and secondary rotation, as you will soon see. The swing plane starts at the ground level where the golf club meets the ball and extends at an angle that intersects the shoulder plane at the top of the swing. Think of it as the plane for the ideal path of the clubhead during the swing.

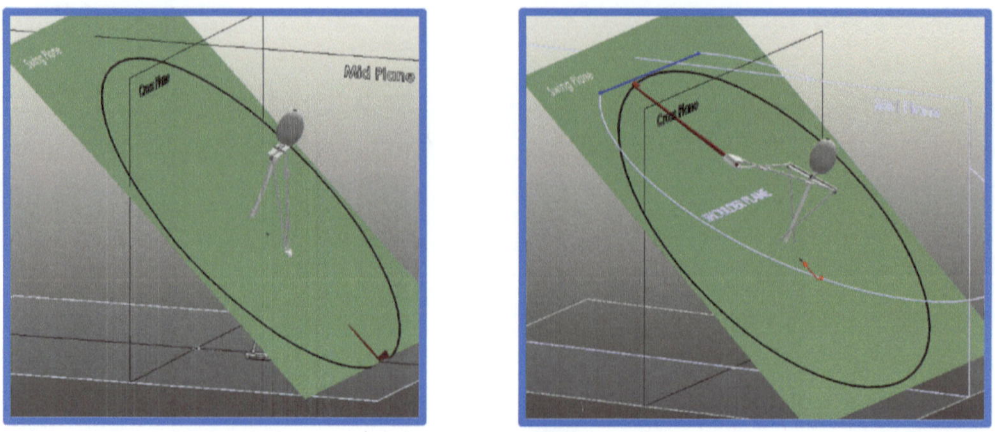

Figure 16: Swing Plane

The Model

Enough about geometry. Let's talk a little bit about the actual model. As I said earlier, rotation is the basis of the PST model presented in this book, which recognizes that the golf swing is not actually a swing but rather a rotation, and to be more precise, the combination of two rotations—primary rotation and secondary rotation, which are tied together using tertiary motion.

So what is primary rotation, secondary rotation, and tertiary motion?

Primary Rotation

Primary rotation is the rotation of the shoulders and club around the centerline of the body, the primary axis. This rotation is completed using your upper torso and your shoulders. A good solid rotation of the shoulders is critical to the ability to hit the ball well.

One of the biggest differences between the swing of a high handicap (HH) golfer and a low handicap (LH) golfer is the use of the upper body (torso) and shoulders during the swing. HH golfers swing their arms a lot, and LH golfers rotate the club using their shoulders.

Primary rotation is simply the rotation around the primary axis during the backswing, downswing, and follow-through.

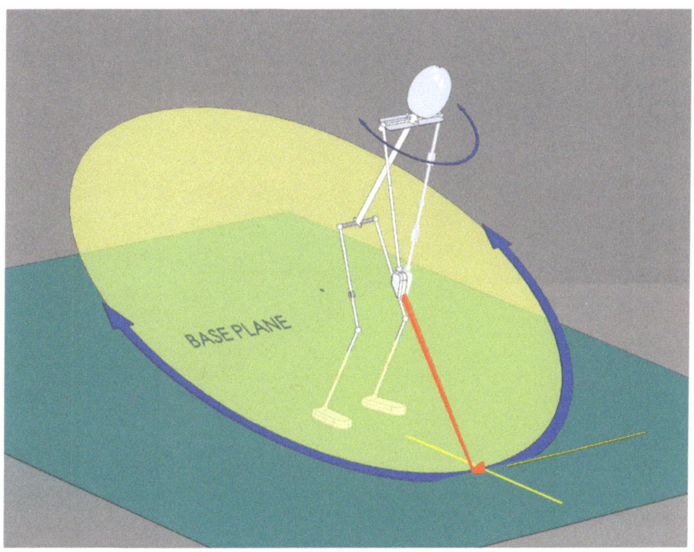

Figure 17: Primary Rotation

If the grip is the cornerstone of a good swing, then primary rotation is the foundation around which a great swing is built. The upper body is very strong and can provide a lot of power and control. Unfortunately, the upper body does not rotate very fast. Chapter 4 explains primary rotation in detail, and Chapter 9 provides an extensive series of step-by-step exercises that can be used to learn and develop primary rotation skills.

Secondary Rotation

We now know that primary rotation is the rotation of the shoulders and club around the centerline of the body, the primary axis. As the club rotates around the body on the backswing, the straight leading arm simultaneously rotates the club in a motion we'll refer to as the secondary rotation.

This is essentially a rotation within a rotation. Specifically, it is the rotation of the leading arm (straight left arm for RH golfers) during the backswing and the rotation of the straight right arm on the follow-through.

As I stated earlier, this is commonly referred to as "wrist rotation," but the wrist is a hinged joint and does not actually rotate. The entire arm rotates, including the wrist and hand and, ultimately, the club.

Secondary rotation is simply the rotation around the leading arm during the backswing, downswing, and follow-through. Remember that for right-handed golfers, the leading arm is the straight left arm, and for left-handed golfers, the leading arm is the straight right arm.

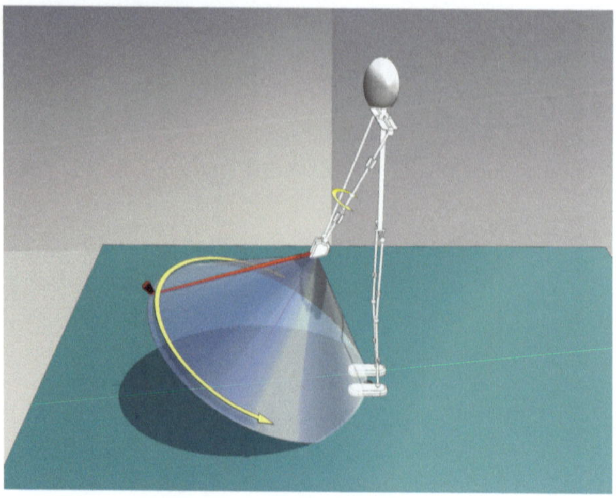

Figure 18: Secondary Rotation

Secondary rotation provides a secondary club path, which is at the base of the rotation cone that is created when you rotate a club around the secondary axis. This is perhaps one of the least understood concepts of the golf swing yet one of the most important when it comes to developing speed of the clubhead and distance.

Primary rotation provides power and control, but secondary rotation provides speed and therefore distance. Chapter 5 explains secondary rotation in detail, and Chapter 10 provides an extensive series of step-by-step exercises which can be used to learn and develop secondary rotation.

Tertiary Motion

Primary rotation is the rotation of the shoulders and club around the centerline of the body while secondary rotation is the rotation of the leading arm (straight left arm for RH golfers) during the backswing. These two motions acting independently are of limited use, but when we tie them together, the result is powerful. How do you tie them together? With some geometry that we will call tertiary motion (i.e., the third motion).

Tertiary motion moves your straight left arm across your chest during the backswing. This is done by shortening the distance between the right shoulder and the wrists by bending the right elbow against the torso during the backswing. This bending of your right elbow (for RH golfers) causes your left arm to move across your chest while it rotates (secondary rotation) in a controlled fashion. This movement also lifts the clubhead from the base plane and into the swing plane.

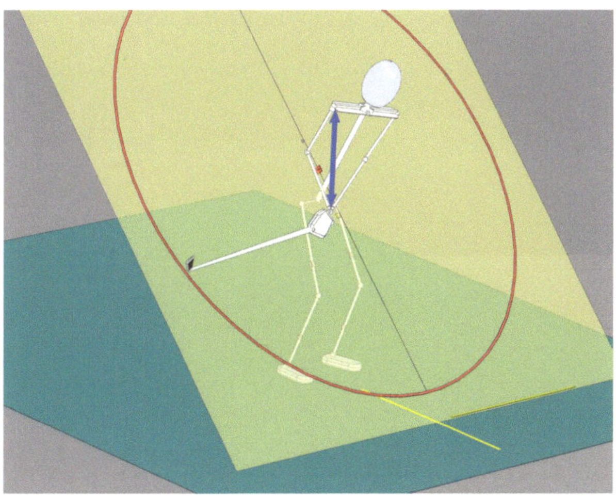

Figure 19: Tertiary Motion

Primary rotation provides power and control, and secondary rotation provides the speed and therefore the distance and tertiary motion ties the two together. Chapter 6 explains tertiary motion in detail, and Chapter 11 provides an extensive series of step-by-step exercises which can be used to learn and develop tertiary motion.

Once you understand all the pieces of the model (i.e., the kinematics of the swing), some useful physics (kinetics) is presented inn Chapter 7 in a way that can be easily understood. All of the pieces of the three-dimensional model are put together into a complete model of the golf swing in Chapter 8.

Chapters 1 through 8 provide knowledge about the golf swing, i.e., understanding the swing.

Chapters 9 through 12 provide step-by-step exercises that will develop the neuromuscular connections in the brain (i.e., hand-eye coordination) needed to put that knowledge to use. This requires repetition and practice. Practicing the wrong stuff can hurt your game. Practicing the right stuff will truly enrich your experience.

Chapters 13 through 15 will put that knowledge and practice to good use and hopefully get you on your journey in the most efficient way. Remember the approach to PST golf, which is to understand and repeat (i.e., the UR method).

Takeaways:

So what did we learn in Chapter 2?

1. The traditional model relies on the two-dimensional model of a pendulum. A more accurate representation is the three-dimensional model, which emphasizes rotation.
2. The PST model breaks down the golf swing into three separate motions: primary rotation, secondary rotation, and tertiary motion. The model is both unique and groundbreaking.
3. Primary rotation provides power and control, and secondary rotation provides the speed and therefore the distance in the swing. Tertiary motion ties the two rotations together.
4. Learning how to hit a golf ball properly not only requires knowledge and understanding but also practice and repetition. Practicing the wrong stuff can hurt your game. Practicing the right stuff will truly enrich your experience. Step-by-step exercises of the right stuff can help you build a great golf swing.

CHAPTER 3
Fundamentals

Gentlemen, this is a football.

—Vince Lombardi

In 1959, Vince Lombardi became head coach of the Green Bay Packers, a struggling American football team that had won only one game the previous season. With Lombardi at the helm, the team's fortunes immediately changed—they posted a 7-5 record, and Lombardi won Coach of the Year. His teams went on to win five NFL championships, including the first two Super Bowls. Lombardi's secret wasn't much of a secret: put *fundamentals* first.

Each year at training camp, Lombardi would start by holding up a ball and saying, "Gentlemen, this is a football."

Lombardi knew that the will to win wasn't enough. To perform at their best, his players needed to know they'd prepared as thoroughly as possible.

Focusing on the fundamentals meant repetition. Although some of his players were the best in the game, Lombardi reviewed basic techniques of blocking and tackling and insisted on intense conditioning and drills.[4]

I don't use this example as a trite way of filling up pages in a book. In my opinion, it's the perfect example of the foundation for good learning—and it's particularly true for learning good golf. A golf swing built on a *shaky* foundation will develop into a *shaky* golf swing.

Lombardi understood the critical reason we begin every new skill by learning the fundamentals. These are the building blocks upon which more advanced knowledge can be built. Often, it's not the fun part or even the most interesting.

But as the old expression goes, *you must learn to walk before you can run.*

The Fundamentals of the Setup

There are many good books about golf written by talented and knowledgeable golf professionals—in particular, Ben Hogan's *Five Lessons: The Modern Fundamentals of Golf.*[5] This book, written by a true master of the sport, is, in my opinion, one of the best books available to beginners and advanced players alike.

The book does an excellent job of laying out the fundamentals of the golf swing, and this chapter will do little more than highlight and add some kinematics to the main concepts Mr. Hogan outlines in his book. I strongly recommend you get a copy of *Five Lessons: The Modern Fundamentals of Golf* and read it.

The two chapters of particular interest are Chapters 1, "The Grip," and 2, "Stance and Posture." The following is my attempt to add extra insight into these chapters.

---

[4] Richard Gunderman, "3 lessons for today's teachers and students from coach Vince Lombardi." The Conversation (December 16, 2019).

[5] Hogan, B., Wind, H. W., and Ravielli, A., *Five lessons: The modern fundamentals of golf.* (NYT Special Services ; Distributed by Atria Books, 2002)

The Grip

Good golf begins with a good grip.

—Ben Hogan

Hogan's dissertation on how to properly grip the club is superb, including the many illustrations and sketches provided in his book. This chapter will highlight items that are particularly important regarding proper grip.

> *The grip is the heartbeat of the action of the golf swing. Logically, it has to be. The player's only contact with the ball is through the clubhead, and his only direct physical contact with the club is through the hands. In the golf swing, the power is originated and generated by the movements of the body. This power is transferred from the player's body to his arms then to his/her hands.*
>
> —Ben Hogan[6]

If you're new to golf, the grip will feel a bit strange at first. A good grip, like almost everything else in golf, requires practice. But it's important, because grip is critical to everything else in the golf swing.

[6] Ibid., 18

Understanding the Wrists

The correct geometry of the leading arm (left arm for RH golfers) is critical if you want to hit the ball properly. Understanding the wrist positions goes a long way to achieving proper geometry of the leading arm and the grip.

Of course, you can't talk about good grip without discussing flat left wrist (FLW). What's a flat left wrist, and why is it important?

Some of this will be covered when we review secondary rotation in Chapter 5. Suffice it to say, we'll touch on it here because of its importance.

Pronation and Supination

Starting with a flat left wrist of the leading arm in the neutral position, rotate the arm clockwise so the palm goes down. This is called pronation. Rotating counterclockwise ninety degrees from the neutral position so the palm faces up is called supination.

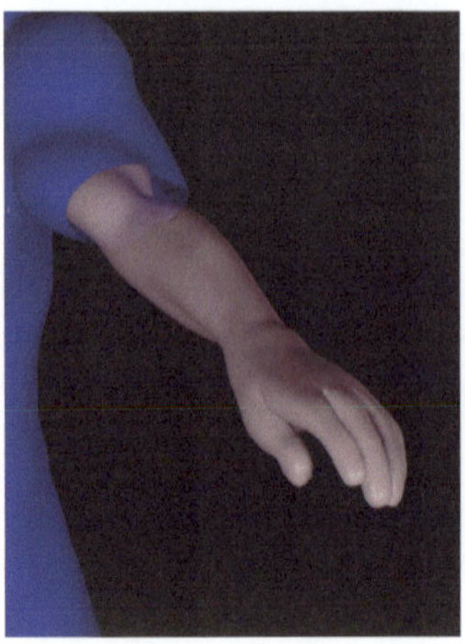

Figure 18: Wrist Down (Pronation)

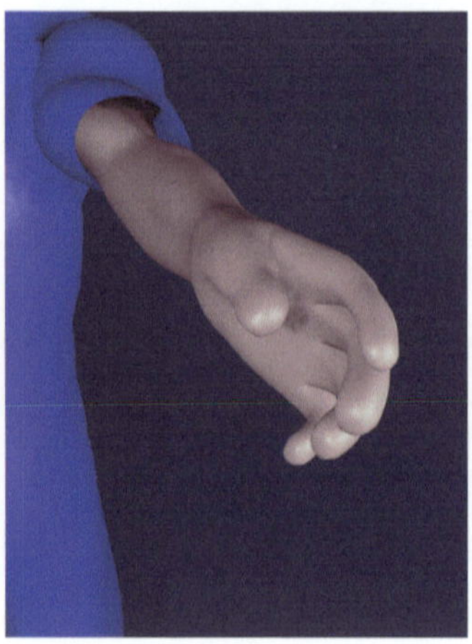

Figure 19: Wrist Neutral

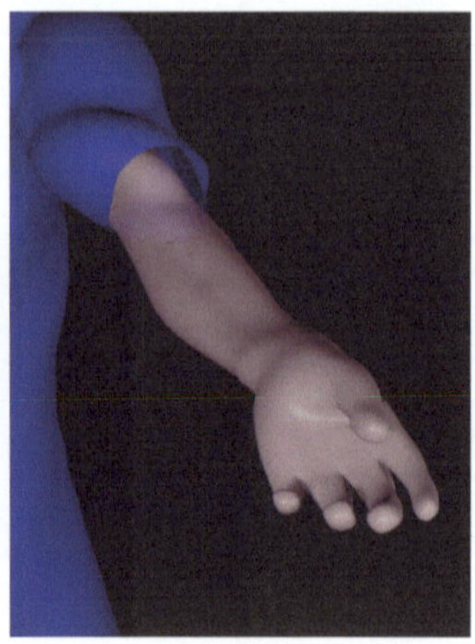

Figure 20: Wrist Up (Supination)

Wrist Hinge Versus Wrist Cock

Hang around a golf course or watch enough golf on TV and you'll hear two terms commonly: "wrist hinge" and "wrist cock." Wrist hinge is the ability to move the wrist in one axis, and wrist cock is the ability of the wrist to move along a different axis.

Wrist Hinge

Hold your left arm straight in front of you with your palm and fingers flat and vertical. Now, move your wrist to the right. This is often referred to as "bowing" the wrist. Now, move your wrist to the left. This is often referred to as "cupping" the wrist. Congratulations—you have just demonstrated wrist hinge!

Wrist hinge is important. In the backswing, the lead wrist (left wrist for RH golfers) should remain flat (no hinging) through the entire backswing and up to impact, while the wrist on the trailing arm (right arm) must hinge to allow the lead wrist to remain flat.

After impact, the lead wrist will start hinging back. The reasons for this will become clear in Chapter 6.

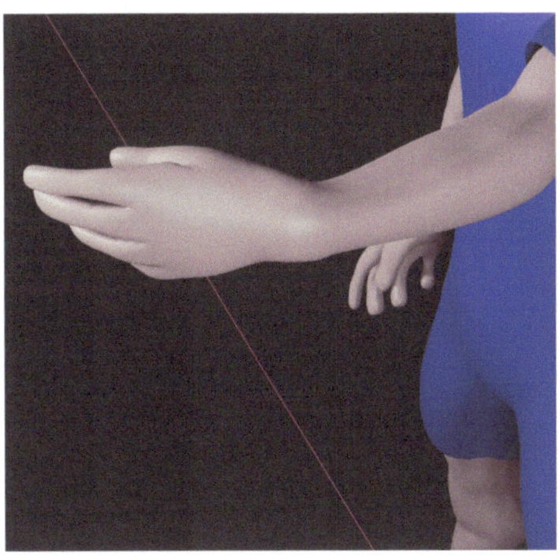

Figure 21: Wrist Hinge In (Flexion)

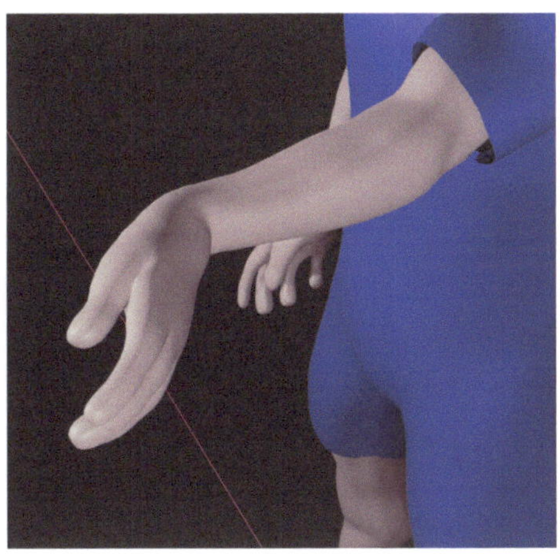

Figure 20: Wrist Hinge Out (Extension)

Wrist Cock

Hold your arm straight in front of you with your palm and fingers flat and vertical. Now, move your wrist up and down. Congratulations—you've just demonstrated wrist cock!

Wrist cock occurs at the top of the backswing as the club changes direction. The momentum of the club at the top of the backswing causes wrist cock in the radial direction (thumb side) as the shoulders and arm reverse direction into the downswing. It can also be used to add extra club speed during the downswing, but this is nominal. Beginner golfers should avoid concentrating on wrist cock, which can mess up the geometry of the golf swing if done improperly.

Wrist cock will occur naturally as you learn to properly transition from the backswing to the downswing.

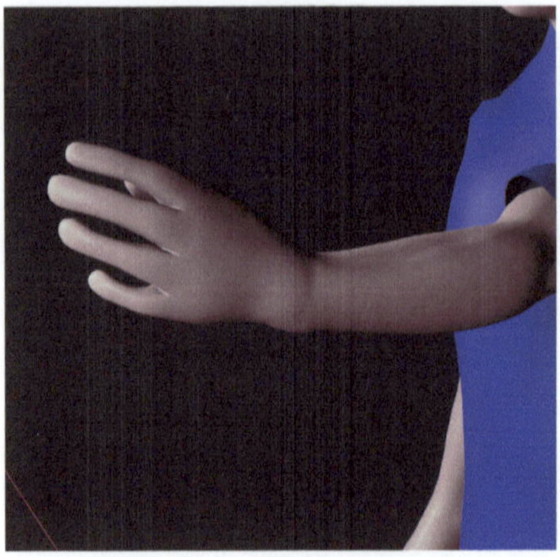

Figure 23: Wrist Cock Up (Radial)

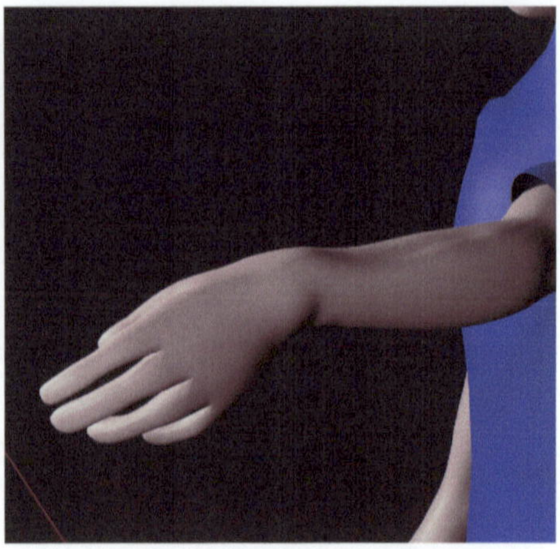

Figure 23: Wrist Cock Down (Ulnar)

Flat Left Wrist

Extend your leading arm (left arm for RH golfers) straight out in front of you. In this position, the left wrist should be flat (i.e., no wrist hinge in [flexion] or wrist hinge out [extension]).

Keeping a flat left wrist (FLW) during the backswing (for RH golfers) is *critical* to keeping the geometry of the swing correct, especially when trying to maintain the club path for secondary rotation, as you will see in Chapter 5.

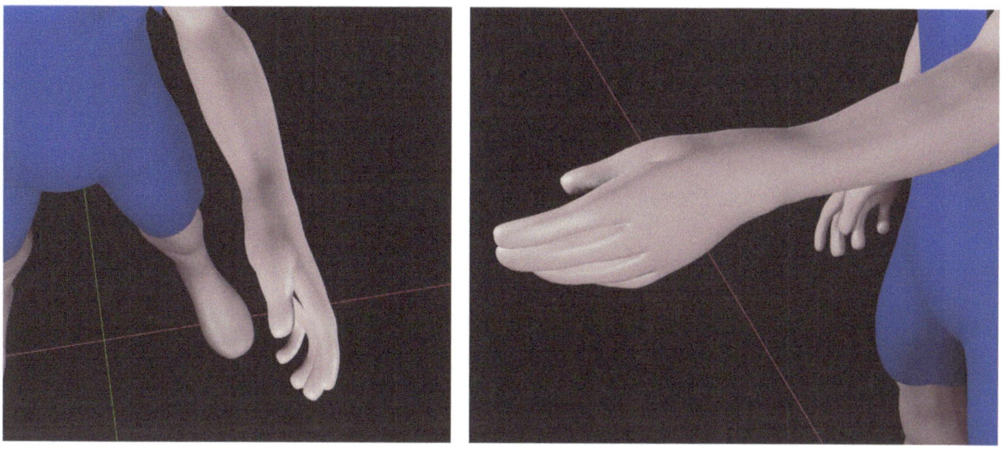

Figure 24: Flat Left Wrist

Establishing a Good Grip

With the left arm extended and a flat left wrist, curl all four fingers in the form of hooks. Hyperextend the arm and point toward the ground with the thumb. The left wrist should be cocked down (ulnar) as far as possible. It should seem like you are pointing to something with your left thumb.

Keep a flat left wrist and lay a club in the curled fingers. The thumb should naturally fall on top of the grip.

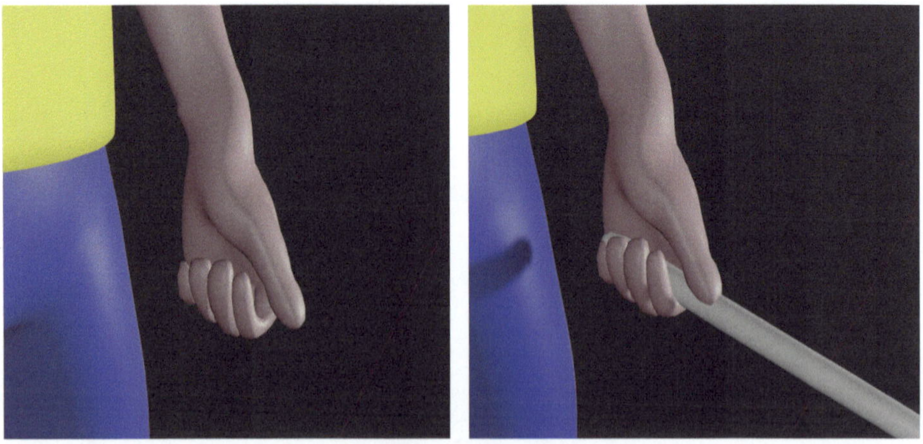

Figure 25: Left Hand Grip

The left arm should be straight (hyperextended), and the left wrist should be in the fully cocked and down (ulnar) position. As you will see in Chapter 5, this provides the smallest swing path and the most stability for secondary rotation.

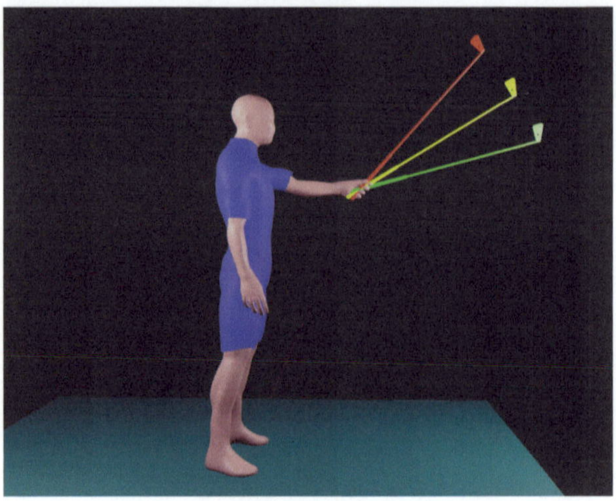

Figure 26: Wrist Position

You should now have the club in the left hand with a light finger grip of the club using all four fingers curled around the shaft and the thumb resting on top of the shaft. The clubhead should be perpendicular to the target line. This is a neutral grip of a club with the right hand.

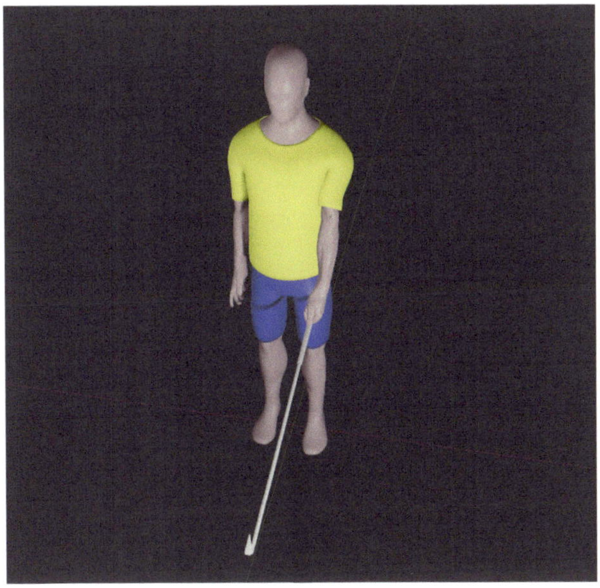

Figure 27: Club Orientation

Similarly, with the right arm extended and with the thumb straight, curl all four fingers in the form of hooks. The right wrist will be *slightly* hinged out (extension).

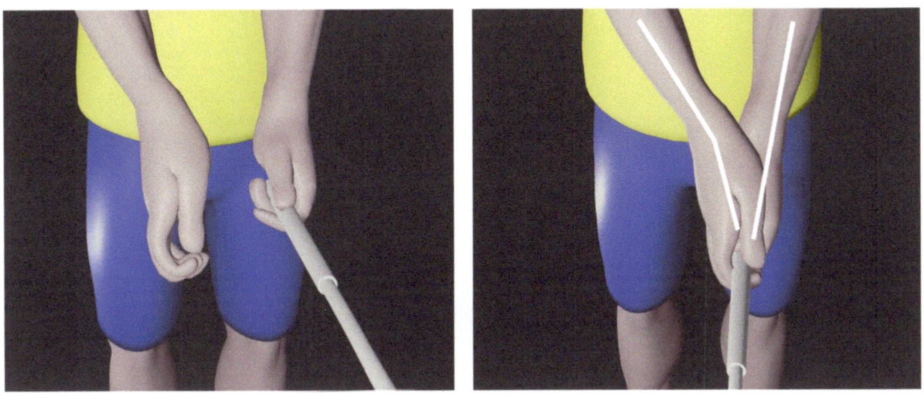

Figure 28: Right Hand Grip

The right hand will need to grip the club in front of the left hand; the right hand will be closer to the clubhead. The idea is to grip the club with both arms *straight*. To do this, you must rotate your right shoulder forward until the right hand is below the left hand.

The illustration below shows the rotation of the shoulders that move the right hand below the left hand to make room for the right hand to grasp the club. Rotating the shoulders allows the left arm to remain straight when grasping the club.

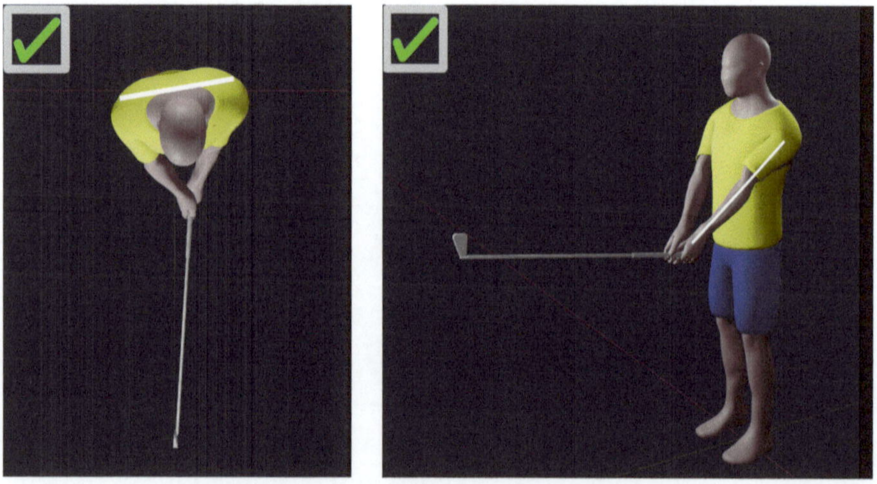

Figure 29: Proper Shoulder Rotation to Accommodate Grip

Many beginner golfers simply bend the leading arm (left arm for RH golfers) with no shoulder rotation to make room for the right hand, and a bent left arm *destroys* the geometry of the swing.

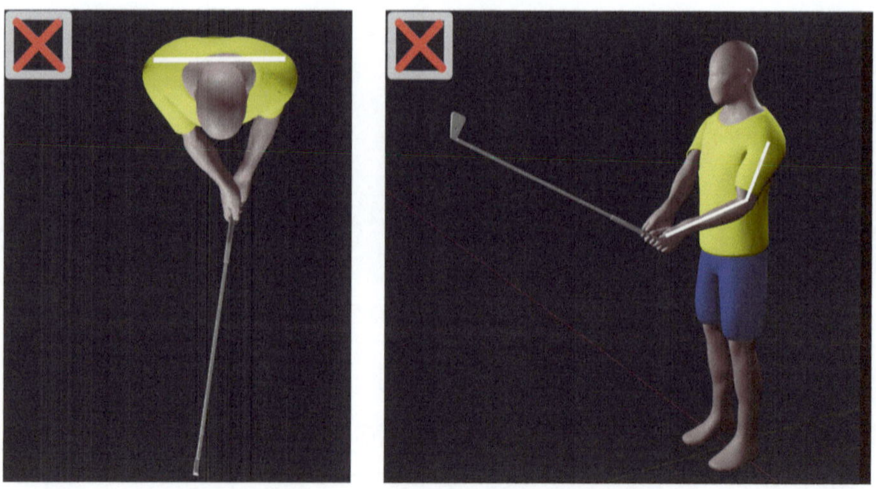

Figure 30: Improper Bending of Elbow to Accommodate Grip

Rotating the shoulders to get a good grip is a key part of setup that allows the golfer to maintain a straight leading arm (left arm for RH golfers) during setup and through the backswing and downswing.

To complete the grip, place the curled index finger, middle finger, and ring finger of the right hand around the club shaft just inside of the left hand, making sure the thumb of the left hand lies in the lifeline of the right hand.

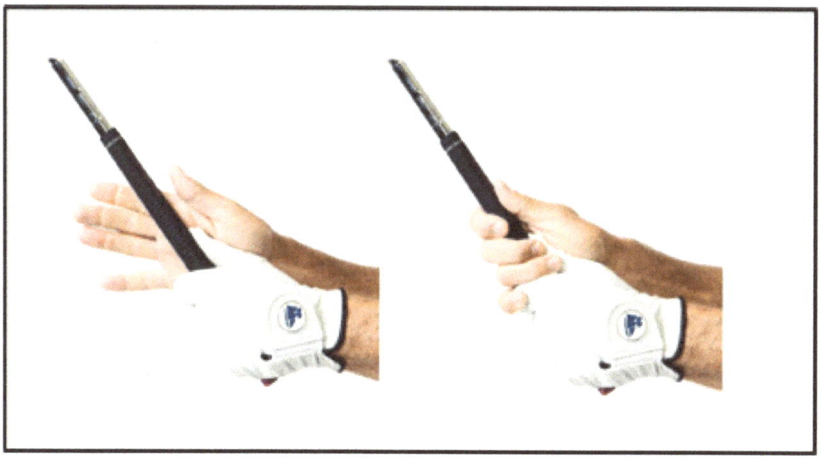

Figure 31: Left Thumb Placement in Lifeline

The pinky finger of the right hand can either overlap the index finger of the left hand or hook the index finger of the left hand.

A good grip must be tight enough to keep the club in position but not so tight as to hinder motion of the leading arm during secondary rotation (more about this in Chapter 5). The grip might feel a bit awkward or cumbersome at first, but it will soon feel natural and comfortable with practice, kind of like a new pair of shoes that needs to be broken in.

Stance and Posture (Good Geometry)

The correct golf setup and stance is key to a correct swing, and understanding the correct geometry of the golf stance goes a long way to establishing the correct setup.

Ben Hogan's dissertation on correct stance and posture is superb and includes many good illustrations and sketches.

> *The proper stance and posture enable a golfer to be perfectly balanced and poised throughout the swing. Only then will his legs, arms, and body be able to carry out their interrelated assignments correctly.*
>
> —Ben Hogan[7]

This book will highlight some of the factors for good posture and stance that are detailed in Mr. Hogan's book and will add additional information regarding the geometry of the setup and how it relates to the rotational aspects of the swing.

You're already aware that the hands and arms are used in golf to connect the club to the shoulders. The rotation of the shoulder around the body is the **primary rotation**.

As your shoulder (connected to the club by the hands and arms) rotates the club back, the straight left arm (for RH golfers) should rotate as you turn due to the geometry of the rotation, hereafter referred to as the **secondary rotation**.

Primary and secondary rotation will be covered in more detail in Chapters 4 and 5 respectively. But with the idea of rotation in mind, let's examine the geometry of the address position in golf.

The primary rotation is around the primary axis (the line through the center of the body and perpendicular to the shoulder plane). When you're standing straight up in the neutral position, the primary axis is perpendicular to the ground.

---

[7] Ibid., 39

However, at setup, you tilt the primary axis at the hips at about 20 to 25 degrees from vertical with respect to the ground (i.e., your spine tilt, aka angle of inclination). This will vary depending on the golfer's physique and club used.

When viewed from the side, here are a couple of points worth noting:

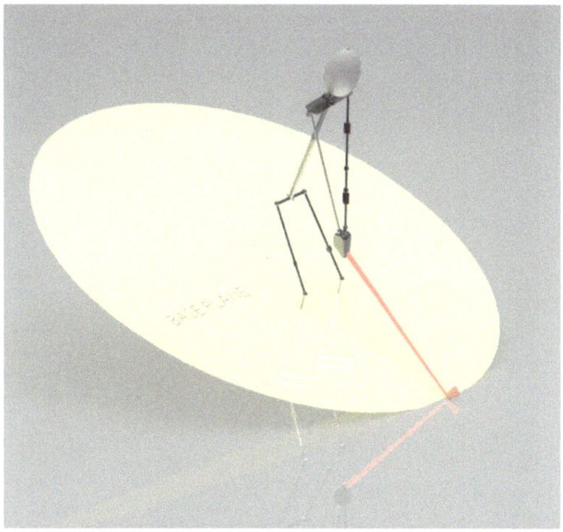

Figure 32: Address Position

1. Tilting of the primary axis is done at the hips and not by bending the back. The back must remain straight or slightly arched to maintain the proper geometry.
2. As you tilt the primary axis (at the hips), the shoulder plane will also tilt (with respect to the ground) by the same amount.
3. When you are standing straight, the primary axis origin is the same as the neutral origin, which is that point on the ground between your feet. However, as you tilt your hips for setup, the primary axis origin changes to a point about twenty-two inches behind the neutral origin *but still on the midplane.*
4. Remember that the cross plane (frontal plane) is the plane perpendicular to the ground that runs through the origin and separates your front half from your back half. As you tilt the primary axis, the buttocks move behind the cross plane, and the shoulders move in front of the cross plane.
5. To accomplish this, the knees must bend slightly. The overall center of mass of the body is still on the cross plane (i.e., between the feet and over the origin). Put another way, the weight of the shoulders leaning forward is balanced by the weight of the buttocks, and the overall effect is a stable setup position.

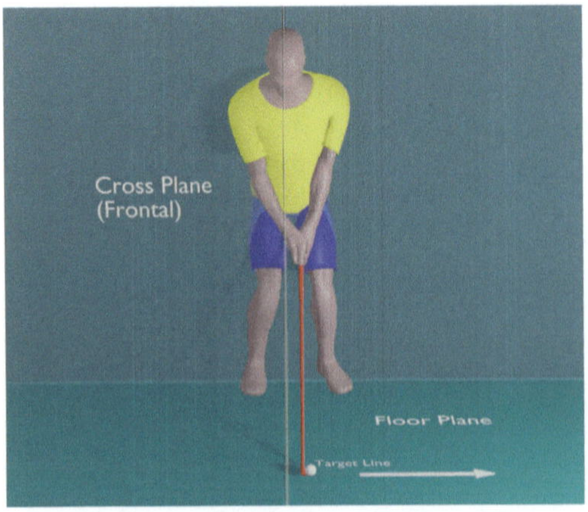

Figure 34: Setup Position/Front View

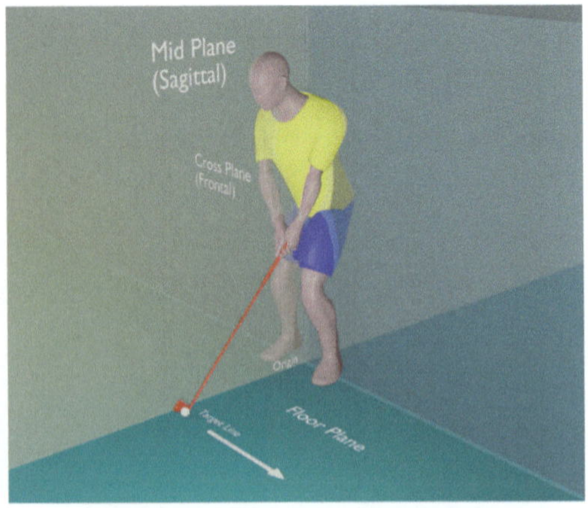

Figure 33: Setup Position/Right Ortho View

When viewed from the front, here are a couple of points worth noting:

1. At setup, both arms should be *straight* and in the form of a V. The inside of the elbow should be pointed out, and the back of the elbow should be pointed into the body.
2. The upper arms should be tight against the upper body.
3. The shoulders should be rotated slightly to accommodate for the grip of the right hand below the left hand.
4. The amount of spine tilt from side to side should be minimal (i.e., do not tilt the primary axis off the midplane). There is some shoulder rotation required to accommodate a proper grip, but do not confuse this with shoulder tilt. We'll discuss the distinction in Chapter 8.
5. The feet would normally be set apart at about shoulder width, slightly wider for longer clubs and slightly narrower for shorter clubs. A stance that is too wide can hinder proper rotation.

Posture

What is posture as it pertains to golf?

Posture is the way you position your body, torso, shoulders, and limbs. So stand up straight, put your shoulders back, stick your chest out, and lift that chin up. Posture describes the way you carry yourself, but it can also describe a certain body position you take, like the posture you should have for a good golf stance.

In theory, good posture seems almost trite, but in practice, most of us can improve our posture. It's a cornerstone to good stance or vice versa; good stance starts with good posture.

Exercise 3a—Good Posture in the Vertical World

Why is this exercise important?

Reinforces good posture

1. Stand straight with your feet shoulder-width apart and arms hanging comfortably by your sides.
2. Your shoulders should be square and your back arched slightly backward (not bowed).
3. Your weight should be evenly distributed on both feet and in the middle of the torso.
4. Your head should be facing forward. Check yourself in a mirror.

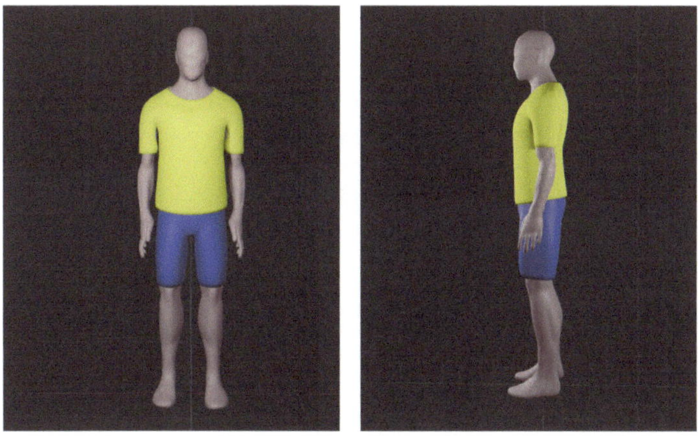

Figure 35: Good Vertical Posture

Remember, the start of a good stance in golf starts with good posture. But wait, there's more!

When we hit a golf ball, we don't hit it standing straight up. We tilt our upper body (torso) by bending at the hips while maintaining good posture.

Repeat the above exercise, but now tilt the upper body (torso) at the hips. If you're like most people, you're probably bending your spine as you tilt your torso. This can really affect the geometry of the golf swing.

To tilt the torso properly, you need to bend at the hips with a straight back. Use a golf club to complete the next exercise.

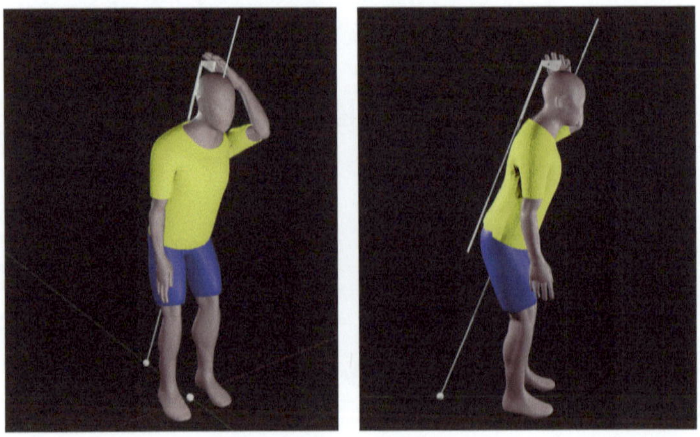

Figure 36: Good Inclined Posture

Exercise 3b—Good Inclined Posture Using a Golf Club with Knees Flexed (Soft Knees)

Why is this exercise important?

Reinforces good posture with a straight back
Reinforces bending at the hips

1. Stand straight with your feet shoulder-width apart and arms hanging comfortably by your sides.
2. Your shoulders should be square and your back arched slightly backward (not bowed).
3. Your head should be facing forward. Check yourself in a mirror for good posture.

4. Take the golf club and put the clubhead on the top of your head with the shaft touching both the back of your head and your tailbone.
5. Now tilt the torso about 25 degrees (from vertical) while keeping the club against the back of your head and your buttocks.
6. Check yourself in a mirror from the side. What do you see?

If the head or the butt are not touching the club as you tilt, you're likely bending your spine instead of tilting at the hips. Make sure you're tilted at the hips at approximately 25 degrees with your back straight and with the back of your head and your butt touching the golf club.

If you are, you're tilting properly at the hips, and the spine will be straight.

Stance

Stance is the way in which someone stands, especially when a particular stance is adopted as in baseball, golf, and other sports. In our case, we'll discuss stance as it pertains to golf.

A good stance is critical to proper rotation and correct execution of the golf swing.

Exercise 3c—Stance with Club

Why is this exercise important?

Reinforces good stance
Illustrates position of the feet

1. Start with good posture. Stand straight with your feet shoulder-width apart and arms hanging comfortably by your sides. Your shoulders should be square and your back arched slightly backward (not bowed).
2. Take your left foot and move it about six inches to the left from centerline (i.e., approximately shoulder width). Your left foot should be slightly open, meaning the toe is pointed out to allow the hip to rotate after impact during follow-through.

3. Take your right foot and move it about six inches to the right from centerline (i.e., approximately shoulder width). The right foot should be perpendicular to the target line, meaning the toe is pointed forward to help limit the hip to rotation during the backswing.
4. Your feet should now be about shoulder-width apart, slightly wider for longer clubs, and your body should be vertical and with good posture.
5. Now tilt your body by thrusting your butt back and shoulders forward while tilting at the hips. Do not allow the back (spine) to bow.
6. Your arms should be hanging vertically at your sides, fingertips pointing slightly in front of your feet.
7. Now let your knees flex some. As you flex your knees, your hands will drop down a few inches. Point the back knee (right knee) toward the midplane again to help limit the hip to rotation during the backswing.
8. Check yourself in a mirror. You should feel like you are in a good, comfortable, and solid stance.

The only thing you're missing at this point is a golf club. Now (finally) grab a midiron (e.g., a 7 iron or 8 iron) and repeat the above exercise. Make sure to hold the club with a good grip.

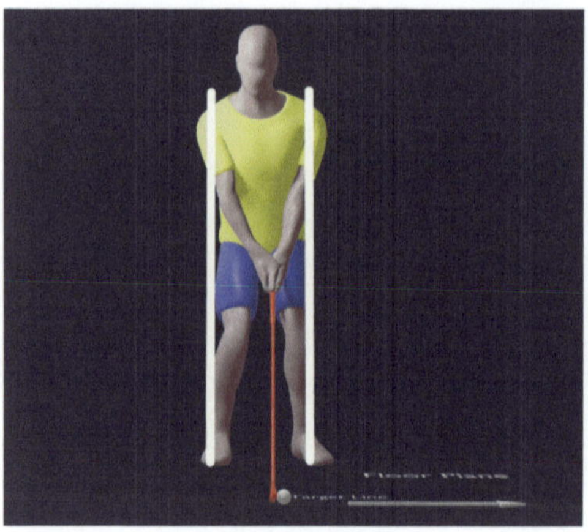

Figure 38: Width of Stance

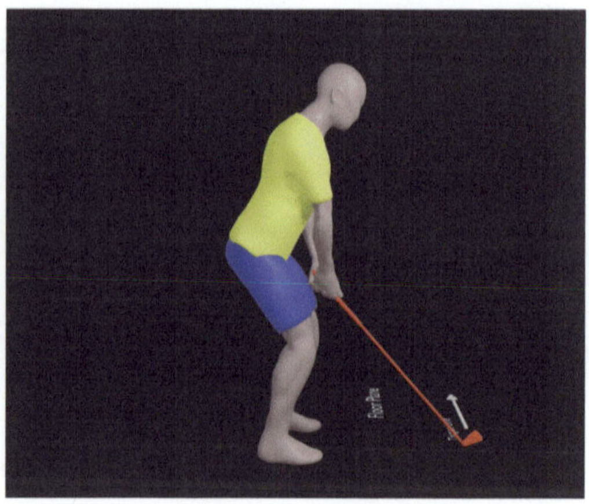

Figure 37: Neutral Stance

Your feet should be about shoulder-width apart, slightly wider for longer clubs and slightly closer for shorter clubs. The back foot should be perpendicular to the target line, and the front foot should be slightly open with respect to the target line.

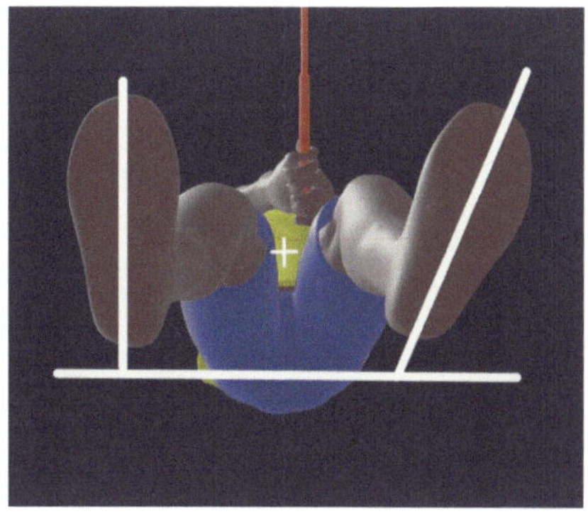

Figure 39: Position of the Feet

The center of mass of the upper body should be centered over the origin located between both feet. The shoulders are in front of the center of gravity, and the buttocks counterbalance the shoulders behind the center of gravity.

Some points worth noting regarding the setup stance with a golf club:

1. The geometry with respect to the midplane will be asymmetric. For example, the left and right side of the body should be about the same except for some shoulder rotation to accommodate the grip.
2. The amount of shoulder tilt (especially for beginner golfers) should be minimal (i.e., do not tilt the primary axis from side to side). Keep the primary axis on the midplane.
3. The longer the club, the more vertical the setup stance and the wider the feet.

Consistent Setup

The setup for a golf shot should be methodical and consistent. Don't expect to consistently hit every shot if you don't consistently set up for each shot. The following is a step-by-step approach to setting up the address after you have determined the shot requirements such as the type of shot and club required.

Setup to Address

Step 1 After determining the club required for the shot, stand erect with good posture (back straight and shoulders square), the club properly gripped with the leading hand (left hand for RH golfers).

Your weight should be over the origin (the midpoint between both feet).

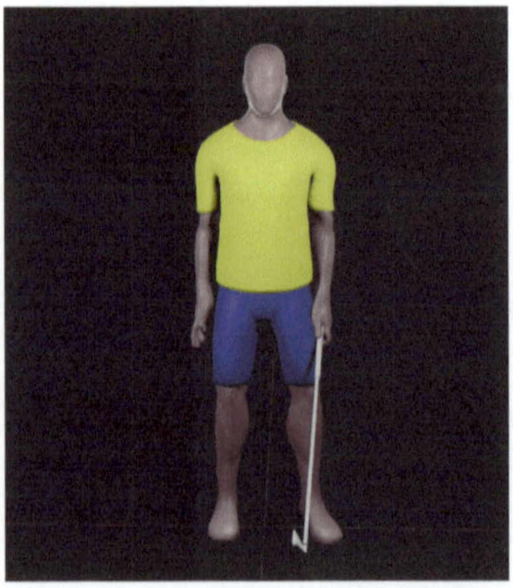

The trailing foot should be perpendicular to the target line, and the leading foot should be slightly open with respect to the target line.

Step 2 Extend your arms straight out in front of you in a V. This forms a triangle, with your shoulders as the base of the triangle.

Remember that the shoulders must rotate slightly around the primary axis to be able to place the right hand in front of the left hand on the club.

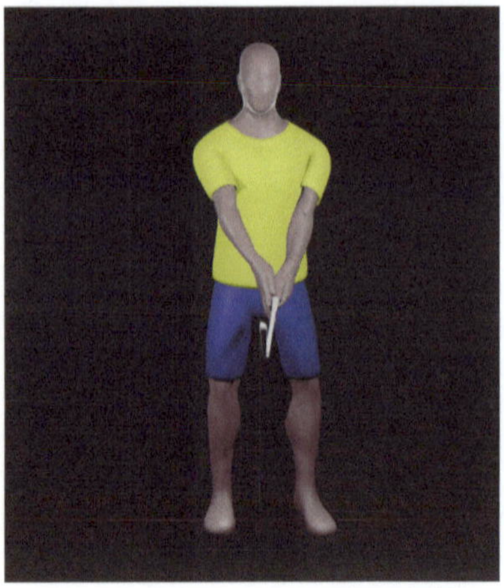

This is the neutral position. Keep your arms *close together*, the inside of your elbows facing upward. The upper arms should be resting comfortably against the sides of the chest.

The clubface should be vertical (i.e., straight up and down).

Step 3 Now tilt your body by thrusting your buttocks back and shoulders forward while tilting at the hips. Maintain your center of gravity over the origin, which is located equidistant between your feet.

Do not allow the back (spine) to bend.

The clubface is perpendicular to the target line.

Step 4 Lower the club by bending the knees until the clubhead is touching the ground.

The center of gravity of the body is still over the origin between the feet.

The clubface is perpendicular to the target line and touching the ground.

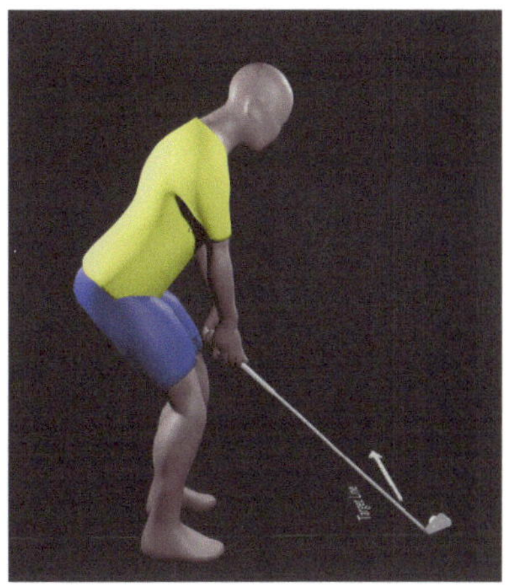

Step 5 The correct grip and setup are critical to establishing the correct geometry for the golf swing, as you will see.

The grip should be neutral.

The weight is evenly distributed side-to-side and front-to-back.

The leading wrist (left wrist for RH golfers) is flat (FLW), and the leading arm is straight (SLA).

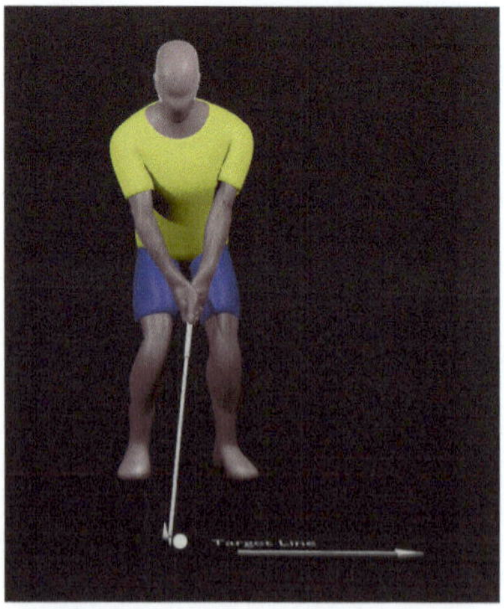

With a good grip and a stable setup, we are now ready to look more closely at primary rotation, which is the foundation of a good swing.

Takeaways:

So what did we learn in Chapter 3?

1. Good golf starts with a good grip.
2. Good posture and good stance are keys to a proper setup and good geometry.
3. The right geometry at setup is key to the right geometry for the rest of the swing.

CHAPTER 4

Primary Rotation

In my introductory chapter, I made a bold claim that the golf swing is not actually a swing at all but rather the combination of three motions: the primary rotation, the secondary rotation, and tertiary motion. To effectively hit a golf ball, these rotations need to be executed correctly and in perfect synchronization.

Revelation #3

Primary rotation provides power and control.

Once you understand the fundamentals of good grip and setup, the next logical step is to understand the primary rotation. If the grip is the cornerstone of the golf swing, primary rotation is the foundation.

But *why* is it so important?

This chapter will explain this and provide a series of easy exercises that will teach you how to properly execute the movement.

"Getting to Know You"

—song by Richard Rodgers

It's All in the Shoulders

The golf ball needs to fly long and straight. To do this, the clubface must contact the ball perpendicular to the target line. The distance is proportional to the speed that the clubhead has when it contacts the ball.

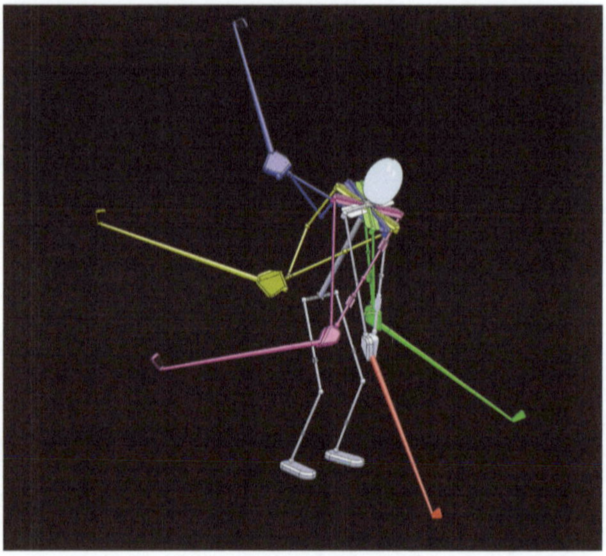

Figure 40: The Shoulders

The clubhead is on one end of the club, and your hands hold the other end. With a proper grip, your arms connect your hands to the shoulders. Your shoulders rotate around your body (the core), which, in turn, rotates your arms, which, in turn, rotate the club around your body.

Much of this chapter deals with teaching your shoulders how to rotate the arms and club around the body. But first, you must teach your arms to do less while simultaneously teaching your shoulders to do *more*.

Remember the friendship between your brain and your arms? Teaching golf based only on swing reinforces that relationship. By realizing that hitting a golf ball is more of a rotation rather than a swing, the emphasis is not on your arms but rather on your shoulders.

Revelation #4

Primary rotation is the rotation of the shoulders and club around the centerline of the body, the primary axis. This rotation is completed using your upper torso and your shoulders. A good solid rotation of the shoulders is critical to the ability to hit the ball well.

The one sure sign of high handicappers is the reliance of arm swinging rather than shoulder rotation during the three seconds it takes to execute a swing. The shoulders (the upper torso) are a big part of the golf rotation (swing). Watch golfers at the range and observe how much shoulder each golfer puts into the swing. The better golfers use a lot of shoulder rotation. Conversely, the high handicapper uses minimal shoulder rotation and plenty of arm swinging.

Figure 41: Stickman

Remember, your brain and arms have had a close friendship since birth. It's only natural that when you pick up a golf club, your arms want to take charge. And why not? Often golf instruction emphasizes how to swing the club.

Keys to Understanding

For this approach—which is different than what you may have been taught—to work for you, there are three key points to understand.

1. To properly hit a golf ball, your shoulders/torso need to rotate the club. Your arms are primarily used in golf to connect the club to your shoulders. The rotation of your shoulders around the body is called the **primary rotation**.
2. Primary rotation provides the power and control of the golf swing. The speed part is achieved with secondary rotation, which will be described in the next chapter.
3. Rotation of your shoulders needs to be a key part of training when learning to hit a golf ball properly. Reteaching the brain to use your shoulders more (and your arms less) is critical—and harder than it sounds.

We'll go through a step-by-step approach, complete with exercises, to master this critical element of the golf swing, but before you head out to the fairway, let's talk about geometry.

Understanding the Geometry

When a golfer stands erect, the centerline of the body corresponds with the primary axis running vertically through your body. The shoulders (which are approximately sixteen inches wide) cross that axis roughly five feet off the ground.

The hip sockets (which are approximately fourteen inches apart) cross the axis of rotation roughly three feet off the ground.

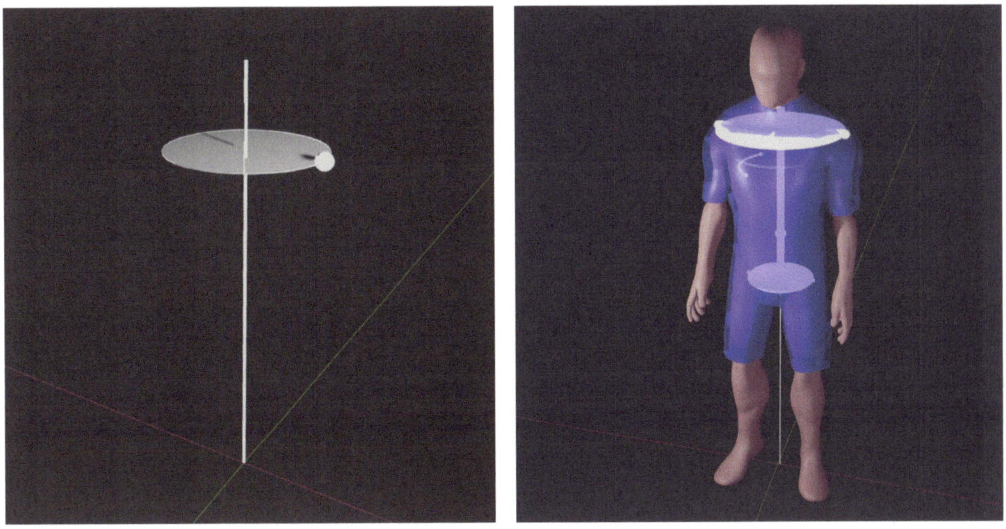

Figure 42: Primary Axis of Rotation

The primary axis of rotation is the line through the center of the body and is perpendicular to the shoulder plane.

When you're standing straight, it doesn't matter, because the axis of rotation is through the entire body. The primary axis origin coincides with the neutral origin. When you tilt at the hips for the address position, the primary axis origin moves behind you to a point of approximately twenty-two inches behind the midplane.

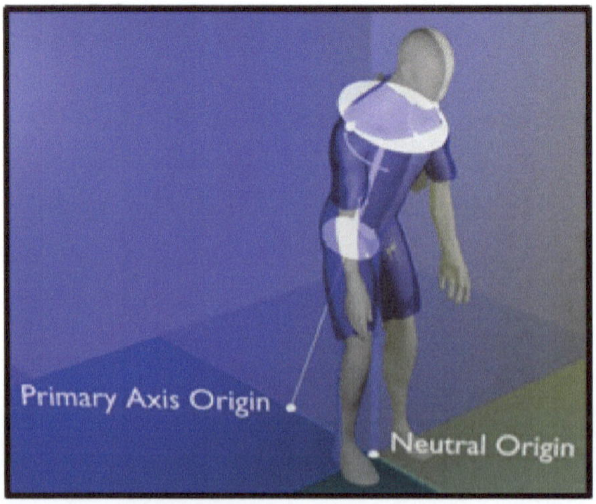

Figure 43: Neutral/Primary Axis Origins

A couple of things worth noting:

1. The neutral origin (between the feet) and the primary axis origin (end of the primary axis) are on the midplane.
2. As you tilt your spine (at the hips) and rotate the primary axis, the neutral axis stays in the same spot, but the primary axis origin moves behind you while remaining on the midplane.
3. There is symmetry between the left side of the body and the right side of the body.

When a golfer is in the setup position, the primary axis is tilted approximately 65 degrees with respect to the ground (i.e., approximately 25 degrees from vertical).

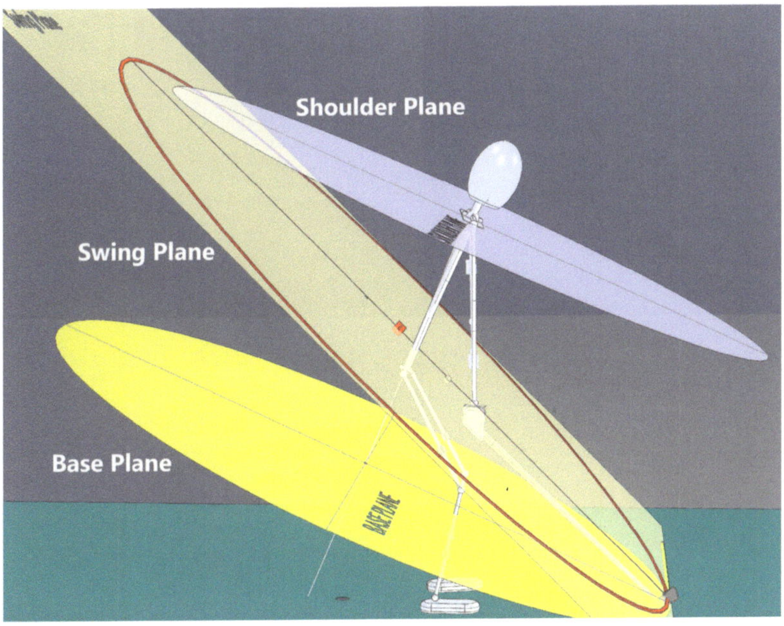

Figure 44: The Planes

This means that the shoulder plane, base plane, and swing plane are also tilted by the same amount, because the shoulder plane and base plane remain perpendicular to the axis of rotation. The amount of tilt may vary somewhat based on the individual golfer's height and the length of the club.

With this basic understanding of the geometry involved, we're now ready for the first exercise demonstrating primary rotation.

Primary Rotation Exercises in the Vertical World

A journey of a thousand miles begins with a single step.

—Lao Tzu

This exercise is the first step in training your shoulders (and untraining your arms), and although it doesn't require a club or a ball (yet), it's extremely important. The exercise involves rotating your shoulders around the center of your body while standing erect.

The first figure represents the top-down view of the body, arms extended in front with the head facing forward. This is the neutral position. The head is facing forward, and the shoulders form the base of a triangle. We will hereafter refer to shoulder rotation during backswing as clockwise with the downswing and follow-through as counterclockwise when viewed from the top.

Figure 45: Neutral V Position

Notice how the rotation of the shoulders around the core traces a semicircle. If you did the impossible and rotated 360 degrees, you'd have a complete circle.

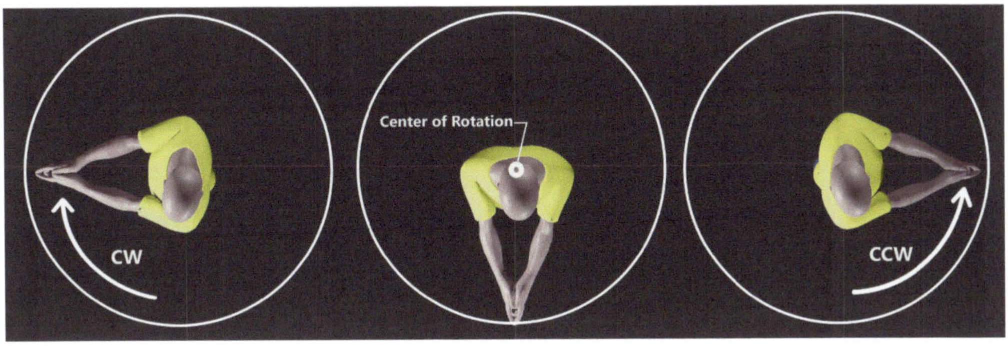

Figure 46: Rotation of the V Position

The following exercise is simple but one of the most important exercises for establishing a good golf swing.

We will start in the vertical world (i.e., standing erect) and then graduate to the inclined world (i.e., at the inclined address position).

Exercise 4a—Primary Rotation (V to V to V) Without Equipment

Training the shoulders to rotate is one of the most fundamental motions to learn in golf.

During this exercise, keep your head still and looking forward. A still head helps maintain the proper geometry from setup through impact. In practice, some head motion is acceptable, but most beginner and many intermediate golfers have too much movement—and *any* movement of the head up or down is detrimental.

Why is this exercise important?

Demonstrates the primary axis of rotation

Trains your brain to use your shoulders and not your arms

1. Stand erect with good posture (back straight and shoulders square). Refer to the previous chapter if you'd like a refresher on proper posture.

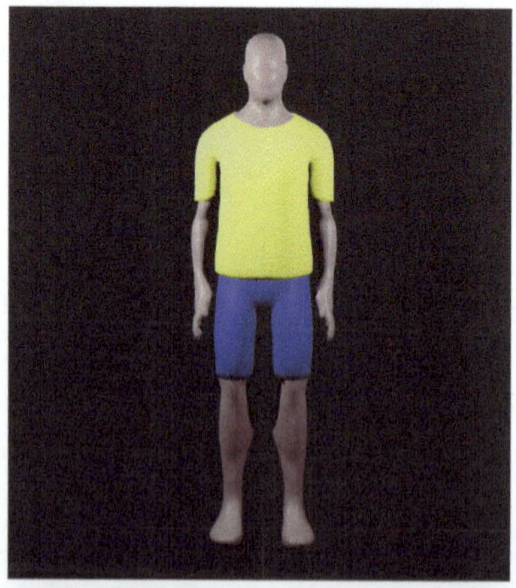

2. Extend your arms straight out in front of you with your hands flat and together, forming a V. This forms a triangle with your shoulders as the base of the triangle. This is the neutral position. Keep your arms as close **together** as possible, and try to keep the inside of your elbows facing upward.

3. *Slowly* rotate the shoulders about 45 degrees clockwise while keeping your head facing forward. Do *not* allow the arms to take over. Make sure the movement is done with your *shoulders only*. If you turn correctly using your shoulders, you'll maintain the V as you turn. Do not bend your elbows.

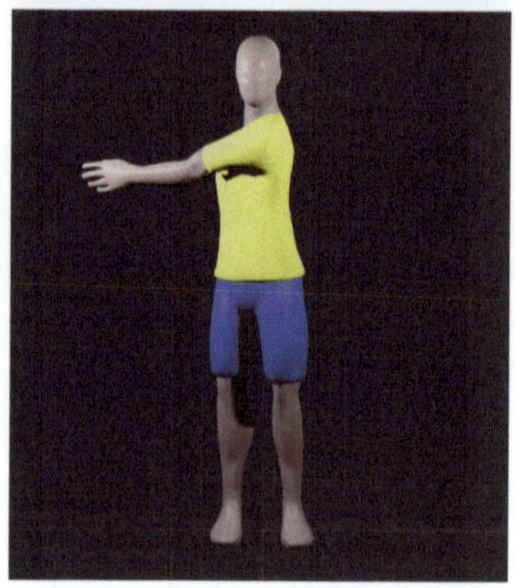

4. Slowly return to the neutral position.

5. *Slowly* rotate your shoulders about 45 degrees counterclockwise while keeping your head facing forward. Don't allow your arms to take over. Make sure the movement is done with your *shoulders only*. If you turn correctly using the shoulders, you'll maintain the V as you turn. Do not bend either elbow.

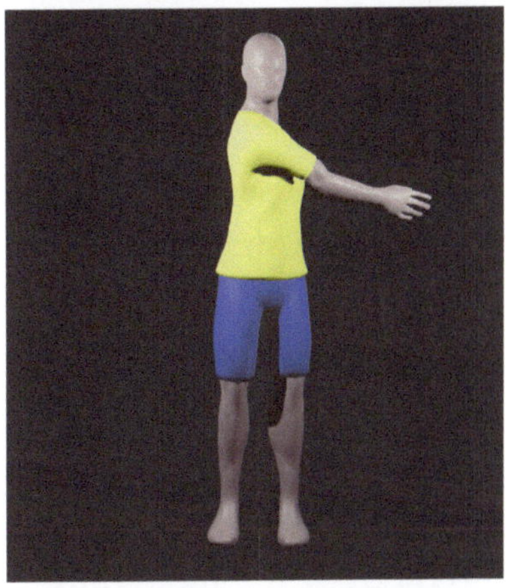

6. Slowly return to the neutral position. Repeat this exercise and gradually work your way up to 90-degree rotation of the shoulders or to the highest degree possible.

Make this exercise a part of your practice routine. As with almost everything in golf, a consistent golf swing begins with repetition.

The deltoid muscle is a large triangular intrinsic shoulder muscle and is among the largest muscle groups in the upper body. These muscles and other muscles in the upper body can develop a significant amount of torque. That's the good news. The bad news is that they do not move particularly fast.

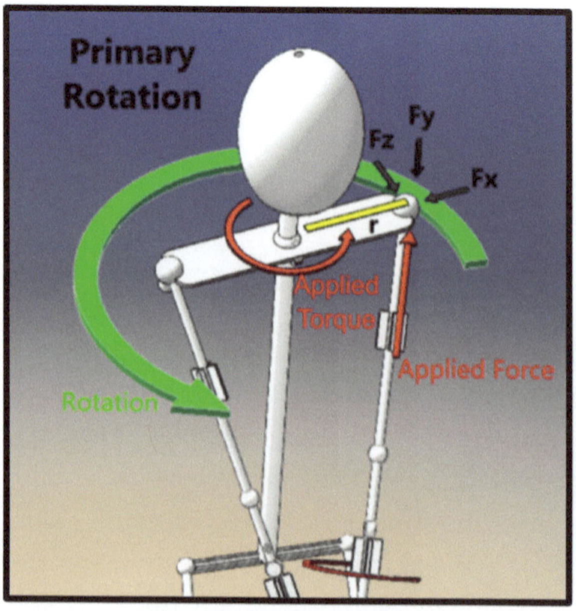

Figure 47: Primary Rotation Torque

As we will see in Chapter 7, torque is a measure of the applied force that can cause an object to rotate around an axis.

In the case of primary rotation, the axis runs through the upper body (the torso). The applied force moves the shoulders, which are connected to the golf club by the arms and hands.

The upper body is very strong and can provide a lot of power and control. However, to use this power, you need to learn to rotate your shoulders effectively.

There two ways to rotate the shoulders around the primary axis (the body):

1. Rotate the shoulders by twisting the legs (lower body).
2. Rotate the shoulders by turning the torso (upper body).

Rotating the shoulders by turning the torso (upper body) is the correct way to rotate the shoulders. This is key to developing the proper torque necessary to strike a golf ball consistently and powerfully.

Notice that the shoulders are rotated 90 degrees in both figures below. The first figure illustrates shoulder rotation by twisting the lower legs (lower body). The second figure illustrates shoulder rotation using the upper body and keeping the lower body still, or quiet.

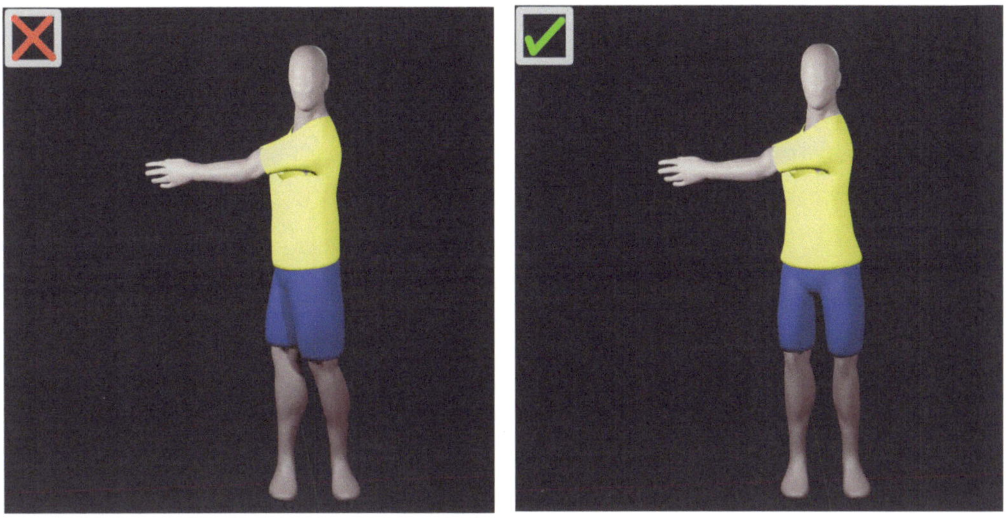

Figure 48: Shoulder Turn

It's important to keep your head still and facing forward as you rotate your shoulders. If you're standing when you do this exercise, keep your feet close together and still during the shoulder rotation.

It's difficult to keep your legs and hips still during the shoulder/chest rotation. As you turn your chest and shoulders, your hips and legs will tend to twist along with the shoulders. The trick is to keep the legs from twisting more than one degree for every three degrees of shoulder turn; for example, on the backswing, the hips' rotation should be about 30 percent of the shoulder rotation.

The best way to demonstrate this is to repeat the shoulder-turn exercise (Exercise 4a) above while sitting down. This works best with a bar stool, but a kitchen chair will do. You'll find that by sitting on the stool, the hips and legs are restricted from turning as the shoulders rotate (while keeping the head facing forward).

Repeat this exercise several times while sitting and then stand up and do the exercise. Be sure to keep your hips and legs from twisting. Remember the movement that occurred while seated. You should repeat this exercise often, both seated and standing.

Though relatively simple, this exercise is important for several reasons:

- There's no arm swinging involved in this exercise. It's all about shoulder rotation.
- This exercise is a constant reminder to the brain that the shoulders are more important than the arms.
- It's a reminder that the head should remain still, steady, and looking forward.
- It reinforces the straight leading arm on the backswing and the straight right arm on the follow-through. We'll deal with bent elbows in the next chapter.
- It is the foundation for the primary rotation. The V shape of the arms will eventually lead to the Y shape of the swing, as we shall see below.

Every practice session should start with this exercise and can even be part of a golf match warm-up routine. Thus far, we've introduced the concept of primary rotation and provided several exercises to demonstrate the movement. Your brain is getting to know your shoulders.

The artist uses a brush; the golfer uses a club!

—Anonymous

We talked about the V shape that results from extending your arms straight out in front of you with your hands flat and together. It's finally time to pick up a golf club.

Exercise 4b—Primary Rotation (V to V to V) with Club (Standing in the Vertical Position)

Why is this exercise important?

Demonstrates the primary axis of rotation
Trains the brain to use the shoulders and not the arms
Develops a sense of club rotation using the shoulders

1. Start with good posture. Stand straight with your feet shoulder-width apart and arms hanging comfortably by your sides. Grab the 8 iron in both hands and remember to hold it with a proper grip. Remember to keep a flat left wrist (FLW) while gripping the club.

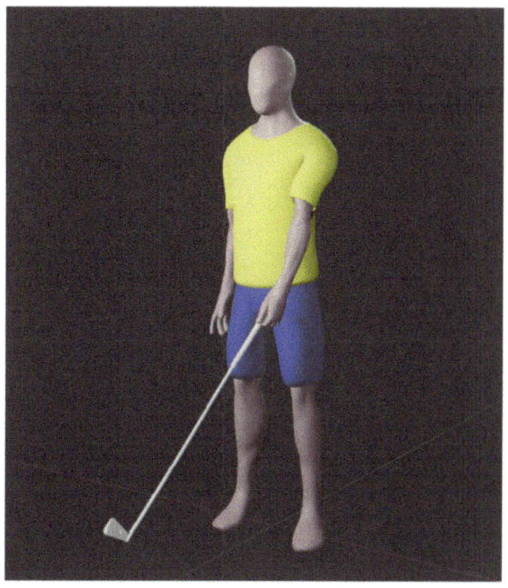

2. With your club in hand, extend your arms out in front of you so that the club is parallel to the ground, your arms forming the top of the Y and the club forming the tail.

   Keep your arms as **close together** as possible, and try to keep the inside of your elbows facing upward. Do not bend your elbows.

   Now, lower your arms until the upper arms are resting against the chest.

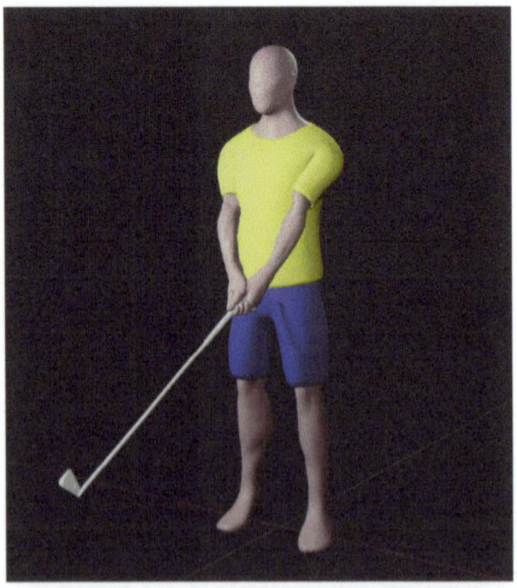

3. *Slowly* rotate the shoulders about 45 degrees clockwise while keeping your head facing forward. Do *not* allow your arms to take over. Make sure the movement is done with your shoulders only. Do not bend either elbow. Note that the clubface will remain vertical during the entire movement.

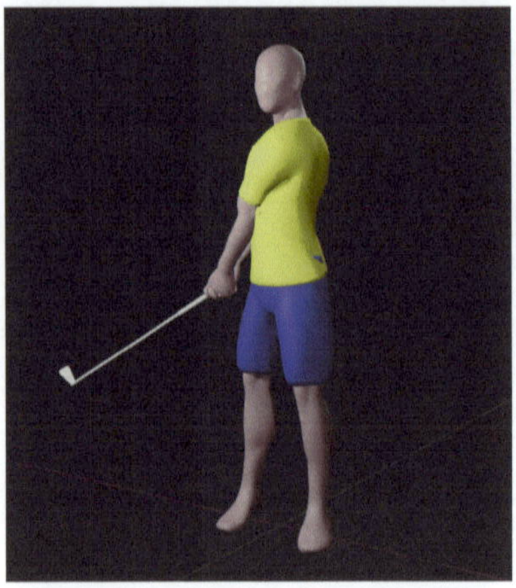

4. Return to the neutral position.

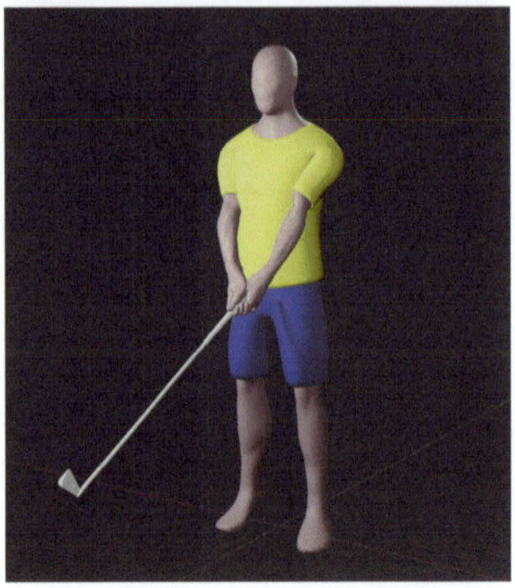

5. *Slowly* rotate the shoulders about 45 degrees counterclockwise while keeping your head facing forward. Do *not* allow your arms to take over. Make sure the movement is done with your shoulders only. Do not bend either elbow. Again, note that the clubface remains vertical.

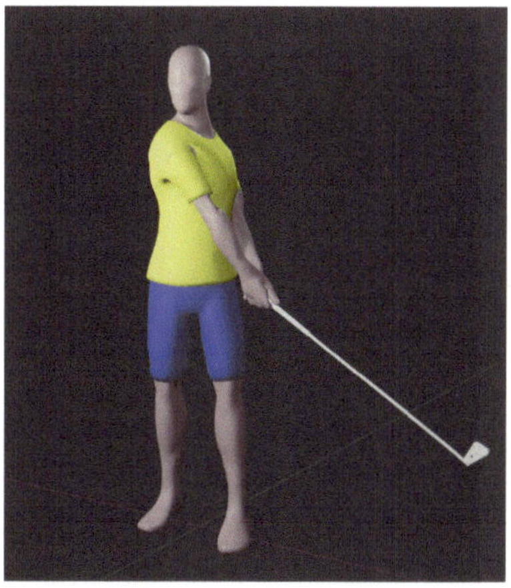

6. Slowly return to the neutral position. Repeat this exercise and gradually work your way up to 90-degree rotation of the shoulders or to the highest degree possible.

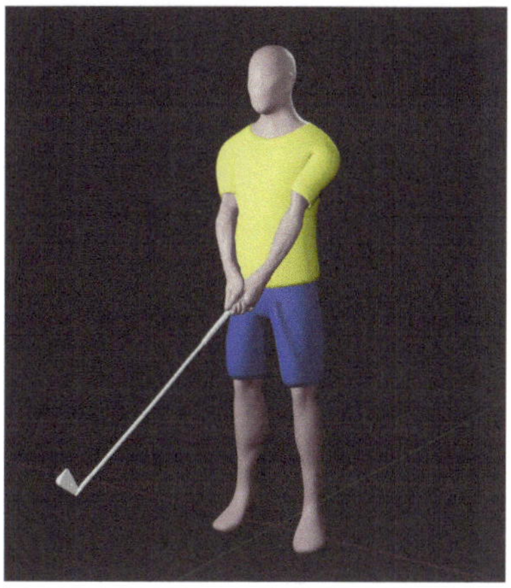

Continue to repeat the exercise and try to feel the shoulder rotation of the club around the body. It may help to do the exercise with your eyes closed, which removes the visual stimulus and lets the mind concentrate on the motions involved.

Repetition of this exercise will train the brain to ignore your arms and to communicate with your shoulders. It's also helpful in stretching and strengthening the shoulder and torso muscles that are critical when executing the swing. You're also now starting to develop a sense of gravity and the weight of the club itself.

With this exercise, you're only rotating 90 degrees in either direction. If you could rotate the full 360 degrees, the clubhead would trace a 360-degree circle. Note that as the club is rotated around the body, the clubface remains perpendicular to the club path, forming the circle on the base plane.

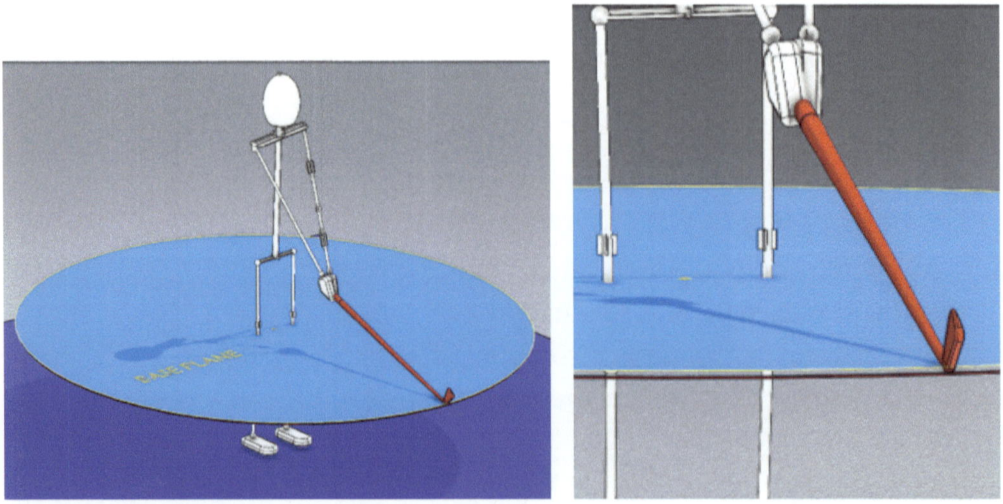

Figure 49: Club Path/Clubface Angle

Keep in mind that the clubface must be perpendicular to the ball at impact during the swing.

We'll continue to expand on this in our discussion of primary rotation, secondary rotation, and the full swing.

Primary Rotation Exercises in the Inclined World

In each exercise above, we were standing (or sitting) in an upright (vertical) position with the axis of rotation in the vertical position (i.e., perpendicular to the floor). We talked about extending our arms straight in front with our hands flat and together to form a V.

It's time to leave the vertical world. We're now ready to tilt the upper body (the axis of rotation) approximately 25 degrees from vertical.

A couple of points to keep in mind:

1. Make sure to bend at your hips and keep your back straight.
2. The geometry with respect to the midplane should be symmetrical (i.e., the left and right side of the body should be about the same).
3. The amount of spine tilt (especially for beginner golfers) should be minimal. Do not tilt the primary axis from side to side. Keep the primary axis on the midplane. It should be noted that there is some shoulder tilt with respect to the ground, which is necessary for a proper grip.

   Repeat Exercise 4b above but in the inclined (address) position. Start this exercise with a good grip and proper setup (see Chapter 3).

Exercise 4c—Primary Rotation (V to V) with Club and Proper Setup

Why is this exercise important?

Demonstrates the primary axis of rotation

Trains the brain to use the shoulder and not the arms

Develops a sense of club rotation on the club path on the base plane around the primary axis

Keeps the clubface perpendicular to the club path

1. Stand erect with good posture (back straight and shoulders square). Refer to Chapter 2 if you would like a refresher.

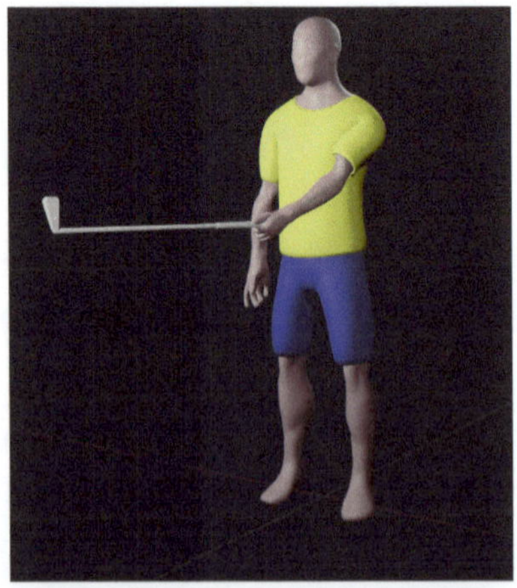

2. With your club in hand, extend your arms out in front of you so that the club is parallel to the ground, your arms forming the top of the Y and the club forming the tail. Keep your arms as close together as possible and try to keep the inside of your elbows facing upward. Do not bend your elbows. Now, lower your arms until the upper arms are against the chest.

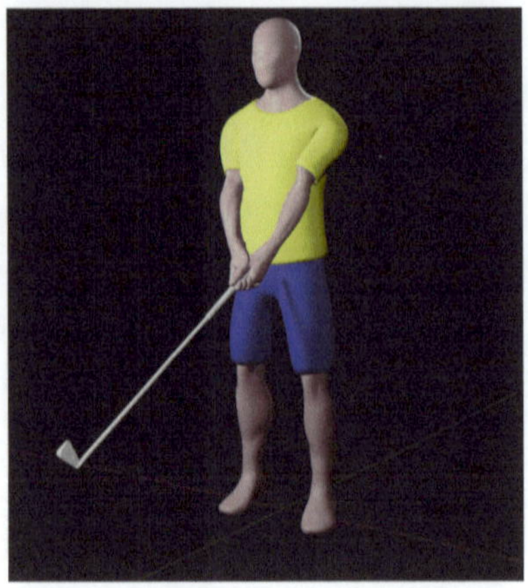

3. Tilt the shoulder plane by bending at the hips to about 25 degrees from the vertical into a good setup position with soft knees (not locked), good posture (shoulders square and back straight), and your hips tilted. As the shoulders go forward, the buttocks go back to maintain the center of gravity.

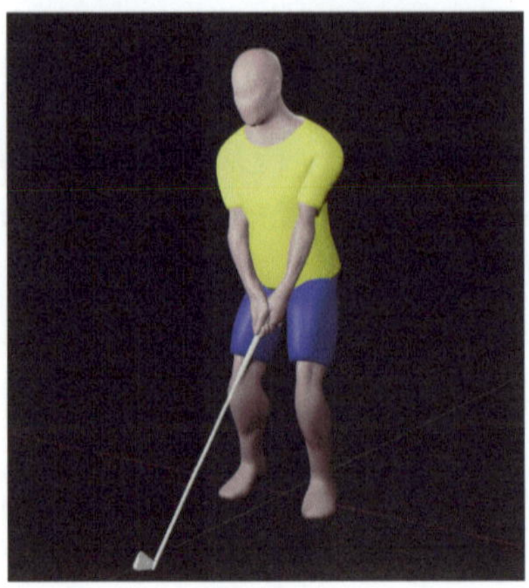

3. *Slowly* rotate the shoulders about 45 degrees clockwise while keeping your head facing forward. Do *not* allow the arms to take over. Make sure the movement is done with your shoulders only, and do not bend your elbows.

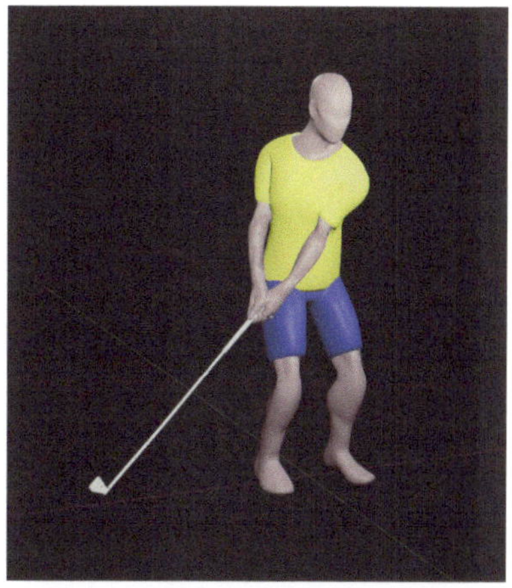

4. Return to the neutral position, brush the ground, and continue through to the left.

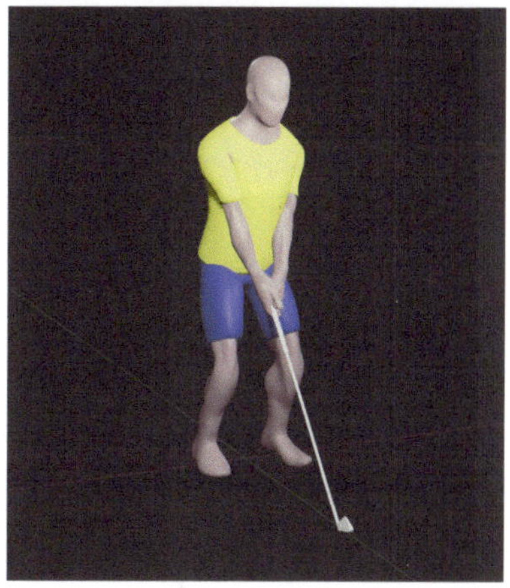

5. Continue rotating your shoulders for about 45 degrees counterclockwise while keeping your head facing forward. Do not allow the arms to take over. Make sure that the movement is done with your shoulders only.

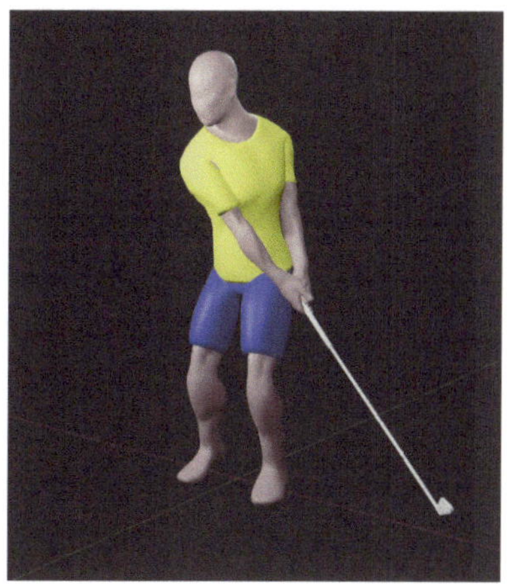

6. Slowly return to the neutral position. Repeat this exercise and gradually work your way up to 90-degree rotation of the shoulders or to the maximum you can do.

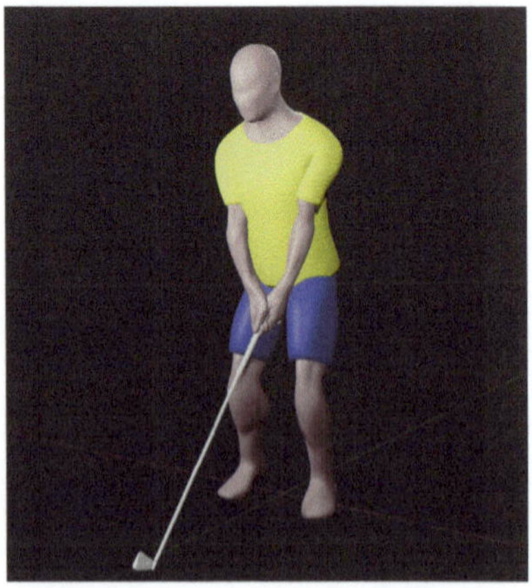

A couple of points worth noting:

1. The exercises so far have been started with shoulder rotation 45 degrees clockwise and 45 degrees counterclockwise for a total of 90 degrees of motion. Most golfers should be able to achieve this level of shoulder rotation without too much effort.
2. Low handicap golfers will rotate their shoulder a full 90 degrees (or more) clockwise and 90 degrees counterclockwise (or more) for an overall shoulder rotation of 180 degrees (or more).
3. Continue to repeat these exercises while gradually increasing your shoulder rotation. Remember to keep your arms straight. The closer to a full 180 degrees, the better, but this may take some time and development if you've not done this in the past.

Though there are plenty of additional exercises to follow in Chapters 9, 10, 11, and 12, all of which will be important, this is probably one of the most important exercises in terms of developing a solid swing.

Do this exercise often and master it. You can vary the amount of backswing from a 45-degree backswing all the way up to a full 90-degree backswing (if you're physically able). Concentrate on keeping your leading arm straight (left arm for RH golfers).

Practice does not make perfect. Only perfect practice makes perfect.

—Vince Lombardi

And so we started this chapter without any equipment and then added a club. It's now time to add a golf ball. With a low iron, repeat Exercise 4c using a golf ball.

Remember, the goal of this exercise is *not* to hit the ball far. This exercise using a ball is all about control and learning to use your shoulders.

A couple of important notes about the V-to-V-to-V exercise when using a ball:

- Do *not* go for distance but rather control. Better to hit the ball straight than far.
- Maintain good posture with a straight back (primary axis). Keep your head looking forward and your eyes on the ball.
- Make sure you're rotating your shoulders throughout the exercise and not allowing your arms to take over. Remember: shoulders, shoulders, shoulders.
- The clubface should remain on the base plane for the entire swing.
- The clubface will not open or close but will remain perpendicular to the base plane for the entire swing.
- Clubhead speed is not particularly fast for this type of swing. Therefore, you won't have much in the way of dynamic forces. This is covered much more in Chapter 7. This chapter is about motion rather than physics (i.e., about the kinematics of the swing).

Your shoulders are important for two reasons: power and control. Notice I *didn't* say speed and control. As you'll see in Chapter 5, speed is more about timing. Control is more important at this point.

Clubface and Club Path During Primary Rotation

It's worth taking some time to think about the path the clubface follows when the club is rotated around the primary axis.

Primary rotation (with no secondary rotation) causes the clubface to move in a semicircle around the upper body. The rotation of the shoulders is about 90 degrees clockwise during the backswing and 90 degrees counterclockwise after impact during the follow-through.

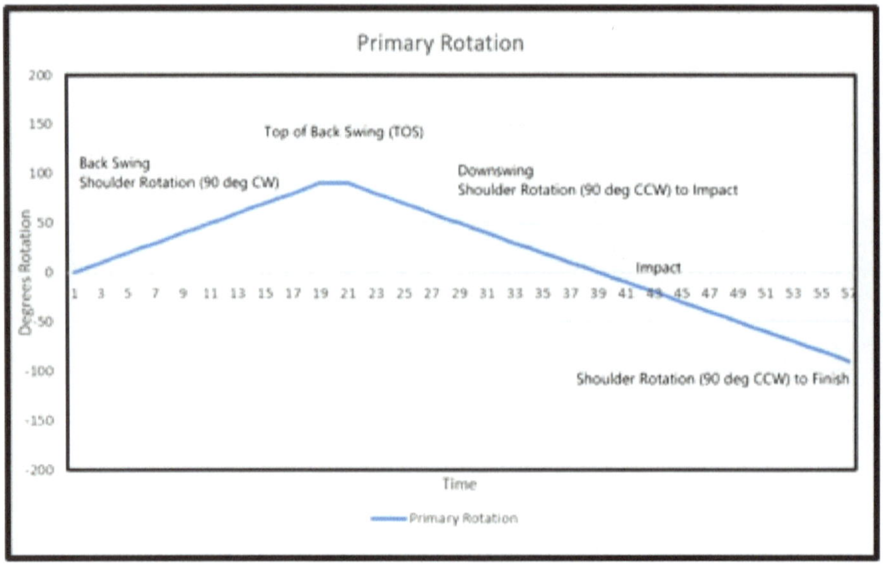

Figure 50: Primary Rotation Graph

When you do this motion with a golf club in your hand, the rotation of the shoulders (primary rotation) causes the clubhead to form a semicircle around the primary axis of rotation (the torso). During a full swing, the rotation of the shoulders is about 90 degrees clockwise during the backswing and 90 degrees counterclockwise after impact during the follow-through.

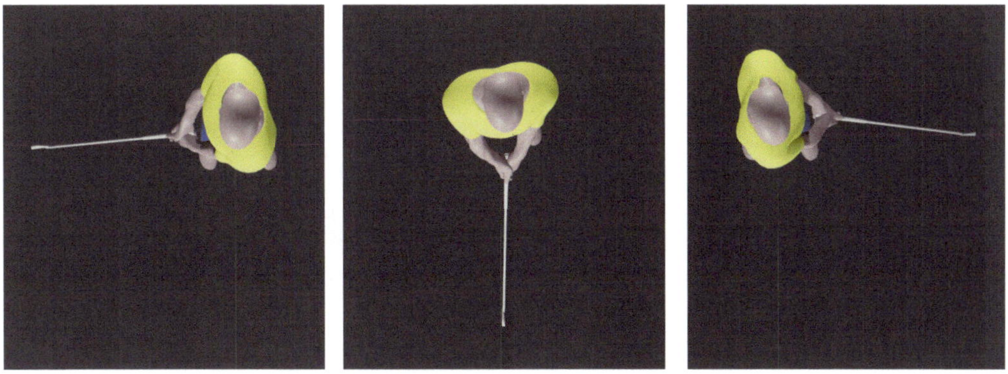

Figure 51: Primary Rotation Club Path

When using only primary rotation of the shoulders, the clubface remains perpendicular to the path during the entire rotation. This is the foundation for putting and chipping, both of which do not require much in the way of clubhead speed but do require good control.

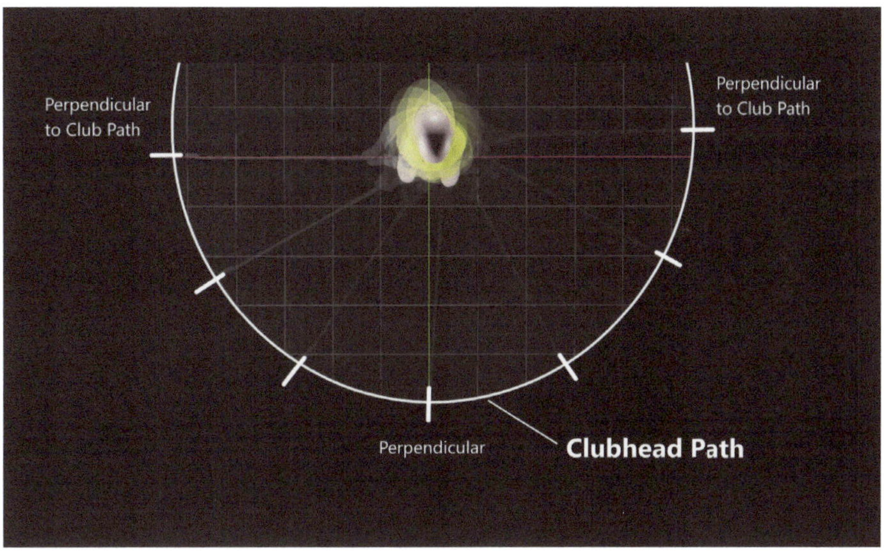

Figure 52: Primary Rotation Clubface Orientation

This chapter focused on primary rotation, which, when done properly, accounts for 180 degrees of motion. It's basically two motions: a 90-degree shoulder-turn clockwise (from neutral) for the backswing and a 90-degree shoulder-turn counterclockwise (from neutral) for the downswing and the follow-through.

The exercises in this chapter focused on learning and understanding primary rotation. To effectively develop this motion requires both understanding and repetition. Chapter 9 provides a series of step-by-step exercises to help with developing primary rotation, which is critical to a good golf swing.

Now with a good understanding of primary rotation and its importance to the swing, we can move on to an explanation of secondary rotation in the next chapter.

Takeaways:

So what did we learn in Chapter 4?

1. You do not swing a club with your arms—you rotate the club with your shoulders and upper body.
2. Primary rotation is the rotation of the shoulders and upper body around the centerline of the body (primary axis). Primary rotation provides power and control.
3. Primary rotation consists of two motions: a 90-degree shoulder-turn clockwise (from neutral) for the backswing and a 90-degree shoulder-turn counterclockwise (from neutral) for the downswing and the follow-through.
4. Rotation of the shoulders (primary rotation) causes the clubhead to form a semicircle around the primary axis of rotation (the torso) on the base plane. When using only primary rotation, the clubface remains perpendicular to the path during the entire rotation.

CHAPTER 5

Secondary Rotation

In Chapter 2, we discussed the importance of good grip and posture, and in the last chapter, we covered primary rotation. Let's move on to the important topic of secondary rotation. Though a critical part of the swing, secondary rotation is often misunderstood and may be the best-kept secret in golf.

Revelation #5

Secondary rotation provides speed and therefore distance.

As you know, primary rotation provides the power and control in the golf swing. Secondary rotation provides the speed. So what is secondary rotation?

Alice thought she had never seen such a curious croquet-ground in her life…the balls were live hedgehogs, [and] the mallets live flamingoes… The chief difficulty Alice found at first was in managing her flamingo: she succeeded in getting its body tucked away, comfortably enough, under her arm, with its legs hanging down, but generally, just as she had got its neck nicely straightened out, and was going to give the hedgehog a blow with its head, it would twist itself round and look up in her face, with such a puzzled expression that she could not help bursting out laughing.

—Lewis Carroll, Alice in Wonderland

Secondary Rotation

As the club rotates around the body on the backswing, the straight leading arm simultaneously rotates the club in a motion we'll refer to as the secondary rotation. This is essentially a rotation within a rotation. Specifically, it is the rotation of the straight leading arm (left arm for RH golfers) during the backswing.

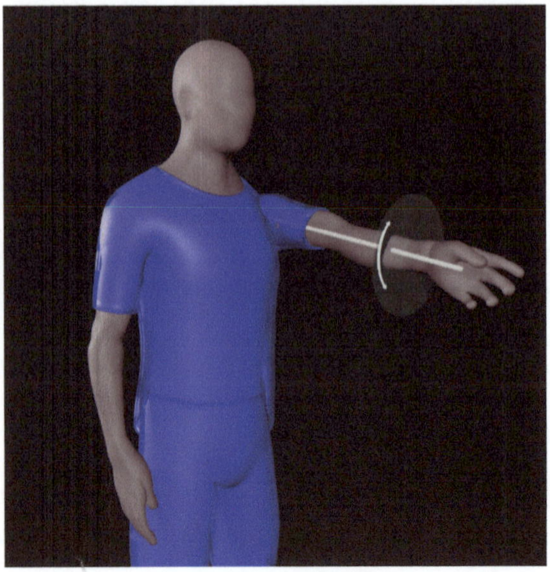

Figure 53: Secondary Rotation

Revelation #6

Secondary rotation is the rotation of the straight leading arm and club around an axis that runs through the leading arm (left arm for RH golfers). Secondary rotation results in a club path whereby the clubface is always perpendicular to the secondary path, which is at the base of the cone resulting from this rotation.

A common misconception in golf is that you rotate the wrist. How many times have you heard the phrase "use more wrist" during golf instruction? The truth is that the wrist joint is an ellipsoidal joint and does not rotate. Ellipsoidal joints enable multidirectional movements but not rotational motion.

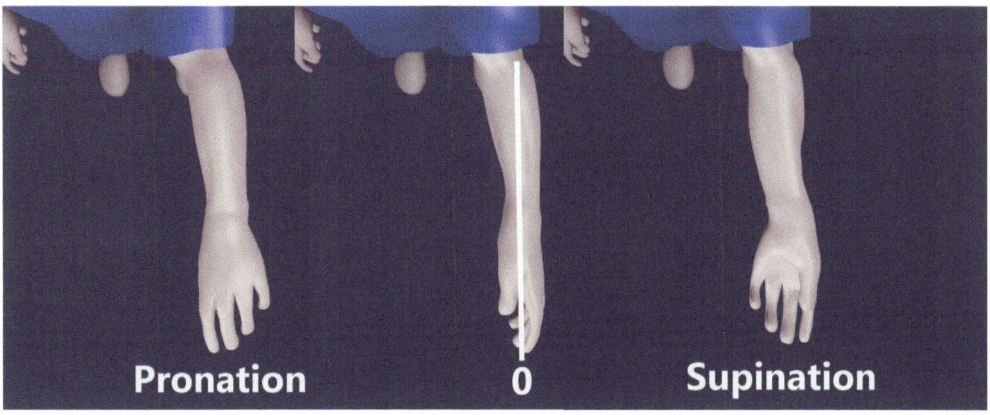

Figure 54: Arm/Wrist Rotation

The wrist can provide extension, flexion, abduction, adduction, and circumduction movement. The term "use more wrist" emphasizes the wrist joint, and many beginner golfers mistakenly believe that they must manipulate their leading wrist during the golf swing to effectively strike the ball. Quite to the contrary, the leading wrist (left wrist for RH golfers) must remain relatively flat (no extension or flexion) during the swing to maintain the proper geometry.

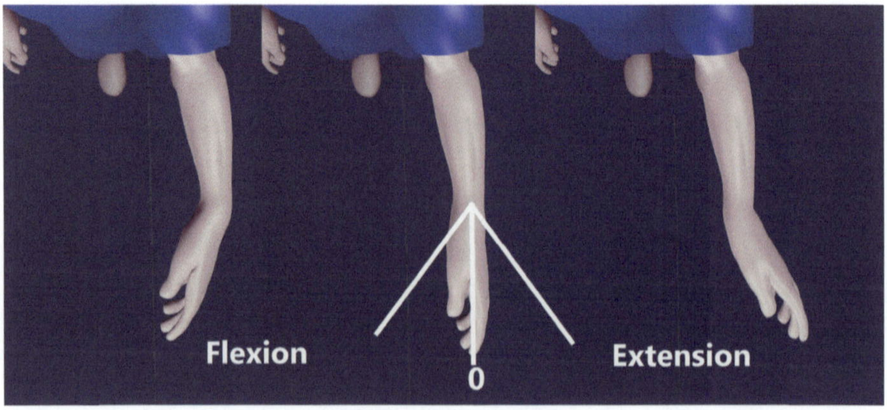

Figure 55: Wrist Hinge

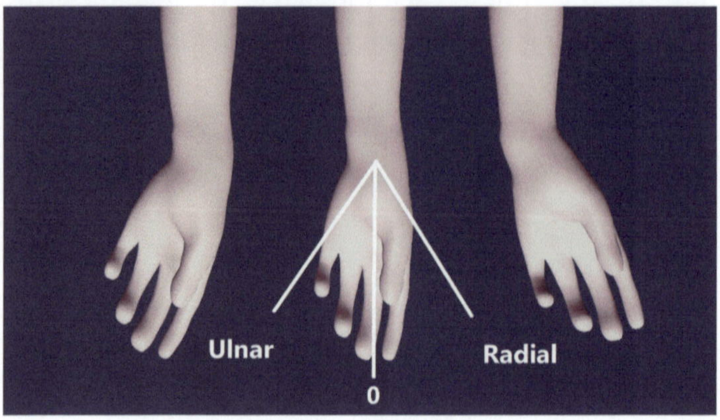

Figure 56: Wrist Cock

The shoulder is a ball-and-socket joint that enables multidirectional rotational motion and movements like backward, forward, and sideways. The only way to rotate the wrists is to rotate the arm. Rotating the straight leading arm (left arm for RH golfers) also rotates the wrist, which is connected to the hand that is holding the golf club.

Secondary Axis of Rotation

Training the *straight* leading arm to rotate around the secondary axis is key to developing speed and distance. The secondary axis of rotation is a line through your straight leading arm on the backswing (RH golfers) and the rotation of the straight right arm on the follow-through (for RH golfers).

During the backswing, you rotate the leading arm clockwise so the palm is facing down, which is referred to as pronation, and on the follow-through, rotating counterclockwise 90 degrees from neutral so the palm faces up is referred to as supination. This rotation is just a little bit tougher to explain and is often misunderstood and poorly explained (or not explained).

We're going to start the explanation with an exercise.

Exercise 5a—Secondary Rotation: The Straight Left Arm (SLA)

Why is this exercise important?

Demonstrates the secondary axis of rotation for the straight left arm

1. Stand facing a wall about arm's length distance away with good posture (back straight and shoulders square).

2. Extend your left arm straight out in front of you to shoulder height. Close your left hand as if you were gripping the golf club. Point to the wall with the tip of your left thumb. It's imperative that you have a flat left wrist. It should be facing to the left.

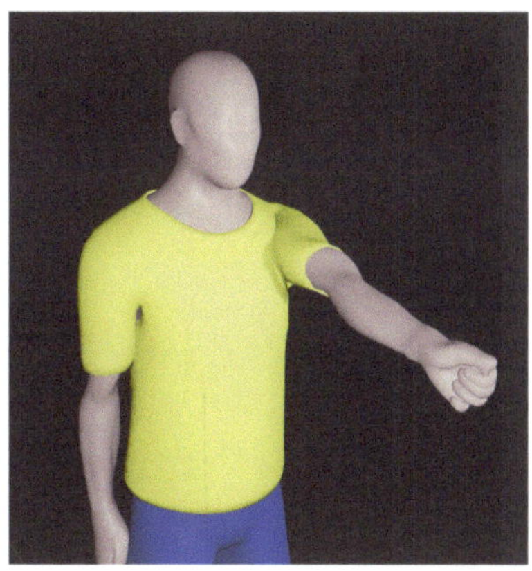

3. While touching the wall lightly with your left thumb, *slowly* rotate the arm about 90 degrees clockwise (as if you were locking a door with a key). Don't allow the wrist to hinge or cock. Make sure you keep a flat left wrist. This movement should finish with the left hand in the pronate position, your palm facing the ground and your flat left wrist facing up.

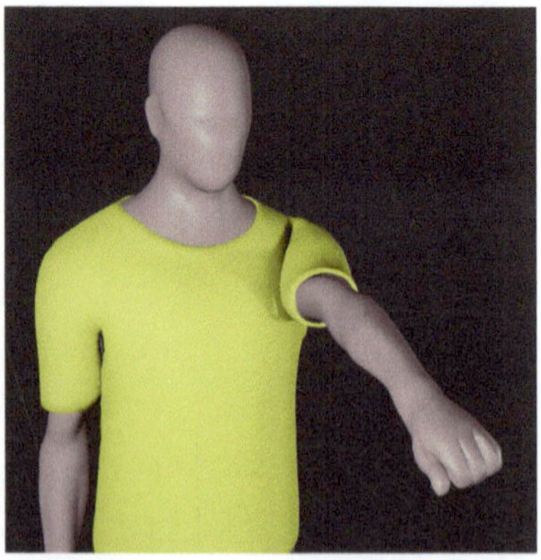

4. Slowly return counterclockwise to the neutral position (flat left wrist facing left).

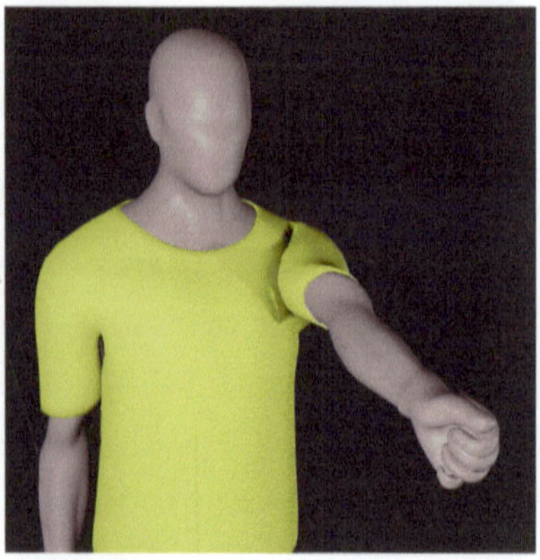

5. Continue touching the wall lightly with your left thumb and *slowly* rotate the arm about 90 degrees counterclockwise (as if you were unlocking a door with a key). Don't allow the wrist to hinge or cock. Make sure that you keep a flat left wrist. The movement should finish with the left hand in the supinate position, your palm facing straight up to the sky and your flat left wrist facing the ground.

6. Slowly return to the neutral position.

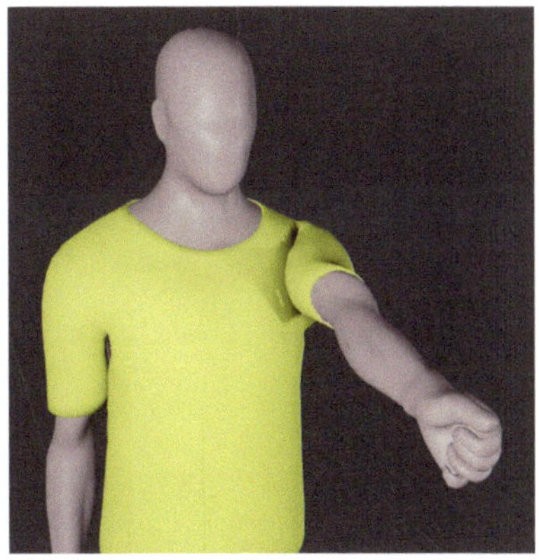

Congratulations! You have just completed one of the most important rotations in golf, second only to the primary rotation—the secondary rotation. As you read further, you'll see why it's so important.

We're going to repeat the exercise with a club, but before we do, let's take a second to reflect on some geometry.

The Importance of Geometry

A cone is a three-dimensional geometric shape that tapers smoothly from a flat base (frequently circular, though not necessarily) to a point called the apex or vertex.

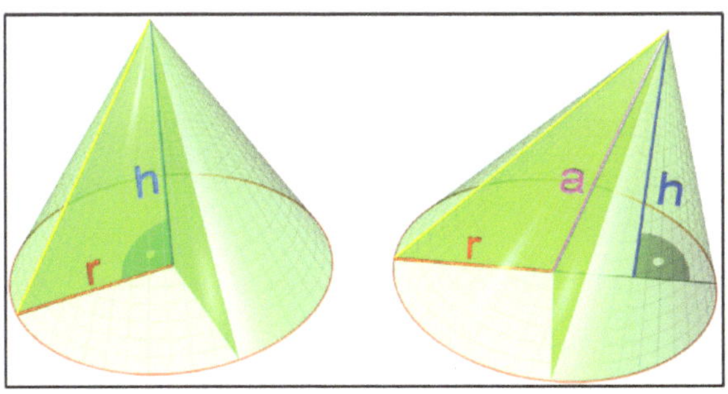

Figure 57: The Cone

In common usage in elementary geometry, cones are assumed to be right circular, where "circular" means that the base is a circle and "right" means that the axis passes through the center of the base at right angles to its plane.

You may have never realized that rotation of the straight left arm (secondary rotation) causes the club to form a cone. **As you rotate your leading arm, the clubhead follows a path that is a semicircle and forms the base of a cone.**

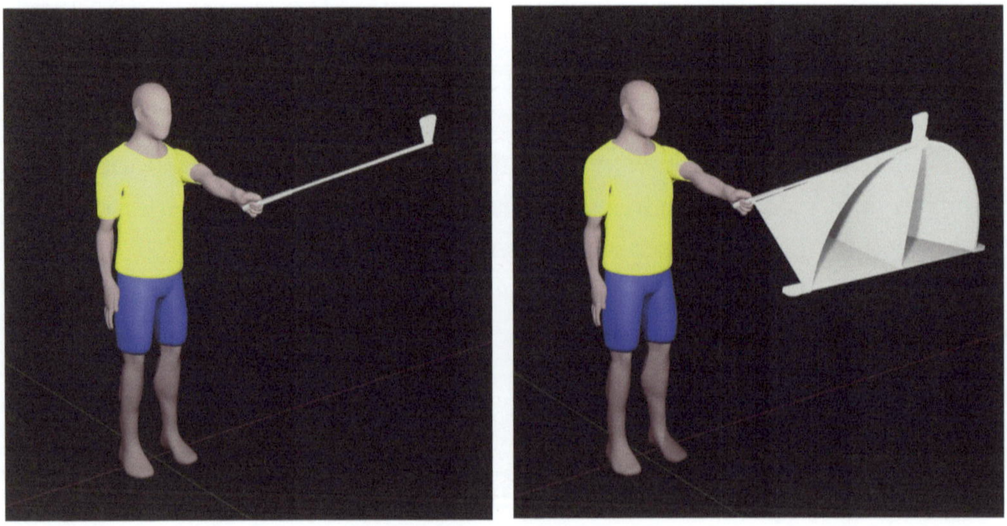

Figure 58: Secondary Rotation of Club

During a full swing, the rotation of the left arm is only about 90 degrees during the backswing and 90 degrees after impact during the follow-through.

We will hereafter refer to rotation of the leading arm during the backswing as clockwise with the backswing and counterclockwise with the downswing and follow-through when viewed from the golfer's perspective. This is illustrated below.

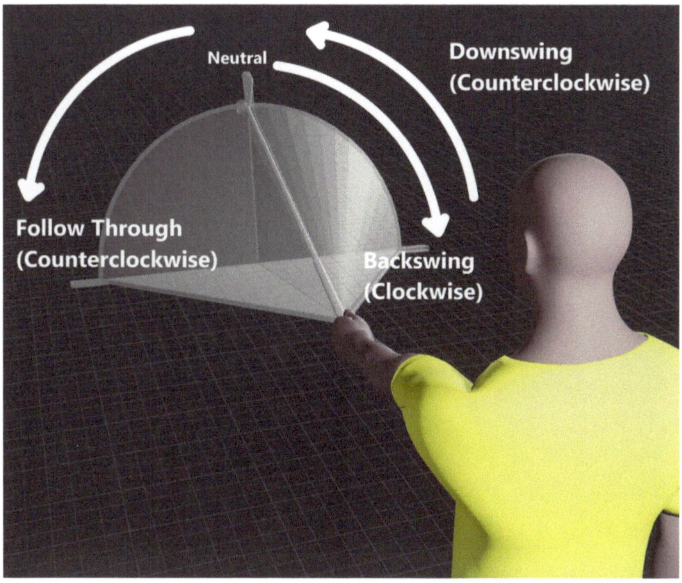

Figure 59: Secondary Rotation Convention

Now that you understand the motion necessary to execute the secondary rotation, let's look at some more of the geometry of that motion. If you repeat the motion in the exercise below with a club and a flat left wrist, you'll find that the rotation of the arm causes the club to trace out a cone.

Exercise 5b—Secondary Rotation: The Straight Left Arm (SLA) with a Club

Why is this exercise important?

Demonstrates the secondary axis of rotation

Demonstrates the path that the clubhead traces as the club rotates from neutral to 90 degrees clockwise and from neutral to 90 degrees counterclockwise

1. Stand in a relaxed vertical position with good posture and your feet slightly apart.

2. Grab a short iron and extend your left arm straight out in front of you just below shoulder level. You must keep a flat left wrist, which should be facing to the left. The clubface should be vertical.

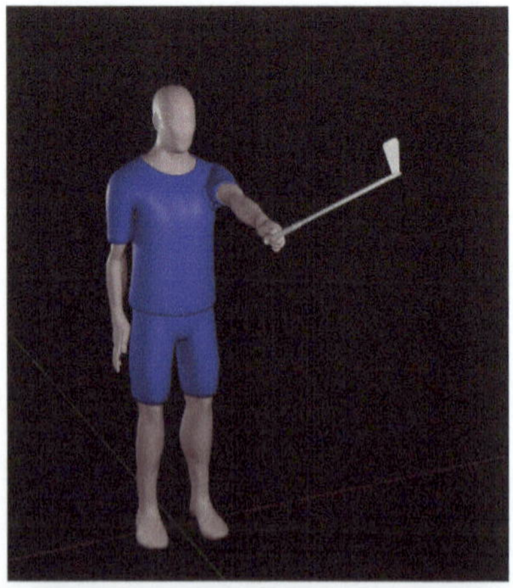

3. *Slowly* rotate the arm about 90 degrees clockwise. Don't allow the wrist to hinge or cock. Make sure you keep a flat left wrist. The movement should finish with the left hand in the pronate position with the flat left wrist facing the sky.

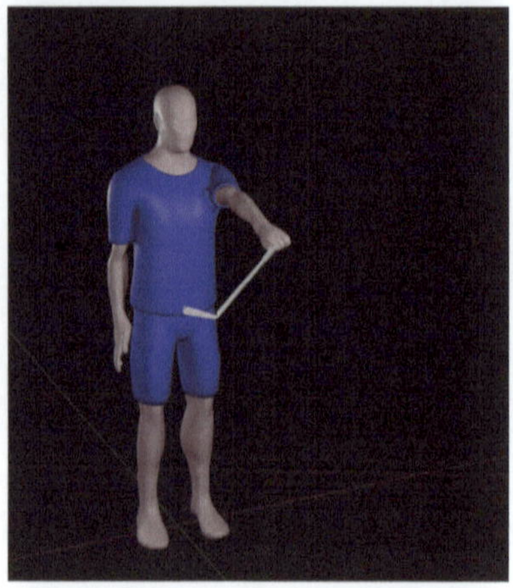

4. *Slowly* return counterclockwise to the neutral position with the flat left wrist facing left.

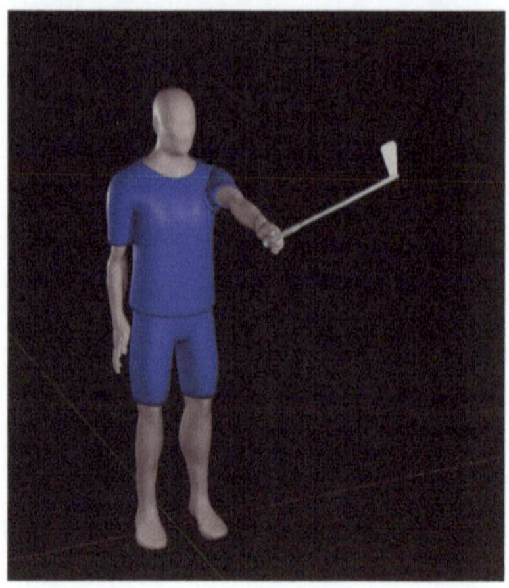

5. *Slowly* rotate the arm about 90 degrees counterclockwise. Don't allow the wrist to hinge or cock. Make sure that you keep a flat left wrist. The movement should finish with the left hand in the supinate position with the flat left wrist facing the ground.

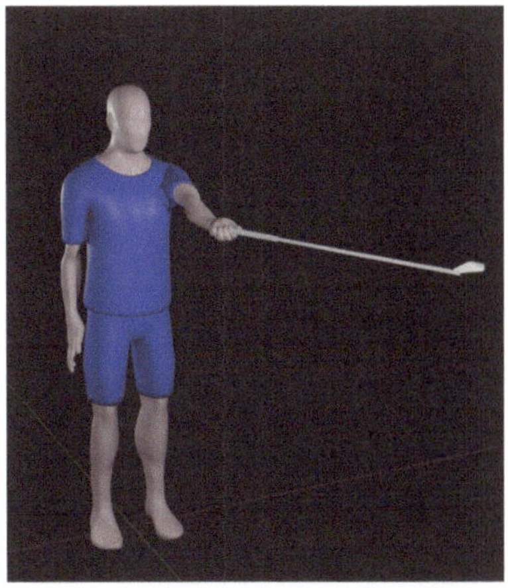

6. *Slowly* return to the neutral position. This exercise should be done slowly so you can observe the clubhead path and orientation during the movement.

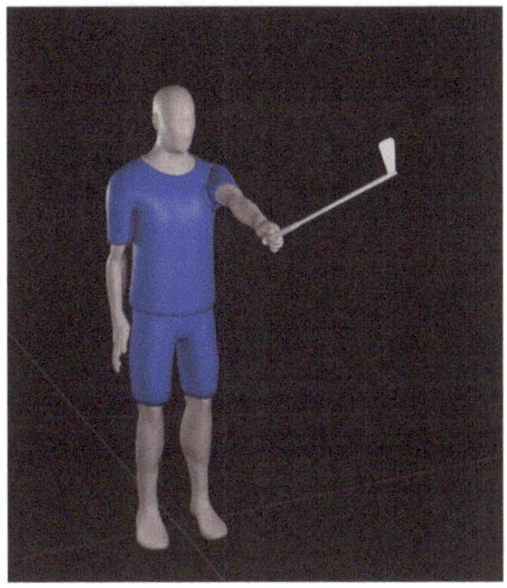

Congratulations! You've just completed the secondary rotation with a club. It's important to keep the wrist flat during the entire exercise. The wrist should be hyperextended and in the ulnar position.

Wrist cock in the radial position helps absorb energy at the top of the backswing and can be used to add some extra club speed during the downswing. However, beginner golfers should avoid concentrating on wrist cock, which can mess up the geometry of the golf swing if done improperly.

By increasing or decreasing the wrist cock, you can increase or decrease the radius (r) of the cone.

Keeping the wrist toward the ulnar deviation position provides the smallest cone radius and the most wrist stability. Put another way, you want to hyperextend the wrist so you feel like you're pointing with your thumb.

For the purposes of the exercises in this chapter, use a flat left wrist (no extension or flexion) and keep the wrist hyperextended with ulnar deviation.

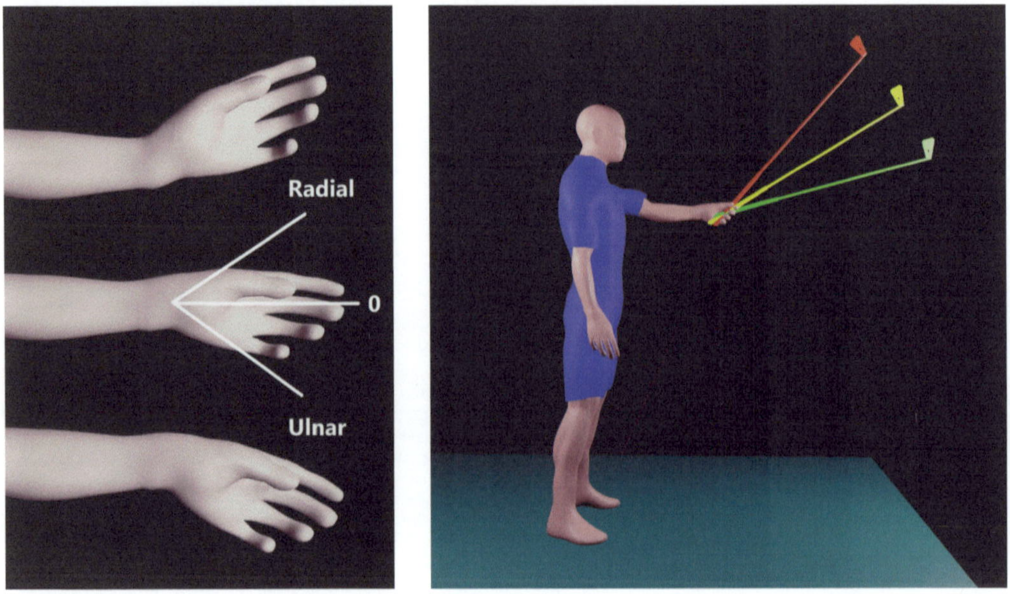

Figure 60: Wrist Position

The leading arm can develop a limited amount of torque. When you turn a doorknob, turn a key in a lock, throw a Frisbee, or rotate a golf club, you use your arm to develop a force called torque. Notice that when you do these activities, you rotate your arm (which rotates the wrist and hand) to turn the doorknob or throw a Frisbee.

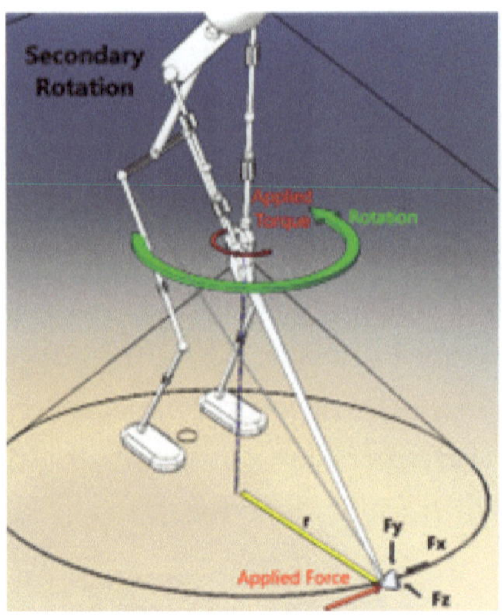

Figure 61: Secondary Rotation Torque

Torque is a measure of the force that can cause an object to rotate about an axis. As you will see in Chapter 7, this is an *applied* force.

In the case of secondary rotation, the axis runs through the straight leading arm. The applied torque rotates the golf club around the secondary axis, which runs through the straight left arm.

The left arm develops a limited amount of torque but can move very fast. *Because this motion can be done so quickly, secondary rotation provides speed and therefore distance, as we will see.*

Now repeat the above exercise in the address position (i.e., in the inclined world).

Exercise 5c—Secondary Rotation: The Straight Left Arm (SLA) with a Club in the Address Position

Why is this exercise important?

Demonstrates the secondary axis of rotation in the inclined position
Demonstrates the path that the clubhead traces as the club travels from neutral to 90 degrees clockwise and from neutral to 90 degrees counterclockwise
Demonstrates the effect of gravity on the motion

1. Stand in a relaxed vertical position with good posture and your feet slightly apart.

2. Grab a short iron and extend your left arm straight out in front of you just below shoulder level. You must keep a flat left wrist, which should be facing to the left. The clubface should be vertical.

   Now tilt the upper body at the hips and flex the knees to get into the proper address position.

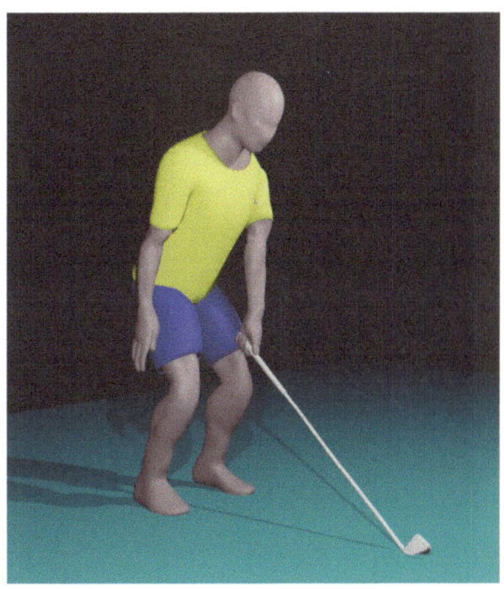

3. As you rotate your shoulders clockwise (primary rotation) about 20 degrees, rotate the straight left arm about 90 degrees clockwise. Don't allow the wrist to hinge or cock. Make sure you keep a flat left wrist.

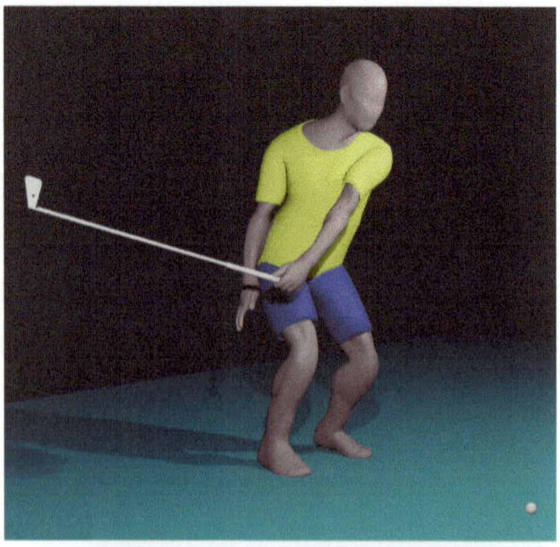

4. *Slowly* rotate your shoulders counterclockwise back to the neutral (address) position as you rotate the straight left arm counterclockwise to the neutral position with your flat left wrist facing left as you reach the address position.

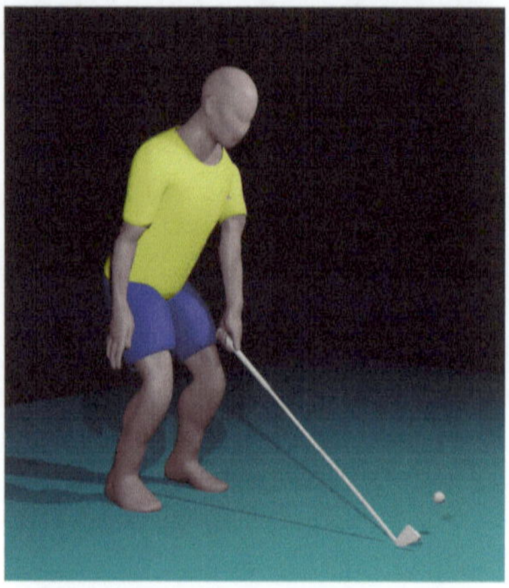

5. Continue to rotate your shoulders counterclockwise past neutral as you *slowly* rotate the left arm about 90 degrees counterclockwise. Don't allow the wrist to hinge or cock. Make sure that you keep a flat left wrist.

   Allow the momentum of the club to finish the swing as you rotate past the neutral position.

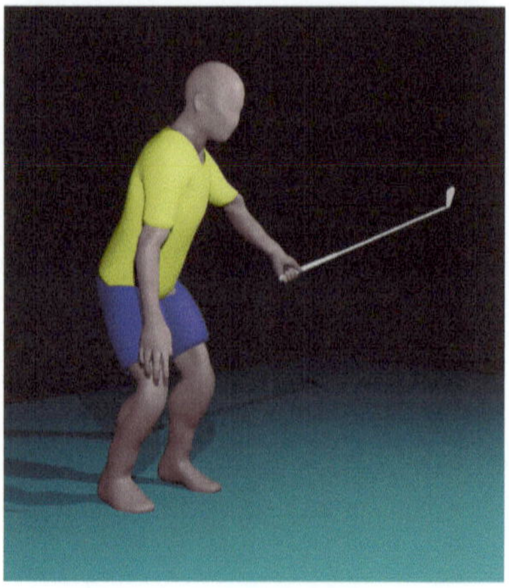

6. *Slowly* return to the neutral position.

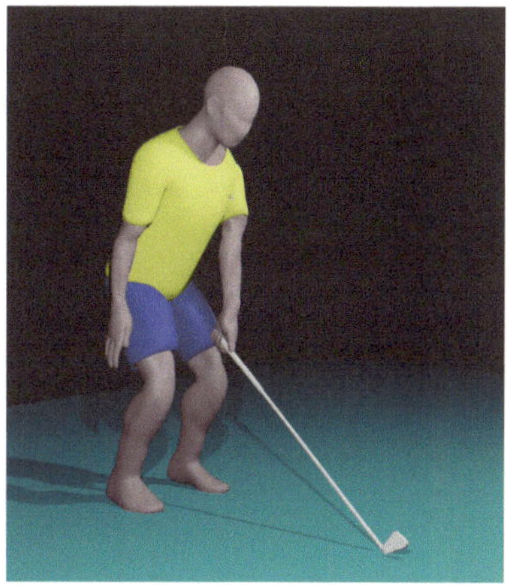

Clubface and Club Path

It's worth taking some time to think about the path that the clubface follows when the club is rotated around a straight left arm. Remember that secondary rotation of the straight left arm causes the club to form a cone. The rotation of the left arm is only about 90 degrees clockwise during the backswing and 90 degrees counterclockwise after impact during the follow-through.

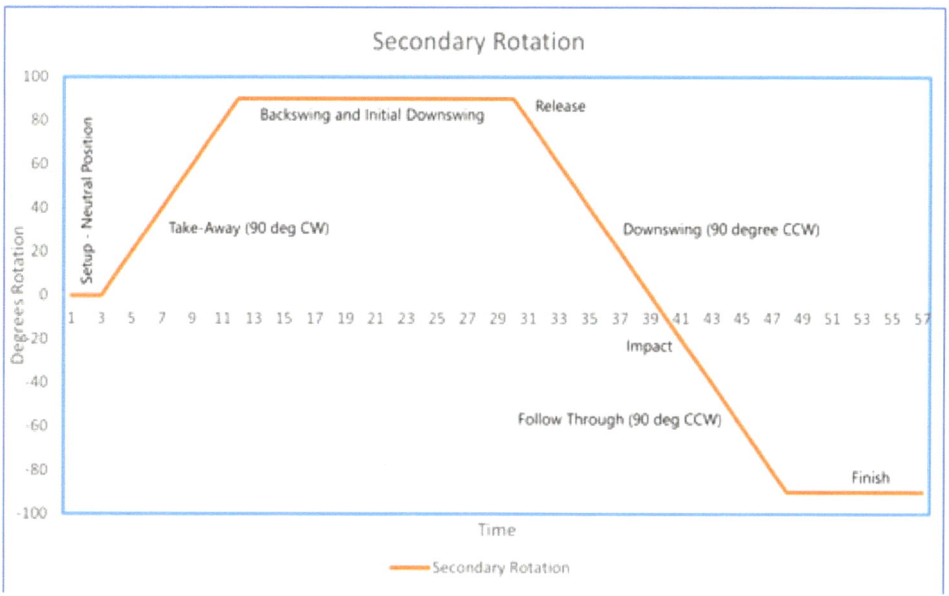

Figure 62: Secondary Rotation Graph

The red line in the graph represents secondary rotation of the straight leading arm. Secondary rotation starts at zero (address position) and, after the initial takeaway, rotates to 90 degrees clockwise during the first part of the backswing.

Secondary rotation is held at 90 degrees as the shoulders initiate the downswing and is held as long as possible until the release. At release, the straight leading arm rotates 90 degrees counterclockwise to impact then continues to rotate an additional 90 degrees counterclockwise to the finish of the swing.

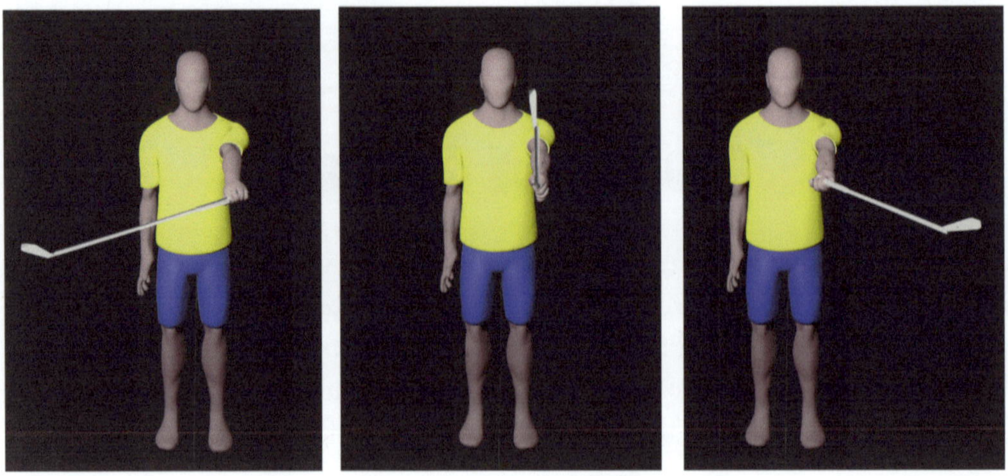

Figure 63: Secondary Rotation Club Path

The club path created by secondary rotation is a semicircular path formed at the base of the cone. The clubface remains perpendicular to this path during the secondary rotation (more about this and the relationship to the primary rotation in Chapter 6).

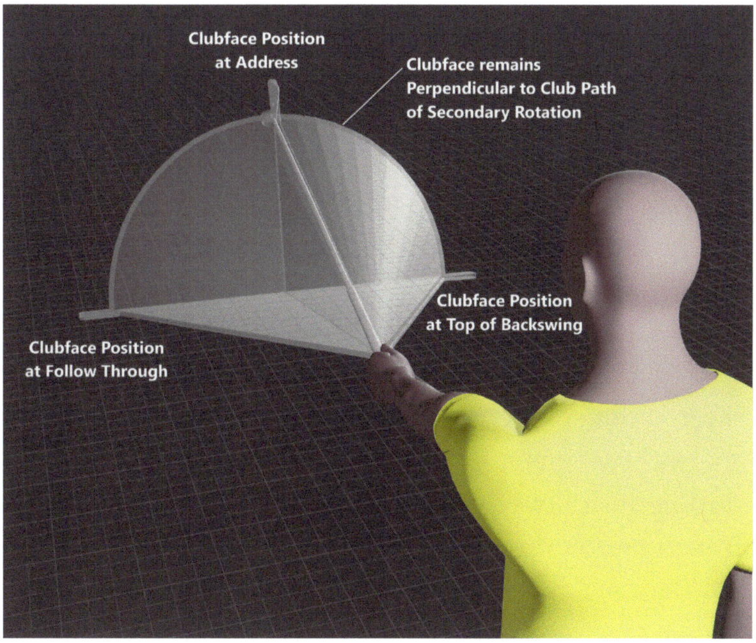

Figure 64: Secondary Rotation Clubface Orientation

So you now have a pretty good understanding of primary rotation, which provides power and control, and secondary rotation, which provides speed and therefore distance. Independently, these two motions are important but limited. Together, they form the basis for a powerful golf swing. Chapter 6 looks at tertiary motion, which is the motion used to synchronize primary and secondary rotation.

Takeaways:

So what did we learn in Chapter 5?

1. Secondary rotation is the rotation of the straight left arm during the backswing and the downswing. Secondary rotation provides speed and therefore distance.
2. Secondary rotation of the straight left arm causes the club to form a cone. The base of the cone is the swing path for this rotation. During a full swing, the rotation of the left arm is only about 90 degrees clockwise during the backswing and 90 degrees counterclockwise after release into impact during the follow-through.
3. The club path created by secondary rotation is a circular path formed at the base of the cone. The clubface remains perpendicular to this path.

CHAPTER 6

Tertiary Motion

In the first few chapters, we covered both primary rotation and secondary rotation. As you'll recall, primary rotation provides power and control in the golf swing while secondary rotation provides speed and therefore distance. These two motions acting independently are of limited use, but when we tie them together, the result is powerful.

When two forces unite, their efficiency double.

—Isaac Newton

Revelation #7

Tertiary Motion provides coordination between primary rotation and secondary rotation. This is done by shortening the distance between the wrists and the trailing shoulder, by bending the trailing elbow against the torso during the backswing.

Remember, if you rotate the club using only primary rotation, the clubhead will travel around the torso on the base plane, and the clubface will remain perpendicular to the club path the entire time. Notice that both arms remain straight

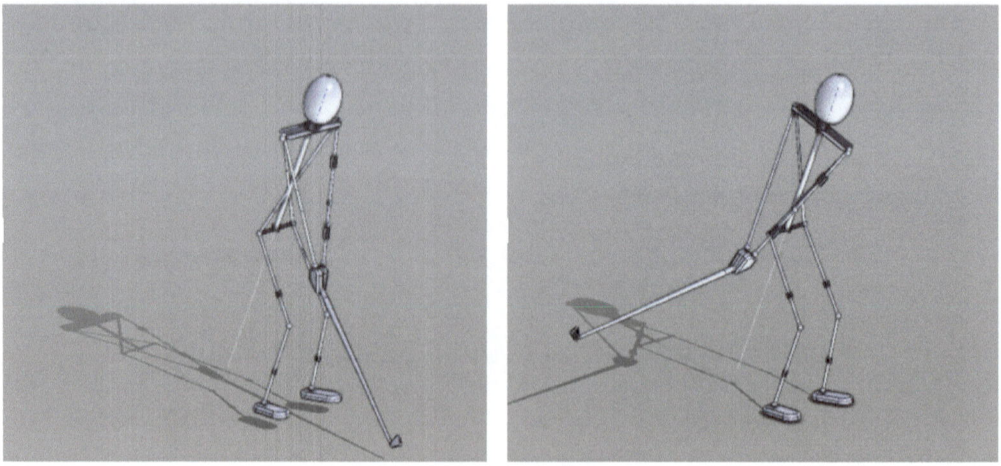

Figure 65: Primary Rotation

This motion makes it easy to control the club and hence the position of the clubface. However, there are some limitations—the torso is powerful but not particularly fast, and maximum travel is limited to about 90 degrees clockwise (backswing) and 90 degrees counterclockwise (follow-through) from the neutral position.

Secondary rotation refers to the rotation of the golf club around your straight left arm, which causes the club path to form a cone. The base of the cone traces a half circle, which is the path the clubhead follows as you rotate your left arm. The clubface remains perpendicular to the path during this motion.

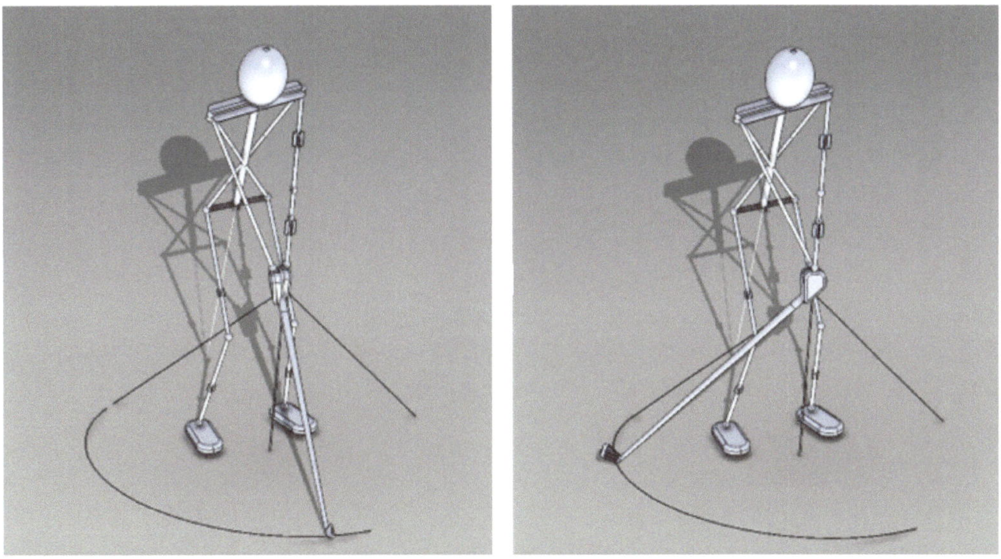

Figure 66: Secondary Rotation

However, when you do this motion with the left (leading) arm only, the club is free-floating in space and hard to control. The rotation of the left arm is about 90 degrees clockwise and 90 degrees counterclockwise from the neutral position.

The straight left arm can only generate a limited amount of torque (applied force), as you will see in Chapter 7, but you can generate a lot of speed with secondary rotation. But by itself, the straight left arm is very hard to control.

Tying It Together

We need a way to tie these two independent rotations together. To do this, we use the trailing arm, elbow, and wrist during the backswing in a motion that connects the primary and secondary rotation. This is referred to as tertiary motion.

Tertiary motion is essentially the third leg of the stool and provides the stability necessary for a good golf swing.

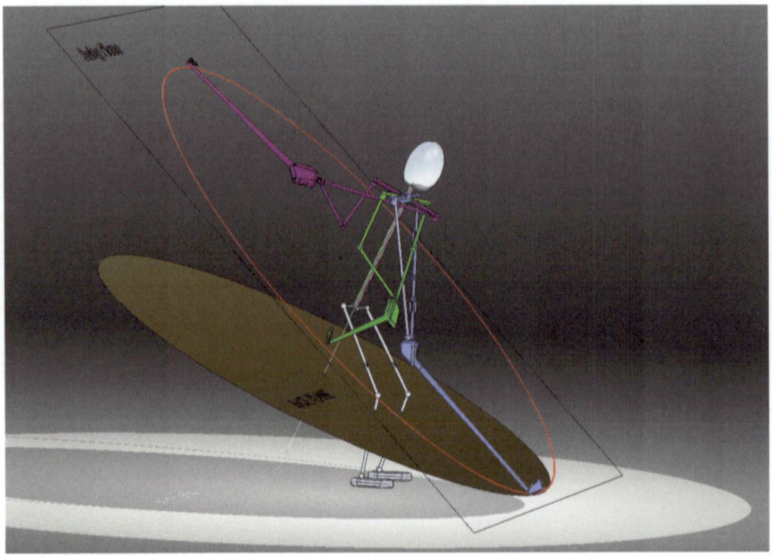

Figure 67: Combined Primary and Secondary Rotation

Revelation #8

Tertiary motion connects primary rotation and secondary rotation together into the coordinated motion necessary to lift the clubhead into the swing plane and rotate the clubface into the proper orientation on the club path.

The *lift* is accomplished by shortening the distance between the hands and the trailing shoulder (right shoulder for RH golfers).

The *rotation* of the leading arm is determined by the amount of the right wrist hinge (extension) to maintain a flat left wrist (FLW) on the leading arm (for RH golfers).

More About Tertiary Motion

Tertiary motion uses the right arm to guide your straight left arm across the chest during the backswing. This is done by shortening the distance between the wrists and the right shoulder by bending the right elbow against the torso during the backswing.

This bending of your right elbow causes your left arm to move across your chest while rotating the leading arm (secondary rotation) in a controlled manner. This movement also lifts the clubhead from the base plane and into the swing plane and orients the clubface onto the club path.

The use of the right arm, elbow, and wrist helps the backswing in three ways:

1. Stability: It's difficult to keep your left arm from wandering around in space without something to tie it down. That something is the right arm.
2. Positioning of the club and clubface: As you bend the right elbow against the right side, it shortens the distance between the right shoulder and the wrist, which lifts the club and clubface from the base plane to the swing plane.
3. Rotation of the secondary axis: As you bend your right arm and elbow against your right side, your right wrist hinges to maintain a flat left wrist on the straight left arm as it rotates around the secondary axis.

Before we continue, let's review some geometry.

There are two types of triangles that help explain this motion: the isosceles triangle and the scalene triangle.

The shortest distance between two points is a straight line.

—Archimedes (c. 287–c. 212 BC),
Greek mathematician, engineer, and inventor

Isosceles Triangle

In an isosceles triangle, the lengths of two of the three sides are equal. So the angles opposite the equal sides are equal. In other words, an isosceles triangle has two equal sides and two equal angles.

The shape of the arms and shoulders in the neutral position approximate an isosceles triangle.

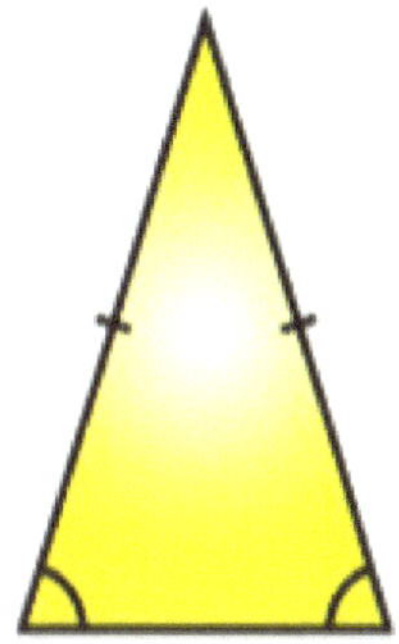

Figure 68: Isosceles Triangle

Scalene Triangle

A scalene triangle has all side lengths of different measures. No side will be equal in length to any of the other sides in such a triangle. In a scalene triangle, all the interior angles are also different. In this figure, you can see how none of the sides are equal in length.

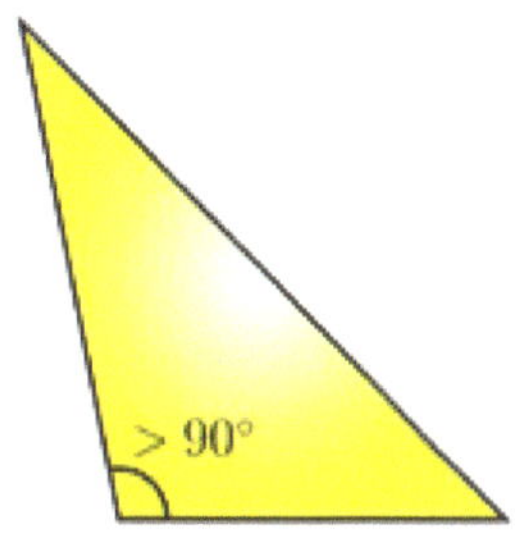

Figure 69: Scalene Triangle

The following table illustrates the changes in geometry as the elbow is bent on the trailing arm during the backswing:

- At Address: The shoulders and arms form an isosceles triangle. The distance between the wrists and the shoulders is about twenty-two inches.
- Takeaway: The shoulders and arms form a scalene triangle. The distance between the wrists and the right shoulder (for RH golfers) has shortened to about sixteen inches.
- Top of Swing: The shoulders and arms form a scalene triangle. The distance between the wrists and the left shoulder (for RH golfers) has shortened to about ten inches.

	ISOSCELES	SCALENE	SCALENE
Distance Between Two Points	**at Address**	**at Takeaway**	**at Top of Swing**
Left Shoulder and Left Wrist	≈ 22 in.	≈ 22 in.	≈ 22 in.
Right Shoulder and Right Wrist	≈ 22 in.	≈ 16 in	≈ 10 in.

At address, the shoulder and the two straight arms approximate an isosceles triangle. The shoulder forms the base of the triangle, and the straight left arm and straight right arm form the sides of the isosceles triangle.

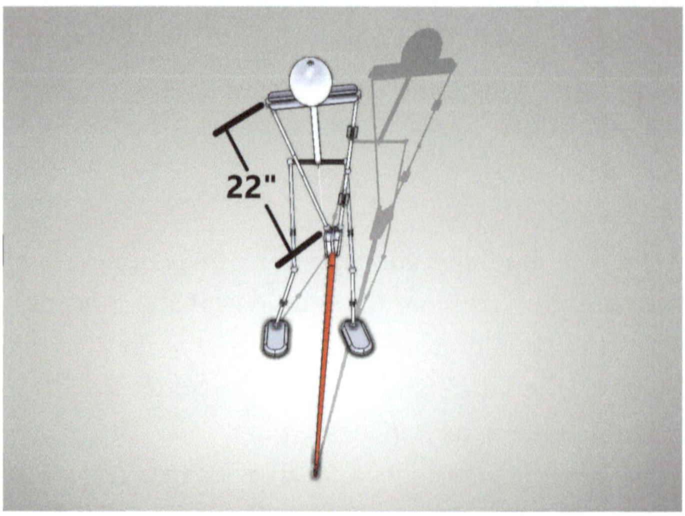

Figure 70: Address Position with Arms Straight

During the initial takeaway, the shoulders still form the base of the triangle, and the straight left arm still forms one side of the triangle. However, the bent right elbow means that the other side of the triangle has been shortened, forming a scalene triangle. The change in the geometry lifts the club and clubface up from the base plane and onto the swing plane.

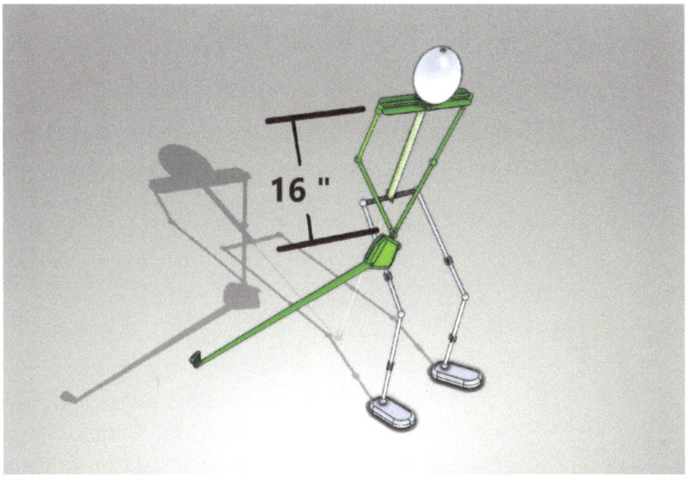

Figure 71: Takeaway with Bent Trailing Arm/Elbow

As the shoulders continue to rotate to the top of the swing during the backswing, the right elbow continues to bend, which shortens the distance between the right shoulder and the hands as the left arm moves across the chest.

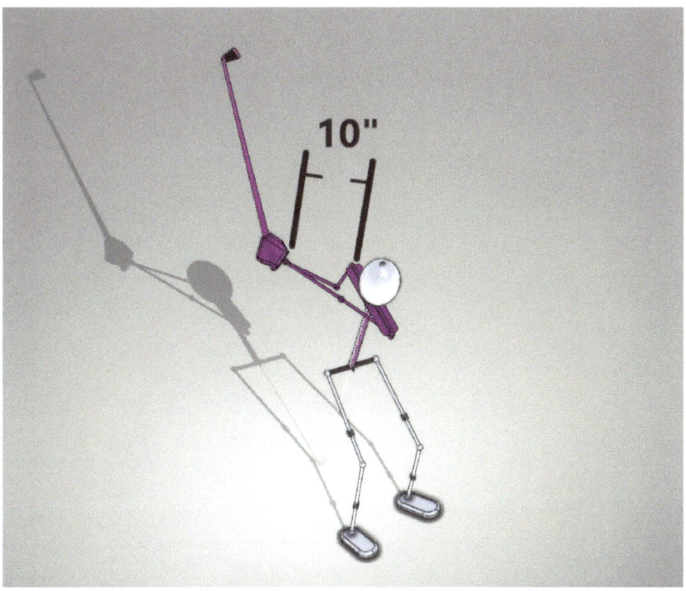

Figure 72: Top of Swing

Address and Initial Takeaway

The shoulders rotate from the neutral position to about 10 degrees clockwise with both arms straight. The club path is on the base plane, and the clubface is perpendicular to the path. The arms and shoulders form an isosceles triangle.

The initial takeaway should consist entirely of primary rotation. Secondary rotation lowers the clubhead; therefore, you must move the club away from the address position to start secondary rotation.

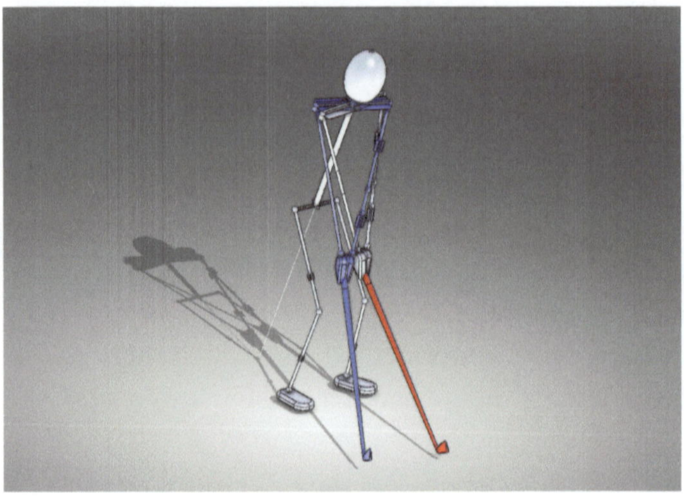

Figure 73: Initial Takeaway

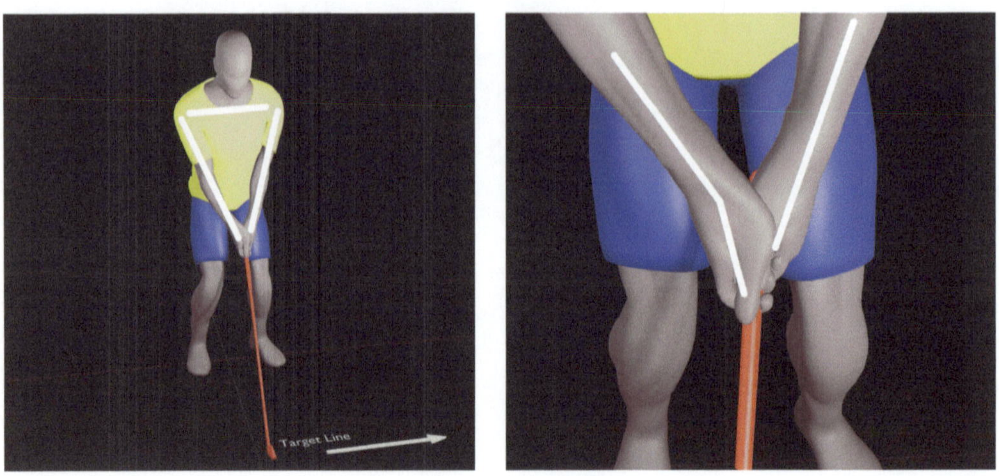

Figure 74: Wrist Position at Address

Both arms are straight. The wrist on the leading arm is flat, and the wrist on the trailing arm is slightly hinged to accommodate a good neutral grip. Notice that the clubface is perpendicular to the target line. The right wrist is hinged slightly out (extension) to maintain a flat left wrist.

Takeaway with Bent Right Arm

As the shoulders rotate about 20 degrees clockwise, the right elbow starts to bend so that the upper right arm is moving against the upper body. The following figures illustrate the initial takeaway with bent elbow and full secondary rotation. The result of this movement lifts the club above the base plane and onto the swing plane.

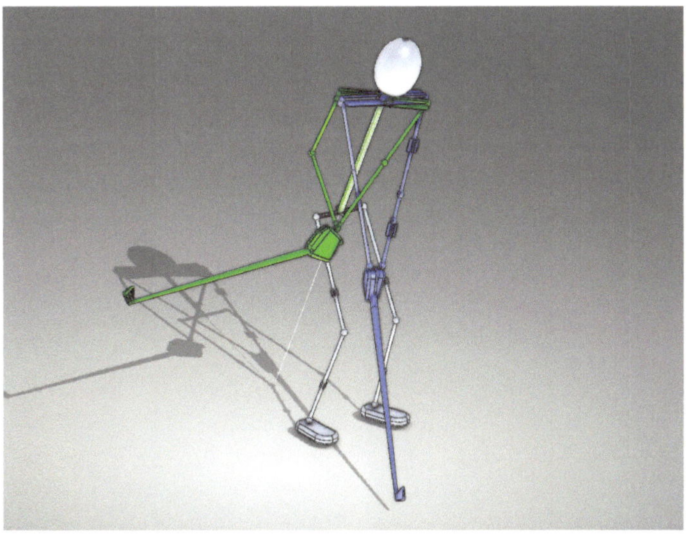

Figure 75: Takeaway

Revelation #9

In the golf swing, the takeaway involves the rotation of the leading arm (straight left arm for RH golfers) 90 degrees clockwise while bending the right elbow into your side and turning your shoulders clockwise during the initial backswing.

As the right elbow bends, the right wrist is hinging (extension) to maintain the flat left wrist on the leading (left) arm. The right wrist continues to hinge out (extension) to maintain the flat left wrist, which, in turn, causes the clubface to continue to open with respect to the swing path.

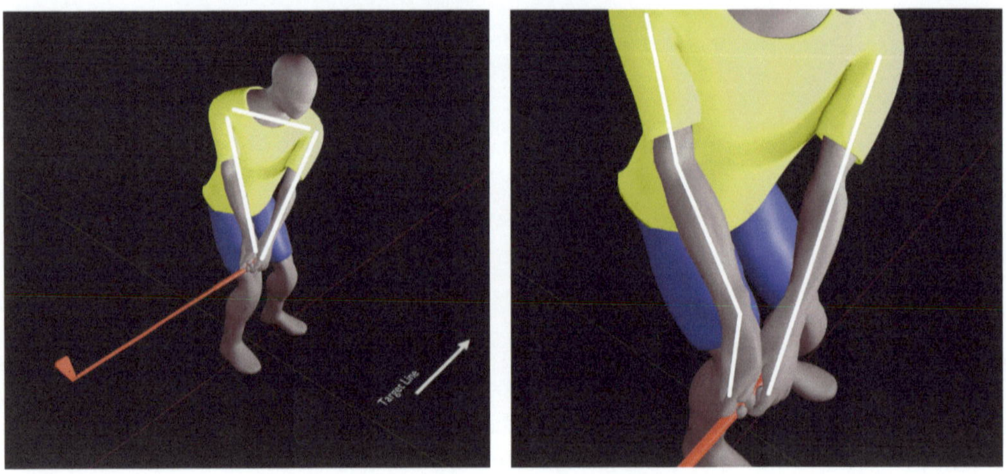

Figure 76: Right Elbow Bend/Right Wrist Hinge at Takeaway

Top of Swing

The shoulders continue to rotate to about 90 degrees clockwise while the left arm remains straight, and the right upper arm stays against the right side as the right elbow continues to bend and the right wrist continues to hinge to maintain a flat left wrist. Bending the elbow shortens the distance between the right shoulder and the wrists even further.

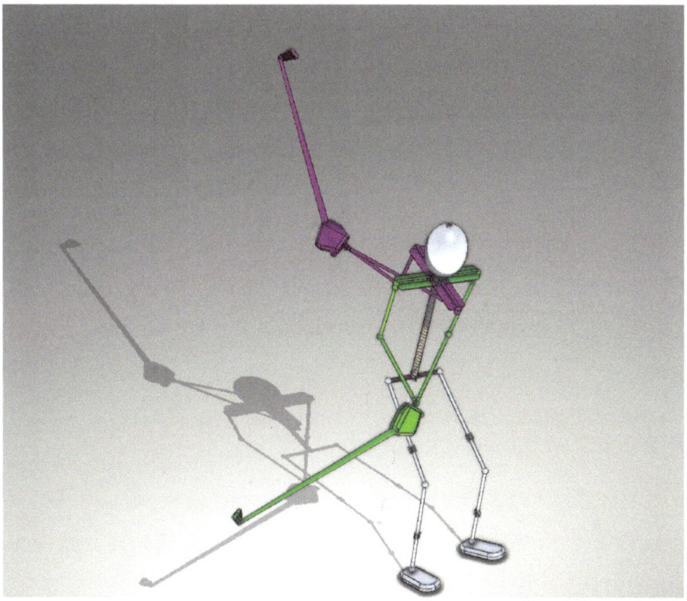

Figure 77: Rotation to the Top of Swing

The illustrations below show the top of the swing with the bent right elbow and hinged right wrist on the trailing arm. To maintain geometry, the right wrist must hinge enough to keep a flat left wrist on the straight leading arm. This results in a club path that is on the swing plane. Notice that the clubface has turned 90 degrees and is tangent to the club path and target line at the top of the swing.

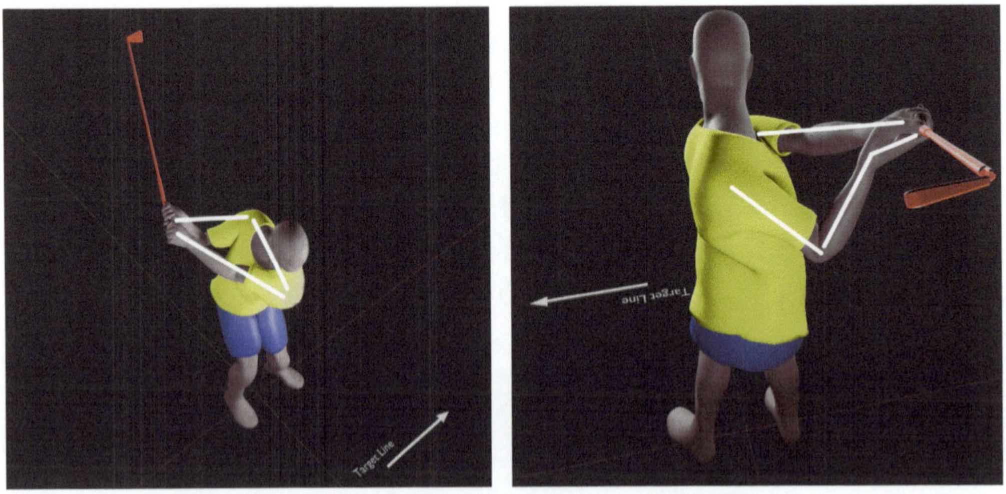

Figure 78: Right Elbow Bend/Right Wrist Hinge at Top of Swing

If we look at the actual dimensions, we see that the distance between the wrist and the right shoulder shortens significantly, about ten inches, during the backswing, while the distance between the left shoulder and wrist remains about the same.

There are some important things worth noting at this point.

- The initial takeaway is done with primary rotation (shoulders only) and no secondary rotation (rotation of the SLA) or tertiary motion (no bending of the right elbow).
- At the end of the takeaway, your right elbow is starting to bend against the right side of your body, and the secondary rotation has completed a full 90 degree clockwise rotation. The distance between the right shoulder and the right wrist has shortened from twenty-two inches to sixteen inches.
- As the primary rotation continues to the top of the swing (approximately 90 degrees of shoulder rotation), there is little additional secondary rotation. However, the straight left arm (SLA) continues to move across the chest. The distance between the right shoulder and right wrist continues to decrease to approximately ten inches at the top of the swing as you bend the right elbow.

The movement of the left arm across the chest allows the club to complete the backswing to the top of the swing in the swing plane. The following figures show the club position resulting from full primary rotation (90 degrees of the shoulders) and full secondary rotation (90 degrees of the straight left arm) with tertiary motion of the left arm across the chest. The clubhead has reached the twelve o'clock position.

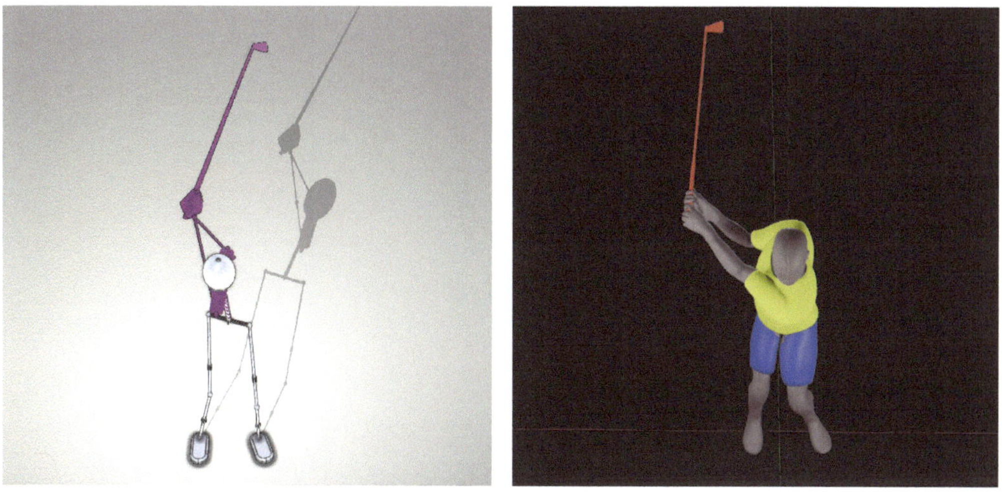

Figure 79: Top of the Swing

At the top of the backswing, there's a pregnant pause as the body reverses direction. This helps to create lag in the downswing. The club has gained momentum in the clockwise direction during the backswing and must now slow down, stop, and change direction to start the downswing. As the club continues past the twelve o'clock position, the hips and shoulders stop and reverse direction.

The downswing essentially reverses the backswing motions. The hips change direction, which, in turn, pull the shoulders, which then pulls the left arm. As you start the downswing, your left shoulder rotates counterclockwise and *pulls* your left arm, which, in turn, *pulls* the golf club back along the natural path on the swing plane.

As the club gains momentum on the downswing, the timing of the straightening of the right arm is critical. This is the release of the club and provides speed from the secondary rotation.

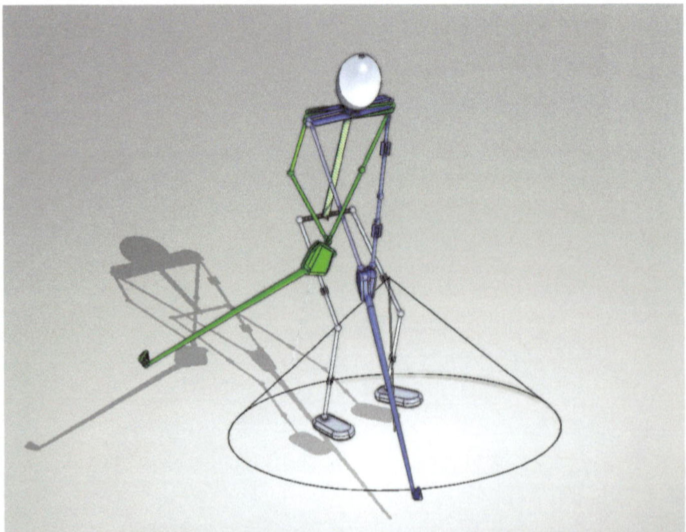

Figure 80: The Release

You don't gain significant distance by speeding up the shoulders and arms during the downswing. This only throws off the tempo and geometry of the swing. The tempo is the timing of each part of the swing. For example, the backswing and downswing may have a count of three. The backswing is on count one and count two and then the downswing to impact is on count three.

Distance is gained by timing the release of the secondary rotation during the downswing with respect to primary rotation of the shoulders.

Often, golfers will start the downswing trying to get the golf club back to the ball by steering it with their hands and arms.

You should rotate the club with your shoulders versus steering the club with your arms and hands. When you use your shoulder to pull the left arm and golf club, the club can find the natural swing path. This results in greater speed and accuracy (more about this in Chapter 7).

Clubface and Club Path

It's again worth taking some time to think about the path that the clubface follows when the club is rotated using both primary rotation and secondary rotation tied together with tertiary motion. The graph below illustrates what happens when you synchronize primary rotation and secondary rotation properly.

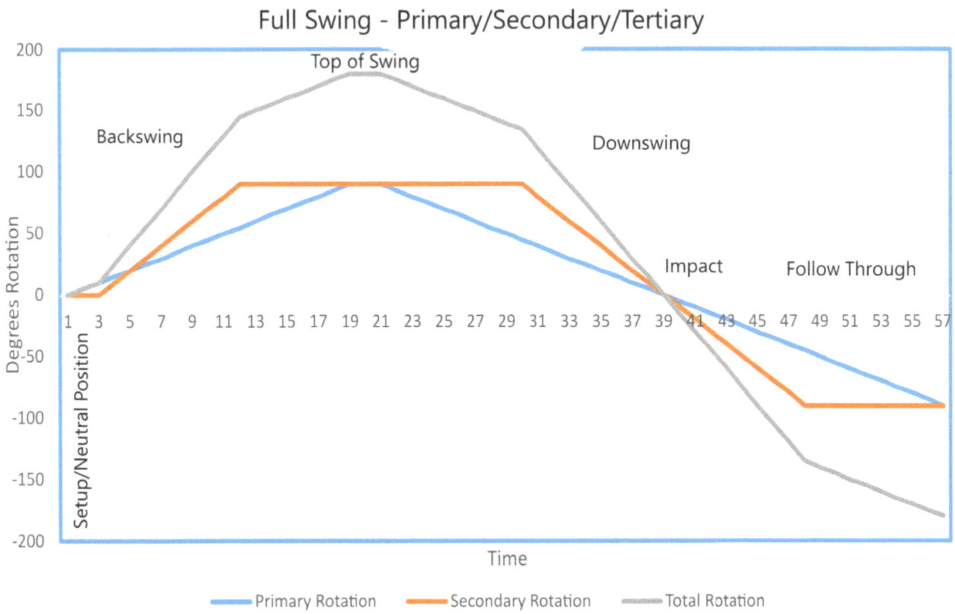

Figure 81: Graph of Combined Primary and Secondary Rotation

The blue line represents primary rotation (shoulder rotation), which starts at zero (address position), rotates 90 degrees clockwise during the backswing, and then is held at 90 degrees for a brief period while the hips change direction to start the downswing. The shoulders then rotate 90 degrees counterclockwise on the downswing to impact, then continue to rotate an additional 90 degrees counterclockwise to the finish of the swing.

The red line represents secondary rotation (straight leading arm), which starts at zero (address position) and, after the initial takeaway, rotates immediately to 90 degrees clockwise during the first part of the backswing, and is held at 90 degrees at the top of the swing. Secondary rotation is held at 90 degrees as the shoulders initiate the downswing. It is held as long as possible until the release, at which point the straight leading arm rotates 90 degrees counterclockwise to impact then continues to rotate an additional 90 degrees counterclockwise to the finish of the swing.

The gray line represents the clubhead position, which is the result of both primary and secondary rotations. The clubhead goes from the six o'clock position (address position) and rotates a full 180 degrees clockwise on the backswing, then changes direction and rotates a full 180 degrees counterclockwise from the top of the swing to impact, then continues to rotate an additional 180 degrees counterclockwise to the finish of the swing.

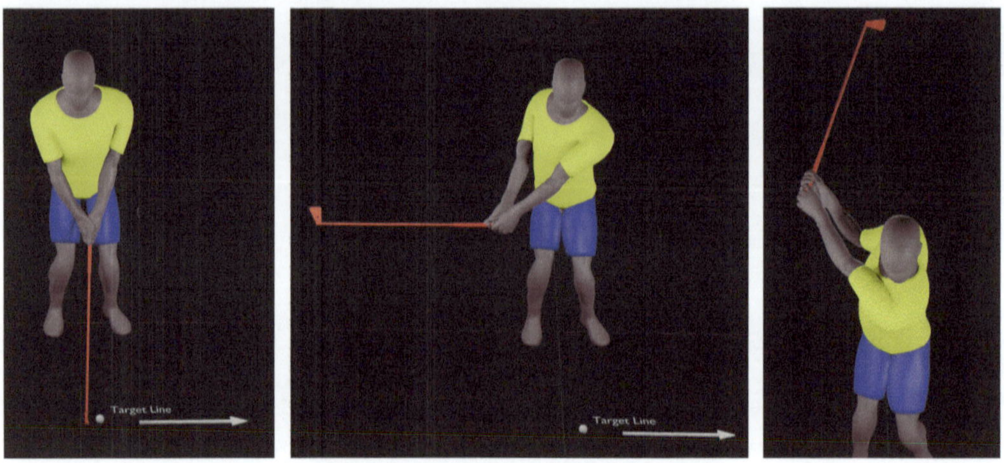

Figure 82: Combined Rotation Club Path

There is additional clubhead rotation that occurs at the top of the swing due to the kinetics of the swing and accompanying wrist cock, which often occurs.

If you remember, when using only primary rotation, the clubface remains perpendicular to the club path. Likewise, when using only secondary rotation, the clubface remains perpendicular to the club path with respect to the secondary axis.

But when you combine the two rotations using tertiary motion, the clubface goes from perpendicular to the club path at address to tangent to the club path at the top of the swing.

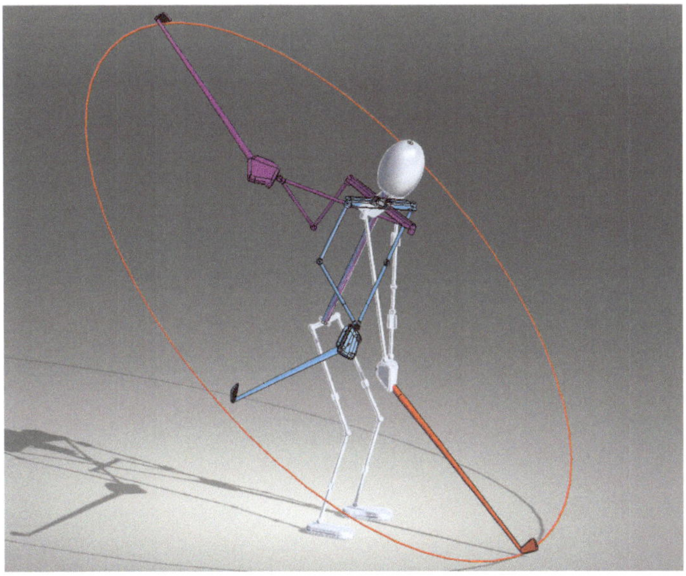

Figure 83: Combined Rotation Clubface Orientation

Primary Rotation Clubface Orientation

Primary rotation is the rotation of the shoulders, arms, and club around the center of the body (see Chapter 4). In the neutral position (center figure below), the shoulders are slightly open to the target line, and the clubface is perpendicular to the club path and the target line. On the backswing, the shoulders rotate 90 degrees clockwise, which rotates the club 90 degrees clockwise (figure on left).

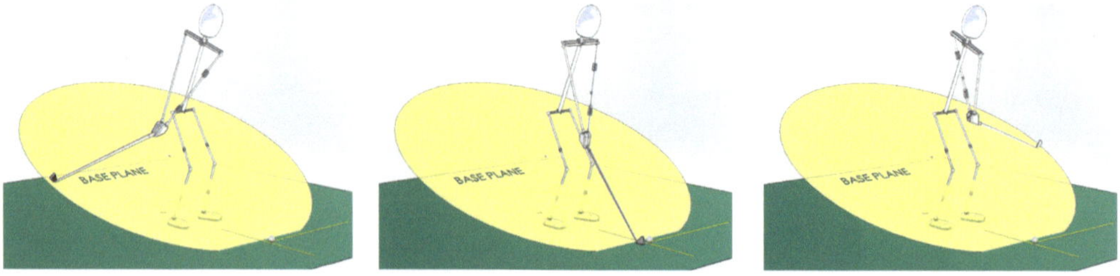

Figure 84: Primary Rotation Clubface Orientation

On the follow-through, the shoulders rotate 90 degrees counterclockwise from neutral, which rotates the club 90 degrees counterclockwise (figure on right). You should note that the clubface stays on the base plane for the entire primary rotation and that the clubface remains perpendicular for the entire motion.

Secondary Rotation Clubface Orientation

Secondary rotation is the rotation of the left arm and club around the center of the straight left arm (see Chapter 5). In the neutral position (center figure), the back of the left hand faces the target line, the clubface is perpendicular to the target line, and the club path is at the base of the cone. On the backswing, the straight left arm rotates 90 degrees clockwise, which rotates the clubhead 90 degrees clockwise along the base of the cone (figure on left).

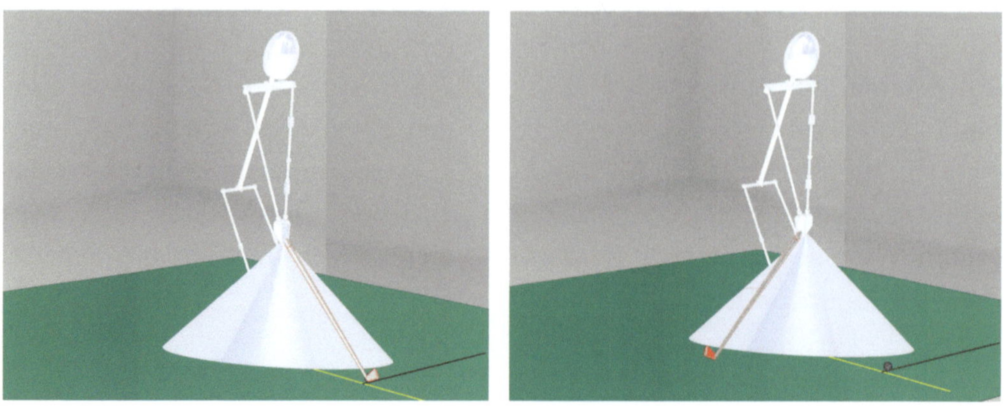

Figure 85: Secondary Rotation Clubface Orientation

On the follow-through, the straight left arm rotates 90 degrees counterclockwise from neutral, which rotates the clubhead 90 degrees counterclockwise along the base of the cone. You should note that the clubface stays on the base of the cone for the entire secondary rotation and that the clubface remains perpendicular through the entire rotation.

Combined Primary and Secondary Rotation Clubface Orientation

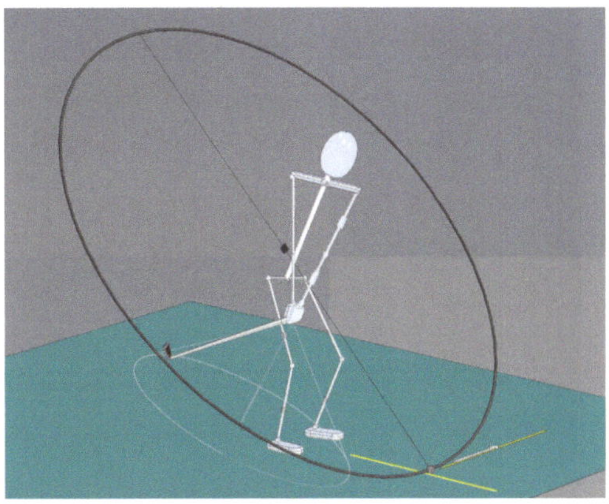

Figure 86: Combined Clubface Orientation

So what happens when we combine primary and secondary rotations? In the neutral position (center figure), the back of the left hand faces the target line, and the clubface is perpendicular to the club path and the target line.

On the backswing, the shoulders rotate clockwise (primary rotation) as the leading arm also rotates clockwise (secondary rotation). But notice that the clubface is no longer perpendicular to the club path. The clubface opens with respect to the club path because of the secondary rotation of the leading arm.

At the top of the swing, the shoulders have rotated 90 degrees clockwise, and the leading arm has also rotated 90 degrees clockwise. The clubface is fully open and tangent to the club path.

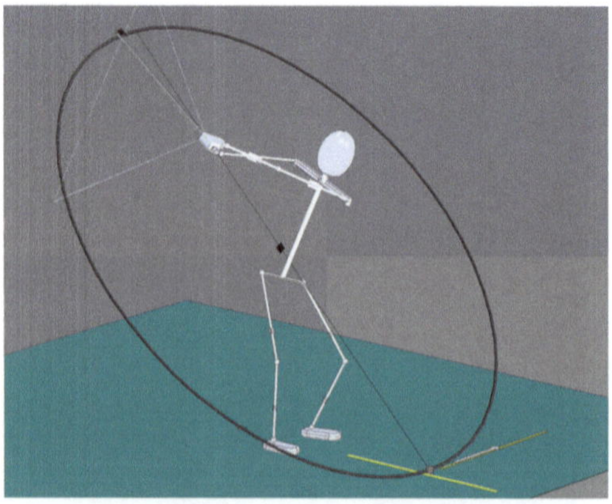

Figure 87: Clubface Orientation at the Top of Swing

On the downswing, the secondary rotation is held as long as possible by maintaining the bent right arm and elbow against the side, which maintains an open clubface during most of the downswing. At release, the secondary rotation starts to unwind as the leading left arm rotates counterclockwise from 90 degrees to 0 degrees (neutral) at impact. At impact, the shoulders (primary rotation) and leading arm (secondary rotation) are in the neutral position (0 degrees), and the clubface is perpendicular to the club path and perpendicular to the target line.

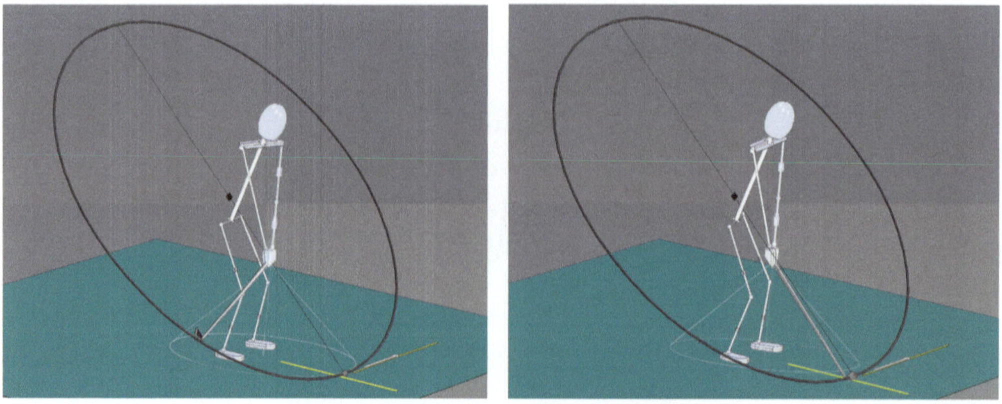

Figure 88: Clubface Orientation During the Downswing

For a straight shot, this is exactly what we want: a clubface that is perpendicular to the club path and the target line at impact.

Remember that the clubhead has a path associated with the primary rotation of the club and a club path associated with the secondary rotation. The *overall* club path is the result of the combination of the primary rotation and the secondary rotation. This relationship is influenced by tertiary motion.

To get the ball to go straight, the clubface must impact the ball perpendicular to the club path (i.e., the target line when addressing the ball with a neutral setup). This means that the clubhead must be perpendicular on the primary rotation club path **and** the clubhead must be perpendicular on the secondary rotation club path at the time of impact. Put another way, the clubface must be in the neutral position (perpendicular position) for both the primary and secondary rotations at the time of impact.

Revelation #10

The full swing is a combination of the primary rotation and the secondary rotation tied together using tertiary motion. The resulting club path is on the swing plane.

The clubface starts perpendicular to the club path (and target line) at the bottom of the swing (address position). During the takeaway, as secondary rotation goes from neutral to 90 degrees, the clubface rotates open with respect to the club path and is tangent to the club path at the top of the swing.

Conversely, the club starts tangent to the club path at the top of the swing and returns to perpendicular at impact as the secondary rotation goes from 90 degrees to neutral after release and into impact.

On the downswing the right arm is used to guide the leading left arm back down the swing plane. The resulting club path, which is on the swing plane, provides a line that is also parallel to the target line at impact. As we will see in Chapter 15, that's great if everything is neutral, meaning a neutral grip, a good setup with shoulders and feet parallel to the target line, and good primary and secondary rotation. This results in a neutral club path with a relatively straight shot and little sidespin.

What happens if we want to hit a draw shot or a fade? Either of these shots requires a certain amount of sidespin. The two main factors that affect ball flight are clubface angle at impact and sidespin.

Clubface Angle and Sidespin

Clubface angle is easy to explain. It is the orientation of the clubface with respect to the target line at impact. There are three possible clubface angles relative to the target line for a particular swing: closed, perpendicular, and open. Thus far, we have focused on a clubface angle that is perpendicular to the target line at impact, which is the desired orientation for a straight shot. As you will see in Chapter 15, we sometimes want to set up the geometry to provide an open or closed clubface at impact for shaping shots.

The three basic club paths are as follows:

1) In-to-In: Has a line that is tangent and parallel to the target line at impact point
2) In-to-Out: Has a line that goes from inside the target line to outside the target line at the impact point
3) Out-to-In: Has a line that goes from outside the target line to inside the target line at the impact point

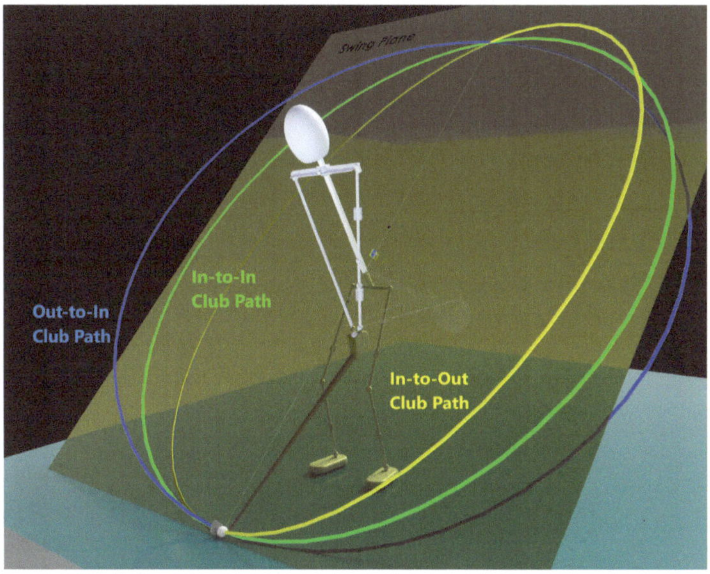

Figure 89: Club Paths

Remember that the full swing club path is a combination of the primary rotation and the secondary rotation tied together using tertiary motion. Tertiary motion determines whether the path is In-to-In, In-to-Out, or Out-to-In.

- If secondary rotation is synchronized perfectly together with primary rotation, the club path is In-to-In.
- If secondary rotation *lags* primary rotation, the club path is In-to-Out.
- If secondary rotation *leads* primary rotation, the club path is Out-to-In.

The following are illustrations of each swing type and the resulting sidespin forces.

In-to-In Club Path

When secondary rotation is synchronized perfectly together with primary rotation, the club path is In-to-In. With proper setup and grip, the clubface returns to the impact position perpendicular to the target line on the swing plane. There is no movement across the target line (in the Y direction) at impact; as a result, there are no shear forces side to side due to friction and, therefore, no side-to-side rotation.

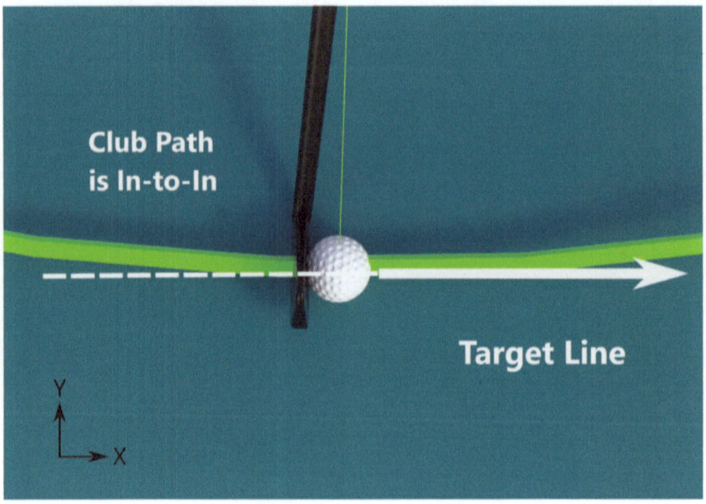

Figure 90: In-to-In Club Path

In-to-Out Club Path

When secondary rotation *lags* primary rotation, the resulting club path is In-to-Out. With proper setup and grip, the clubface returns to the impact position across the target line and slightly *below* the swing plane. The clubface is moving along the target line (in the X direction) and across the target line (in the Y direction) at impact; therefore, there are shear forces side to side due to friction and movement in the negative Y direction. The result is a counter-clockwise rotation, which we call sidespin.

Figure 91: In-to-Out Club Path

Out-to-In Club Path

When secondary rotation *leads* primary rotation, the resulting club path is Out-to-In. With proper setup and grip, the clubface returns to the impact position across the target line and slightly above the swing plane. The clubface is moving along the target line (in the X direction) and across the target line (in the Y direction) at impact; therefore, there are shear forces side to side due to friction and movement in the positive Y direction. The result is a clockwise rotation (sidespin).

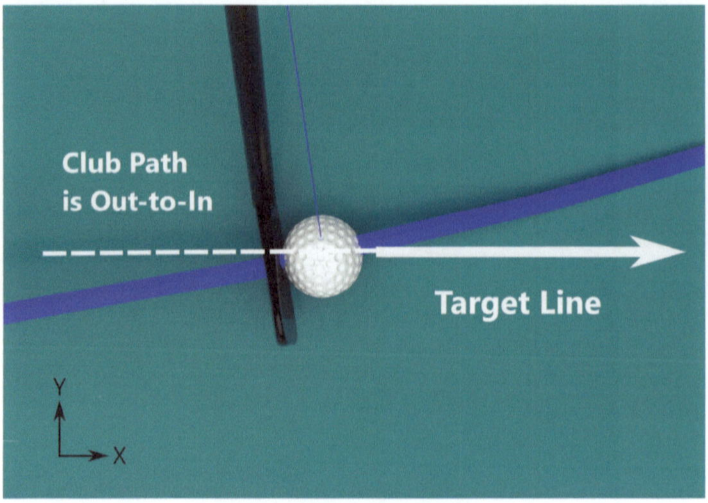

Figure 92: Out-to-In Club Path

We have now discussed the three major motions used in the golf swing. Primary rotation provides the power and control, secondary rotation provides the speed and distance, and tertiary motion ties the two together. The combination gives us three possible club paths.

Revelation #11

The two main factors that affect ball flight are **clubface angle at impact and sidespin**. The clubface angle and sidespin are determined by the club path. The club path is the result of primary rotation and secondary rotation tied together using tertiary motion.

The three club paths are as follows:

1) In-to-In has a line that is tangential to the target line at impact point and produces no ball spin, which results when primary rotation is perfectly synchronized with secondary rotation.

2) In-to-Out has a line that goes from inside the target lin e to outside the target line at the impact point, which produces counterclockwise ball spin as a result of secondary rotation lagging primary rotation.

3) Out-to-In has a line that goes from outside the target line to inside the target line at the impact point, which produces clockwise ball spin as a result of secondary rotation leading primary rotation.

By now, we have a solid understanding of the kinematics of the golf swing. The golf swing is comprised of some distinct motions with specific geometries that move together with proper timing. Before we put all the pieces together in Chapter 8, the next chapter will introduce a little bit of the physics, aka the kinetics of the golf swing.

Takeaways:

So what did we learn in Chapter 6?

1. The swing is a combination of the primary rotation and the secondary rotation tied together using tertiary motion. The resulting club path is on the swing plane. The amount of secondary rotation determines if the clubface is perpendicular to the club path, tangent to the club path, or somewhere in between.
2. Tertiary motion decreases the distance between the right shoulder and the hands by bending the right elbow and arm. This motion synchronizes the primary rotation (shoulder rotation) and secondary rotation (rotation of the straight left arm). Bending the right elbow during the backswing lifts the clubhead from the base plane and onto the swing plane and provides the proper orientation of the clubface during the backswing.
3. The two main factors that affect ball flight are clubface angle at impact and sidespin. The clubface angle and sidespin are determined by the club path, which results from the timing between primary rotation and secondary rotation.

CHAPTER 7

Time for Some Physics

In Chapter 1, Revelation #2 states that if you don't get the kinematics of the golf swing right, the physics of the golf swing doesn't matter. You should now understand the kinematics—the motions involved—so it's time to layer in some physics.

For every action, there is an equal and opposite reaction.

—Sir Isaac Newton

There are numerous books that deal with the physics of golf, and they all have equations, data, and information that can become quickly complex. The information in these books may be accurate, but it isn't necessarily relevant, and it can certainly be hard to understand. This book presents a simple equation and some well-defined concepts regarding rotational forces that are both useful and pertinent to the golf swing.

Newton's second law of motion describes the relationship between an object's mass and the amount of force needed to accelerate it. It's often stated as F = MA, which means the force (F) acting on an object is equal to the mass (M) of an object times the acceleration (A) of the object.

Newton's laws of motion are three basic laws of classical mechanics that describe the relationship between the motion of an object and the forces acting on it. These laws can be paraphrased as follows:

- A body remains at rest or in motion at a constant speed in a straight line unless acted upon by a force.
- When a body is acted upon by a force, the time rate of change of its momentum equals the force (F = MA).
- If two bodies exert forces on each other, these forces have the same magnitude but act in opposite directions.

It is interesting to note that the first references to golf were in the historic town of St. Andrews, Scotland in 1552. It was over one hundred years later that Isaac Newton first stated his theories in his *Philosophiæ Naturalis Principia Mathematica* (*Mathematical Principles of Natural Philosophy*), originally published in 1687.[8]

Newton used these laws to investigate and explain the motion of many physical objects and systems, which laid the foundation for modern classical mechanics. This chapter is all about classical mechanics and golf.

---

[8] "Wikimedia Foundation. (2024, June 10). Newton's laws of Motion. Wikipedia. https://en.wikipedia.org/wiki/Newton%27s_laws_of_motion

Figure 93: Newtonian Physics

Even if physics wasn't your favorite class in school, bear with me through this chapter. The following discussion will be relatively simple, avoid equations where possible, and hopefully be useful for improving your understanding of the kinetics of the golf swing.

Kinetics: a branch of science that deals with the effects of forces upon the motions of material bodies or with changes in a physical system. [9]

Don't confuse kinetics with kinematics. We have thus far been discussing kinematics, the branch of mechanics concerned with the *motion* of objects without reference to the *forces* that cause the motion.

Now we will be discussing kinetics which is the effects of forces upon the motions of material bodies. Kinematics has to do with geometry, and kinetics has to do with energy. I wish that the words were not so similar, but please don't blame me. I don't make up the words; I just try to explain them.

---

[9] "Merriam-Webster. (n.d.-b). *Kinetics definition & meaning*. Merriam-Webster. https://www.merriam-webster.com/dictionary/kinetics

Newton himself never wrote or formulated the equation F = MA, and he never said, "Force equals mass times acceleration." Instead, he said, "The force on an object is equal to the rate of change of the object's momentum," where momentum is the product of mass times velocity. Let's take a quick look at Newton's three basic laws of classical mechanics as they pertain to golf.

1. **A body remains at rest or in motion at a constant speed in a straight line unless acted upon by a force.**
   The ball is at rest on the tee, on the fairway, on the green, or in some less desirable location (like in the woods). It will stay there forever until acted on by a force. You either pick it up, or you hit it with the head of a golf club. The only other force acting on the ball is the gravity that is holding it in place.

2. **When a body is acted upon by a force, the time rate of change of its momentum equals the force (F = MA).**
   The head of the golf club has mass. This varies from club to club, and for comparison, the average 8-iron head weighs about 275 grams (about 10 oz.), and the average driver weighs about 200 grams (about 7 oz.). A golf ball weighs about 45 grams (1.6 oz.).

   At address, the club is at rest and not able to deliver much force. You step up to the ball and address it. "Hello, ball, how are you?" Sorry, that was the wrong address!

   You rotate the club to the top of the swing. The clubhead stops at the top and changes direction. What happens on the way down to the ball?

   Remember that torque is a measure of the force that can cause an object to rotate about an axis. Just as force is what causes an object to accelerate in linear kinematics, torque is what causes an object to acquire angular acceleration on the downswing.

   Initially, torque applied by the shoulders pulls the club back along a circular path, which is hopefully on the swing plane. As the shoulders rotate (primary rotation), the clubhead starts to accelerate and gain velocity and momentum.

As the club approaches the bottom of the downswing, the speed of the clubhead due to primary rotation is relatively small because the shoulders are powerful but do not move very fast; the amount of acceleration and velocity are limited. Professional golfers will use the shoulders (primary rotation) to rotate the club back around the body (primary axis) but hold the release (secondary rotation) as long as possible. When we *hold* the release as long as possible, the clubhead must rotate quickly along the secondary path to get to the neutral position at impact.

The mass of the clubhead is constant, but the *speed* of the clubhead increases dramatically during secondary rotation. Torque supplied by the leading arm (SLA) powers this motion.

The velocity at impact due to *both* primary rotation and secondary rotation is now quite high. The contribution to total energy delivered by the clubhead to the ball at impact is the sum of energy delivered by primary rotation and the energy delivered by secondary rotation. The amount of energy delivered by secondary rotation is quite high, because the velocity of secondary rotation is high.

Remember that force = mass × acceleration:

$$F = MA$$

In *translational* physics (linear motion), force = mass × acceleration, which is also expressed as mass × (velocity ÷ time). This means if you increase the external energy to a system (i.e., add force to a given mass), it will accelerate, which increases the object's velocity.

For *rotational* physics, if you increase the energy to a system (i.e., apply torque to an object with a fixed inertia), the object's angular acceleration (and therefore tangential acceleration and velocity) will increase, which will increase the object's angular (and tangential) velocity.

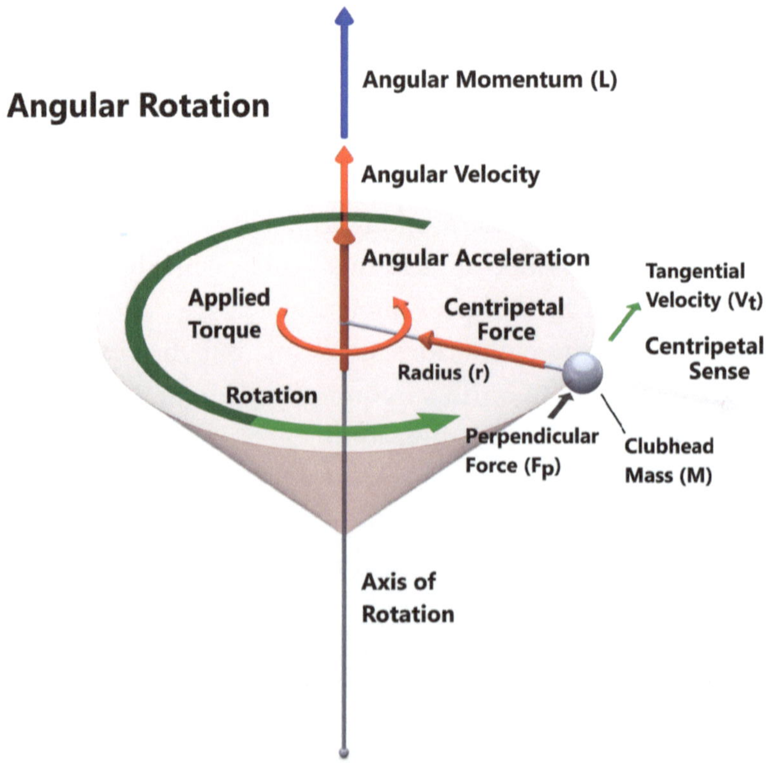

Figure 94: Rotational Motion

Bottom line, the clubhead will gain additional velocity and momentum in a very short period. Wow! Seems like a lot, but if you are patient, there are some good illustrations to follow that will help to explain all of this.

And finally, there is Newton's third law of motion:

3. **If two bodies exert forces on each other, these forces have the same magnitude but opposite directions.**
The clubhead has gained momentum prior to impact while the ball rests patiently on the ground. At impact, a significant amount of energy is transferred from the clubhead to the ball.

Mass (clubhead) × Velocity (clubhead) = Mass (ball) × Velocity (ball)

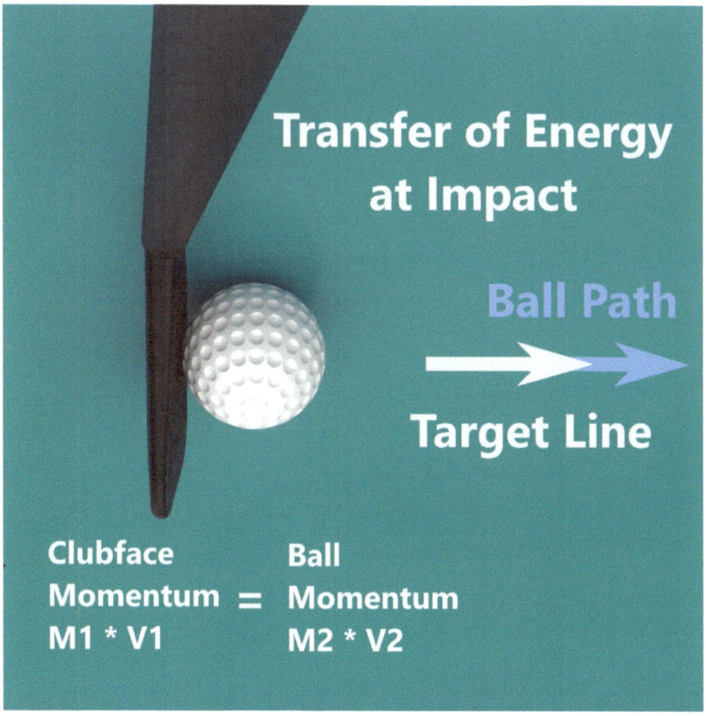

Figure 95: Transfer of Energy at Impact

There are many factors that determine how much energy is transferred, but ultimately, the speed of the clubhead is the most important factor, and speed equates to distance. The higher the clubhead velocity, the faster the ball will travel if struck properly.

So how does this all apply to the golf swing? We know that the distance a ball will travel is directly related to the energy that is transferred from the clubhead to the ball at impact. That energy is supplied by the golfer.

Revelation #12

There are three forces that affect the golf swing: applied force, centripetal force, and gravity. Applied force is supplied by the golfer when they apply torque using the upper body (primary torque) and leading arm (secondary torque). Centripetal force is a radial force resulting from rotation. Gravity is a force that attracts a body toward the center of the earth.

Applied Force—Primary Rotation

An applied force is a force that acts from the outside (i.e., applied to the golf club). In our case, the source of this applied force has two components: primary torque and secondary torque.

Primary torque is the result of rotating the upper body, which, in turn, rotates the shoulder around the primary axis.

Your upper body and shoulders (the core) supply the torque. The arms are attached to the shoulder, and the club is attached to the arms. Therefore, the torque of the upper body is used to rotate the arms and club around the body. The upper body is easy to control and powerful and can provide quite a bit of torque but at relatively slow speed.

Remember Revelation #3: primary rotation provides power and control. The applied torque provides the force that rotates the left shoulder, which rotates counterclockwise on the downswing.

$$F \text{ (force)} = T \text{ (torque)} \div r \text{ (radius)}$$

The applied force can be broken down into the x-axis component (Fx), the y-axis component (Fy), and the z-axis component (Fz). As the shoulders, left arm, and club rotate (primary rotation), the clubhead starts to accelerate and gain momentum.

As the club approaches the bottom of the downswing, the speed of the clubhead is limited because the shoulders can only rotate so fast. Some swing types like putting and chipping use only primary rotation because accuracy is more important than distance. The momentum of the clubhead at impact does not need to be very big; therefore, the speed of the clubhead can be relatively small.

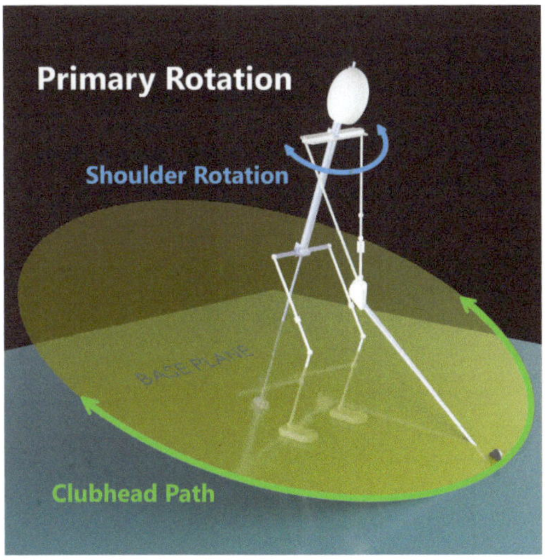

Figure 97: Primary Rotation

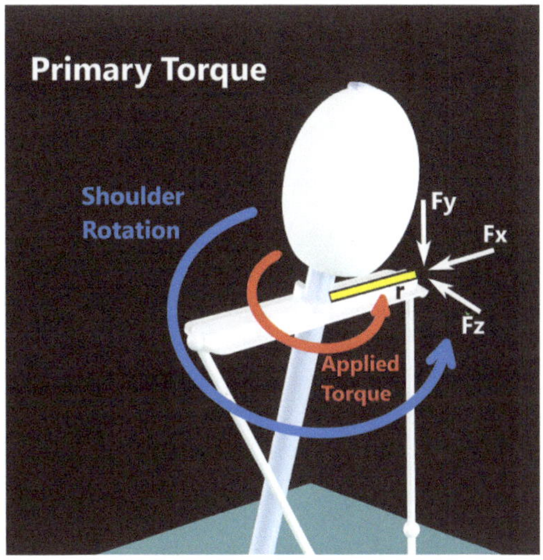

Figure 96: Torque from Primary Rotation

Applied Force—Secondary Rotation

The other applied force is the torque that is provided by the leading arm (the infamous straight left arm). This left arm rotation, though not as powerful as the shoulders, can still provide the torque to power secondary rotation. The motion of the leading arm is hard to control. What the leading arm lacks in power and control is made up for by the ability to gain speed quickly.

Remember Revelation #5: secondary rotation provides speed and therefore distance. The applied torque from the leading arm (SLA) provides the force that rotates the club around the secondary axis.

The force provided by this rotation can be broken down into the x-axis component (Fx), the y-axis component (Fy), and the z-axis component (Fz). The left arm rotation causes the left hand, wrist, and club to rotate collectively as the clubhead accelerates and gains velocity and momentum.

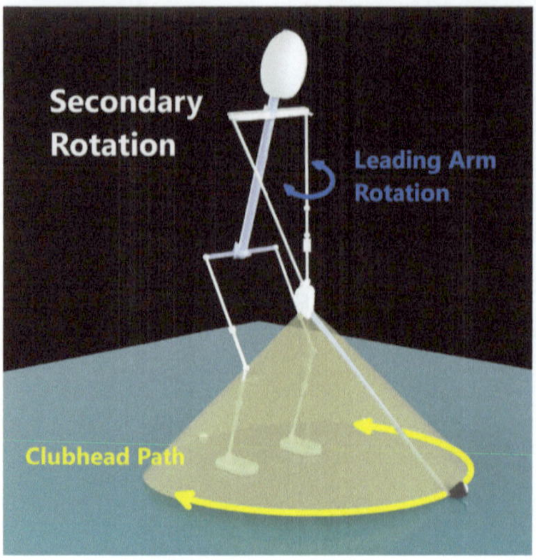

Figure 99: Secondary Rotation

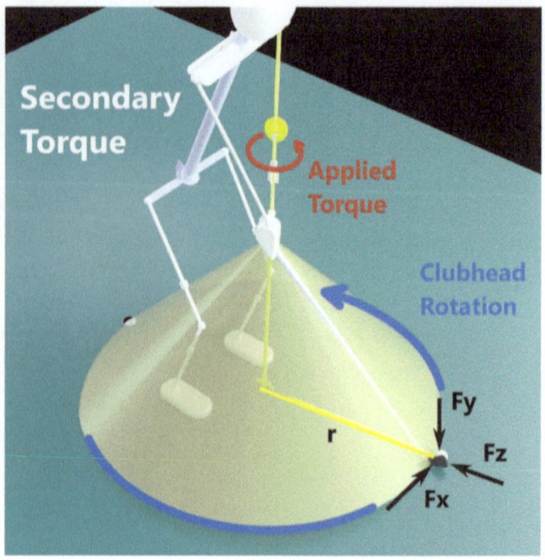

Figure 98: Torque from Secondary Rotation

If the golfer holds the release as long as possible on the downswing, the clubhead must rotate quickly along the secondary path to get to the neutral position at impact.

Some swing types use both primary and secondary rotation because distance becomes important. Clubhead speed is necessary to get distance. Secondary rotation is needed to get clubhead speed.

Applied Force—Primary and Secondary Rotation Combined

When both primary and secondary rotation are used as with the full swing, the combined momentum provided at impact is the sum of the momentum from both. Another way of stating this is that the energy delivered to the ball at impact results from the applied force provided by shoulder torque and the applied force provided by the leading arm torque.

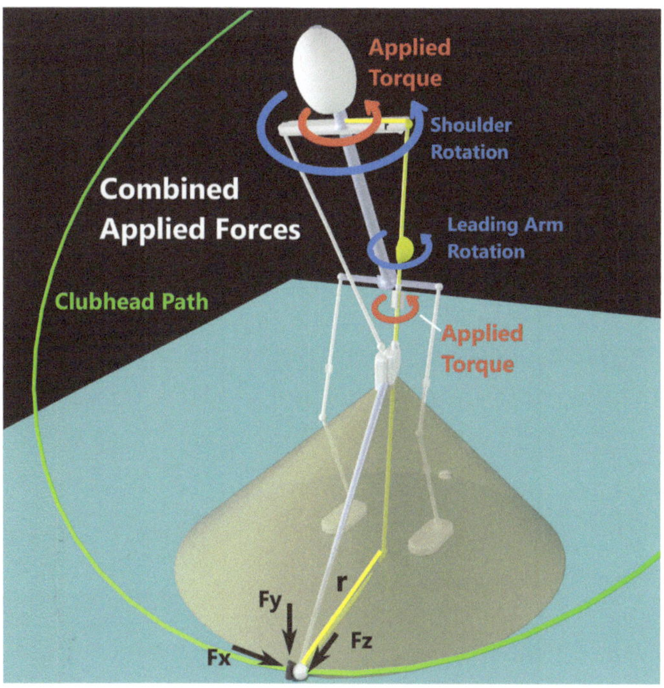

Figure 100: Combined Forces of the Swing

This brings us full circle to Newton's third law:

If two bodies exert forces on each other, these forces have the same magnitude but opposite directions.

The equivalent of Newton's law (F = MA) for rotational forces is:

$$\text{Torque} = Cmr^2\alpha.$$

Here, torque (T) is analogous to force, angular acceleration (α) is analogous to linear acceleration, and Cmr2 is analogous to the moment of inertia for a golf club, where C will be a constant for a given golf club and would be less than 1 (assuming m is the mass of the golf club and not of just the head). Admittedly this is a little geeky but stay with me.

In the golf swing, the mass of a given club is constant, and the radius from the axis is known. We supply the torque by rotating the upper body (primary rotation) and rotating the leading arm (secondary rotation). The speed of the clubhead at impact can be derived from the angular acceleration:

$$\text{Angular acceleration } \alpha = \text{Torque} \div m \times r^2$$

Here, m is the mass of the club, and r is the radius from the rotational axis to the clubhead.

Tangential acceleration (linear acceleration) is related to angular acceleration:

$$\text{Acceleration (tangential)} = \text{Acceleration (angular)} \times \text{radius}$$

You apply torque to get the club to move around the body. The upper body can supply quite a bit of torque but not so much speed. The leading arm can provide a lot of speed but not as much torque.

Two important points worth noting from this brief physics discussion:

1. Ball Path: The path the golf ball will take is determined by the orientation of the clubface at the time of impact.
2. Ball Speed: The distance a golf ball travels after impact is directly a function of clubhead velocity at impact.

We have just discussed the applied forces supplied by the body, which provides the energy delivered to the ball at impact. Now let's look at the other two forces: centripetal force and gravity.

Centripetal and Gravitational Force

Force is required to make an object move, and force acts differently on objects depending on the type of motion it exhibits. In the case of rotational motion, a special force comes into the picture. That is centripetal force, which literally means "center seeking."

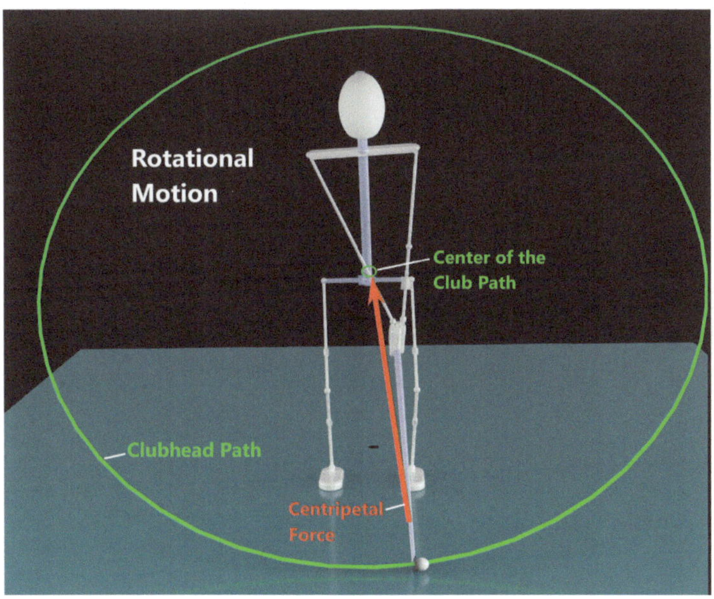

Figure 101: Centripetal Force

Centripetal force is a net force that acts on an object to keep it moving along a circular path. You will often hear the term "centrifugal force" when referring to the golf swing. Centrifugal force is not a real force at all but rather a perceived effect of rotational motion.

The more accurate term would be centrifugal sense, which is the *perception* an object is moving away from the center of the circle. There is no outward force. It is just the perception that an object is moving away from you during rotation. In reality, the object is trying to move in a straight line and is being restrained by a real force called centripetal force, which is a radial force that acts toward the center of the rotation.

A big myth in golf is the belief that centripetal force and gravity provide a lot of the energy to the golf ball at impact. Centripetal forces generated during the swing are radial forces and perpendicular to the club path. Therefore, they do not provide any significant energy to the ball at impact. However, these are real forces and cannot be totally ignored since they do influence the clubhead path.

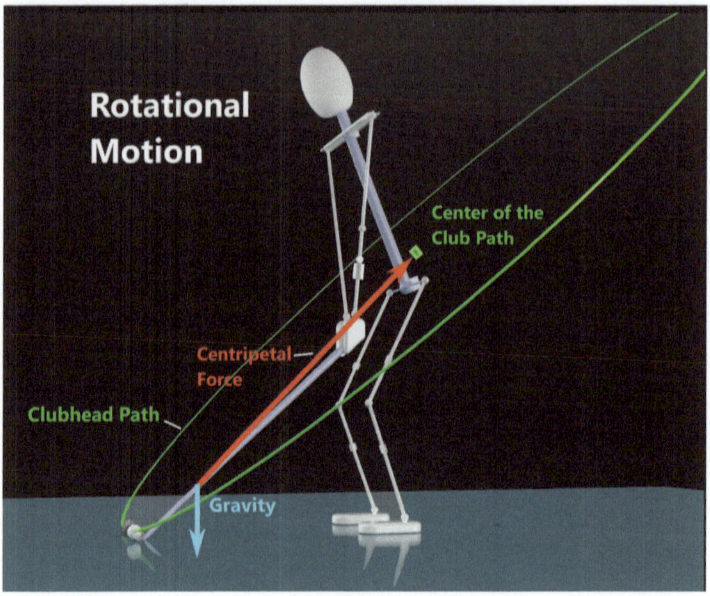

Figure 102: Centripetal Force and Gravity

It is worth noting a couple of things about gravity and centripetal force.

1. Gravity is always present and always pulling the club straight down, regardless of what part of the swing you are in.
2. Centripetal force is only present while the club is in motion (rotating), and it is proportional to the speed of rotation. In other words, the faster the clubhead speed, the larger the force. The direction of the force is radial and toward the center of the circle.
3. Primary rotation has a club path on the base plane around the center of the body, and the club is affected by gravity and centripetal force.
4. Secondary rotation has a club path perpendicular to the secondary axis (SLA), and the club is affected by gravity and centripetal force.
5. The actual golf swing is a combination of both primary rotation and secondary rotation. The effect of gravity is still always the same and pulling the club down. Centripetal force is the combination of primary-rotation centripetal force and secondary-rotation centripetal force and will change depending on what part of the swing you are in.

Remember that the *applied* forces (shoulder and left arm torque) described above provide the energy to move the clubhead along the club path. You must supply energy (i.e., torque) to drive the golf club mass around the rotational axis at an acceleration.

Why is this important?

Speed translates to distance. For a given golf club, you apply torque to get the clubhead to move around the body. With everything else constant, you can only increase the speed by applying more torque or by changing the timing between primary and secondary rotation.

Clubhead/Club Path

When you rotate an object around an axis, the object will try to rotate on a specific path. Think of this path as the path of least resistance, which we'll call the natural path.

Revelation #13

When you rotate a club around the axis, there is an optimum path, the natural path which is on the swing plane. In the case of the golf swing, the path is the combination of the combined primary rotation and the secondary rotation.

If you rotate a ball on the end of a string around an axis, it will find its natural path. The same applies to the head of a golf club. If you replace the string with a shaft, the head of the golf club can be manipulated away from the natural path if other applied forces are exerted on the club shaft.

We learned that the proper combination of rotations results in a club path that is on the swing plane. This club path can be thought of as the natural path that the head of the golf club would follow if it were not manipulated or steered away from this path.

The goal of a good golf swing is to rotate the head of the golf club on the swing plane along its natural path. The primary rotation has a semicircular path that is along the base plane. The secondary rotation also has a semicircular path around the secondary axis (straight left arm) and is at the base of the cone.

The actual swing path is a combination of both the primary swing path and the secondary swing path.

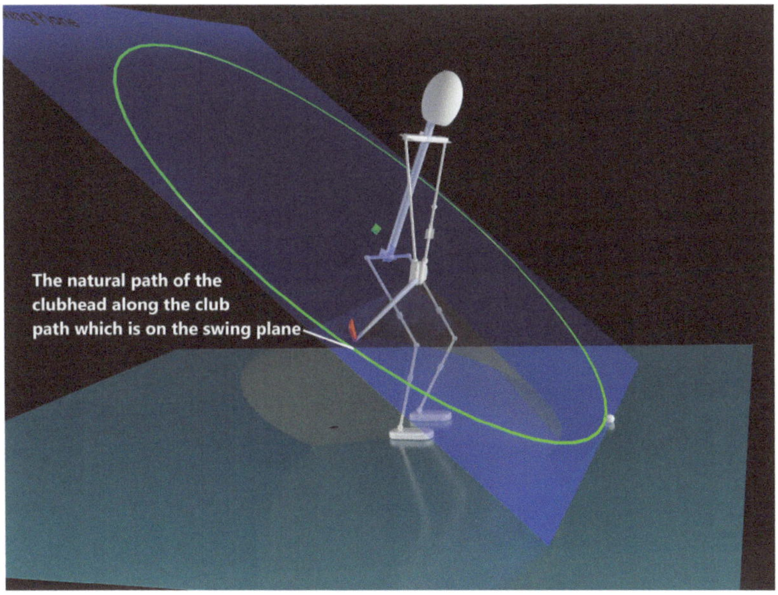

Figure 103: The Natural Clubhead Path

As you guide the clubhead to the top of the swing, you store energy in the torso, kind of like winding up a spring, which can be used to apply force on the downswing. If the downswing is executed properly, the club is pulled back along the swing plane on the natural path of the clubhead to impact.

The previous chapters examined the kinematics of these motions, and this chapter has focused on the kinetics of these motions, but let's look at a few of the key dynamics of these motions.

Pulling Versus Steering

At the top of the backswing, energy has been stored (potential energy) in the torso. The club and clubhead, which have gained momentum in a clockwise direction, must slow, and this builds up additional forces in the torso as the clubhead comes to a stop. At the top of the swing, after stopping, the torso must now reverse direction and start to rotate counterclockwise.

If done properly, the counterclockwise rotation of the torso causes the left shoulder to pull the club and clubhead back along the natural club swing path. This is a critical concept.

May not an ass know when the cart draws the horse?

—William Shakespeare, King Lear

If you've ever pulled a child in a wagon, you know it's much easier to pull the wagon along a path with the wagon handle than it is to push the wagon along the same path with the handle. Not to say that it's impossible to push the wagon along that path, but it requires a lot of extra steering to accomplish the task. Any slight misalignment, and the wagon will veer off course. If you pull the wagon, it will easily follow a natural path.

The same concept applies during the downswing. If you use your shoulders to pull the club around the body, the clubhead is more apt to fall into its natural path. However, if you start the downswing with your arms instead of your shoulders, you're pushing the club and clubhead and you must carefully steer it along the swing path. It's not impossible to do but very difficult, and the chances of keeping the clubhead on the natural path and returning it to the point of impact correctly with the right clubhead alignment are slim.

This is one of the big differentiators between a high handicap golfer and a low handicap golfer. High handicap golfers tend to start the downswing with their arms. They then need to steer the clubhead back to impact, resulting in loss of speed (thus distance) and improper clubhead alignment (accuracy).

This chapter has addressed some of the key elements of physics as they relate to the effects of forces upon the motions of the golf swing. There is a wealth of knowledge and understanding of the golf swing in terms of angular motion that is quite fascinating.

It is now time to apply the knowledge we have gained into understanding the swing.

If knowledge is power, knowing what we don't know is wisdom.

—Adam M. Grant, Think Again: The Power of Knowing What You Don't Know

Takeaways:

So what did we learn in Chapter 7?

1. The geometry of the golf swing needs to be correct, otherwise the kinetics (the study of forces) don't really matter.
2. There are three forces associated with the golf swing:
   a. Applied forces created by the torso and leading arm
   b. Centripetal force, which is created by rotation of the club
   c. Gravitational force

   Applied forces provide the energy delivered to the ball. Centripetal force and gravity can affect the swing path.
3. On the downswing, the shoulders pull the leading arm, club, and clubhead back along the natural swing path. Use your leading shoulder to pull the club around the body.

CHAPTER 8
Putting It All Together

The proper order of things is often a mystery to me.

—Lewis Carroll, author

I claim that the golf swing is not actually a swing at all but rather the combination of two rotations: the primary rotation and the secondary rotation. To effectively hit a golf ball, both rotations need to be executed correctly and in perfect synchronization.

In Chinese mythology, yin and yang were born from chaos when the universe was first created, and they are believed to exist in harmony at the center of the earth. The simple meaning of yin and yang is, "You complete me."

However, there is more to it. It is also about balance. The other meaning would be, "You balance me out." In Chinese philosophy, yin and yang represent two equal entities that complement each other and should be considered together.

The primary rotation and the secondary rotation are the yin and yang of golf. When these two rotations exist in harmony, they are the center of the golf swing. Individually, they do very little, but together, in balance, they complete—and complement—each other.

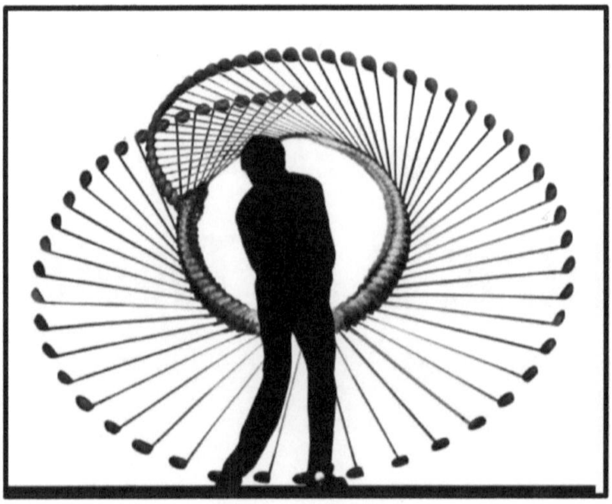

Figure 104: The Full Swing

It is worth taking a second to pause here and reflect on a few things. Building a good golf swing involves learning (and understanding) all the pieces and then putting those pieces together carefully and in a step-by-step fashion.

The main concepts presented so far include:

- Grip
- Setup
- Primary rotation
- Secondary rotation
- Tertiary motion
- The kinetics of the swing

The golf ball needs to fly long and straight. To do this, the clubface must contact the ball perpendicular to the target. The direction the ball travels is a function of the angle of the clubface to the target line as the clubface contacts the ball. The distance the ball travels is proportional to the speed of the clubface as it contacts the ball. We're now going to assemble the pieces.

In real life, the golf swing is not a series of discrete steps but rather one continuous fluid motion. The average swing time for a pro is 0.60 to 0.90 seconds, and the average swing time for an amateur is 0.75 to 1.20 seconds. The golf-swing tempo is the time it takes to get your club from the address to the top of the backswing and back down to impact, and that ratio is typically two to one.

Back Rotation and Forward Rotation

Backswing and downswing are well established terms in golf, though the more accurate alternate description could also be back rotation and forward rotation.

However, for purposes of continuity, I'll use the colloquialism "backswing" to refer to the primary rotation and secondary rotation from the address position to the top of the swing (clockwise rotation) and the colloquialism "downswing" to refer to the motion from the top of the swing (counterclockwise rotation) to impact.

Breaking the swing into discrete steps makes it easier to explain and to understand the full swing.

Revelation #14

The full swing is a combination of 90-degree rotations:

- **Backswing is 90 degrees clockwise rotation of the primary rotation (shoulders) and 90 degrees clockwise rotation of the secondary rotation (straight left arm) to the top of swing.**
- **Downswing is 90 degrees counterclockwise rotation of the primary rotation (shoulders) and 90 degrees counterclockwise rotation of the secondary rotation (straight left arm) to impact (the inflection point).**
- **Follow-through is 90 degrees counterclockwise rotation of the primary rotation (shoulders) and 90 degrees counterclockwise rotation of the secondary rotation (straight leading arm) to the finish.**

We're going to divide the full swing into ten steps, many of which use some combination of primary rotation and secondary rotation.

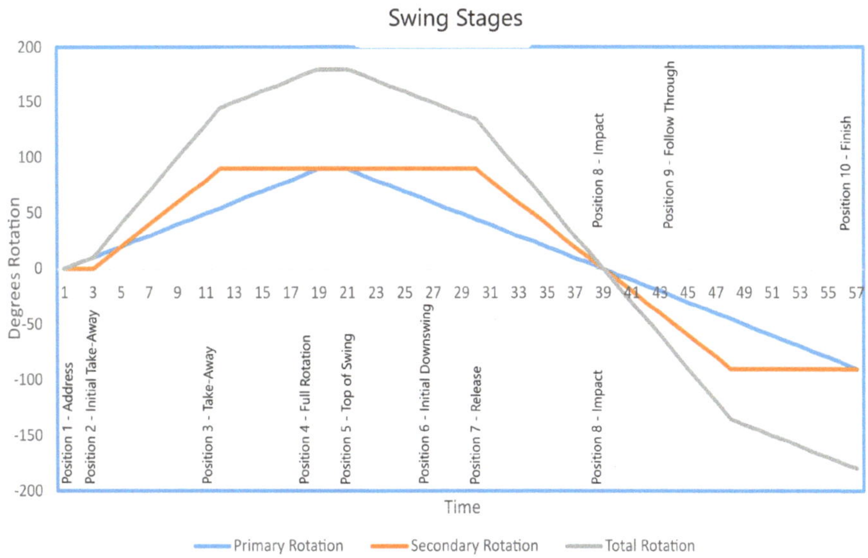

Figure 105: The Swing Stages

Step 1: Address Position
Step 2: Initial Takeaway (Primary Rotation CW)
Step 3: Takeaway (Primary Rotation and Secondary Rotation CW)
Step 4: Full Rotation to Top of Swing (Primary Rotation and Secondary Rotation CW)
Step 5: Top of Backswing
Step 6: Initial Downswing (Primary Rotation CCW)
Step 7: Release (Primary Rotation and Secondary Rotation CCW)
Step 8: Impact
Step 9: Follow-Through (Primary Rotation and Secondary Rotation CCW)
Step 10: Finish Position

Each of the steps listed above are described on the following pages. The relative rotation at each position is given in degrees from address (the neutral position), which is considered 0 degrees.

The backswing is considered clockwise (CW) and the downswing and follow-through are considered counterclockwise (CCW). The percentages are representative and will vary depending on many things, such as club type, skill level, age, etc., but are provided as a general guide.

Step 1: Address

Primary Rotation: +5 degrees
Secondary Rotation (red): 0 degrees
Hip Orientation (blue): 0 degrees
Clubface Location: six o'clock

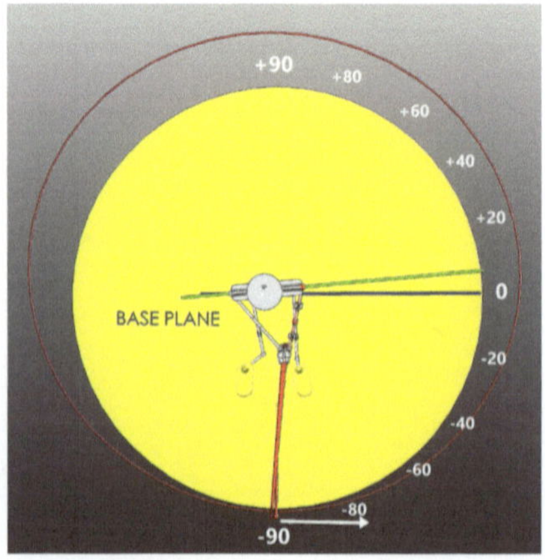

Figure 106: Step 1/Address

The green line represents the shoulder rotation. The blue line represents hip rotation.

The hips and feet are parallel to the target line (cross plane). Both arms are straight (forming the V). The shoulders are rotated slightly to allow for a good grip and a straight leading arm.

The clubface is on the base plane and perpendicular to the target line.

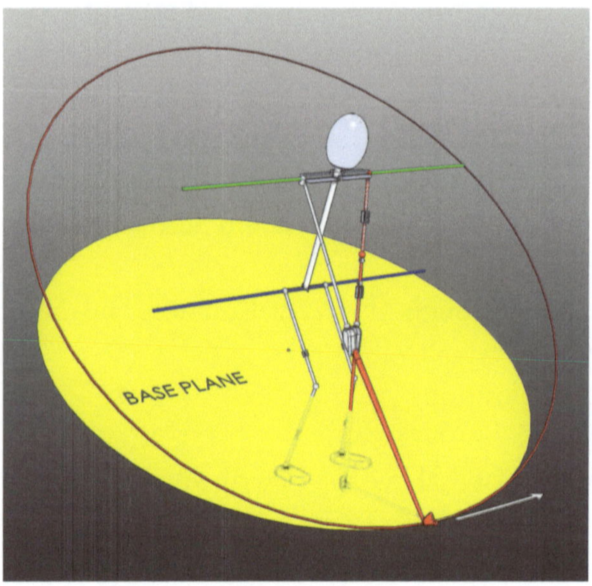

Figure 107: Address

Step 2: Initial Takeaway (Primary Rotation CW)

Primary Rotation (green): from +5 to –15 degrees
Secondary Rotation (red): 0 degrees
Hip Rotation (blue): 0 degrees
Clubface Location: from six to seven o'clock

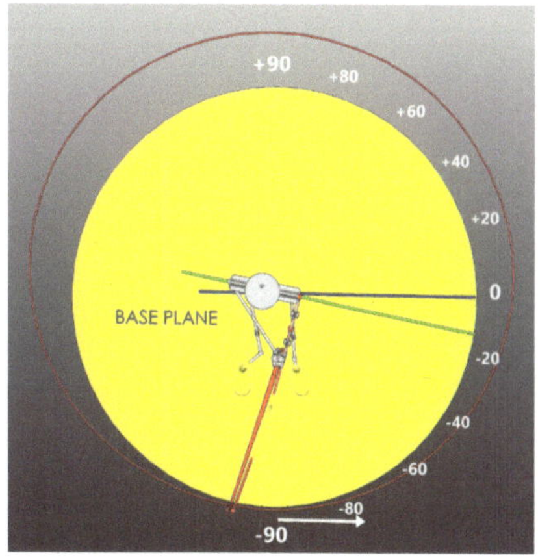

Figure 108: Step 2/Initial Takeaway

The initial takeaway consists entirely of primary rotation. You can't start secondary rotation until you have moved the clubhead away from the address position and off the ground.

The shoulders and arms start to rotate the club away from the ball. Keep both arms relatively straight (forming the V). The hips have not moved and are still parallel to the target line. The knee on the right leg is pointed slightly inward toward the midplane and is restraining the hips from moving during the backswing.

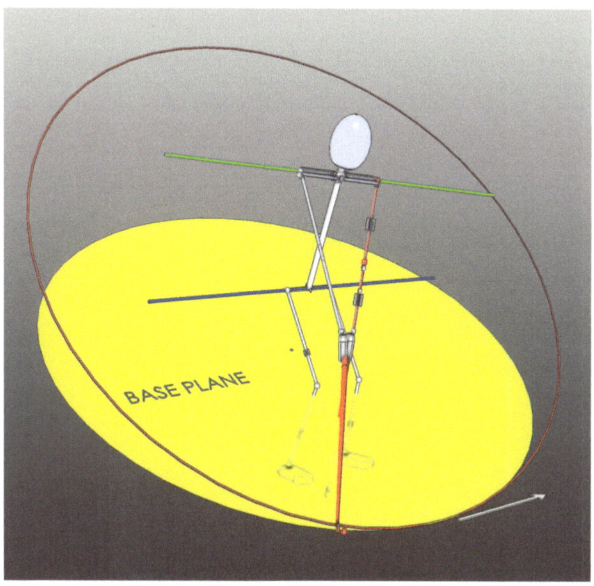

Figure 109: Initial Takeaway

The clubface is still on the base plane and perpendicular to the club path. As you move the club away with the shoulders and straight arms, the clubface will remain on the base plane, and the clubface will be perpendicular to a circular path.

Step 3: Takeaway (Primary Rotation CW and Secondary Rotation CW)

Primary Rotation (green): from –15 to –45 degrees
Secondary Rotation (red): from 0 to –60 degrees
Hip Rotation (blue): from 0 to –25 degrees
Clubface Location: from seven o'clock to eight thirty

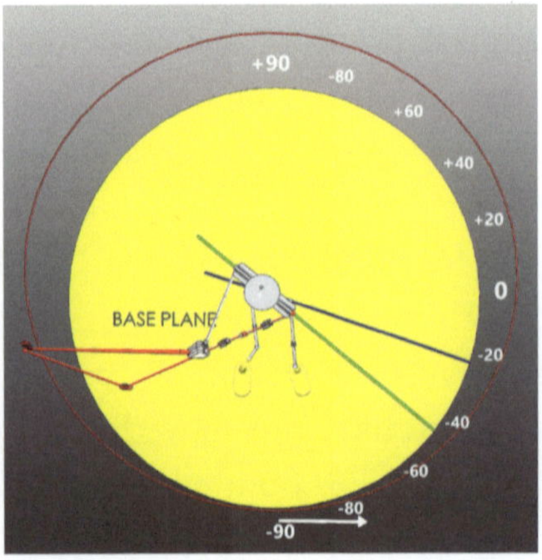

Figure 110: Step 3/Takeaway

Shortly after the primary rotation has started, the secondary rotation begins. As the shoulders continue to rotate the club away from the ball (primary rotation), the right elbow moves in against the right side as the straight left arm rotates (secondary rotation). The secondary rotation is completed well before the primary rotation stops at the top of the swing.

As a rule of thumb, the elbow should be against the side of the body (i.e., secondary rotation clockwise completed) before the shoulders (primary rotation) have turned 45 degrees. The wrist hinge of the trailing wrist (right wrist) on the takeaway should be enough to maintain the flat left wrist.

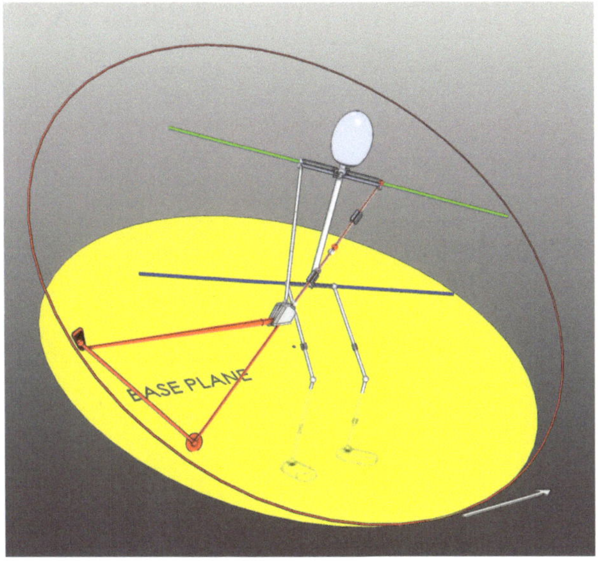

Figure 111: Takeaway

The knee on the right leg is still pointed slightly inward toward the mid-plane and continues to limit hip movement. But as the upper body rotates, the hips start to start to move but lag the shoulders. The right foot is perpendicular to the target line, and the right leg remains relatively locked in place as the left leg bends slightly inward to permit the upper body to rotate.

Note: You should feel as if the shoulder turn is rotating the arms, which results in the clockwise rotation around the primary axis of rotation (center of body). This motion will continue until the elbow is nearly against the right side (at approximately 45 degrees of rotation), at which point the shoulders will continue to rotate to full rotation (approximately 90 degrees) to the top of the backswing.

Remember from Chapter 4 that the bending of the right elbow against the side guides the straight left arm to rotate and to move across the chest, thereby lifting the clubface into the swing plane and following a club path along the swing plane. The clubface is no longer on the base plane.

Step 4: Full Rotation to Top of Swing (Primary Rotation and Secondary Rotation CW)

Primary Rotation (green): from –45 to –85 degrees
Secondary Rotation (yellow): from –60 to –90 degrees
Hip Rotation (blue): from –25 to –40 degrees
Clubface Location: from eight thirty to eleven thirty

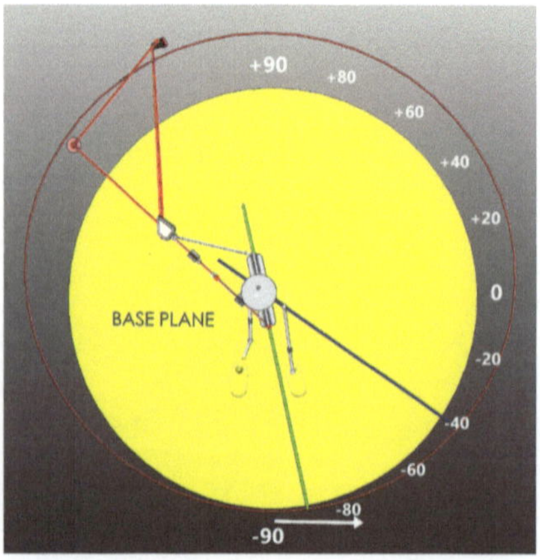

Figure 112: Step 4/Full Rotation to Top of Swing

As the shoulders continue to rotate back, the arms, hands, and club are rotated back around the center of the body (primary axis of rotation).

The right arm, elbow, and wrist guide the straight left arm across your chest during the backswing. This is done by shortening the distance between the right shoulder and the wrists by bending the right elbow against the body during the backswing.

Note that at the top of the swing, the *left* arm is still relatively straight but has rotated a full 90 degrees, and the *right* elbow will be against the right side. The eyes are still looking down at the ball. The clubface should be behind the shoulders and on the swing plane, roughly tangent to the club path and parallel to the target line.

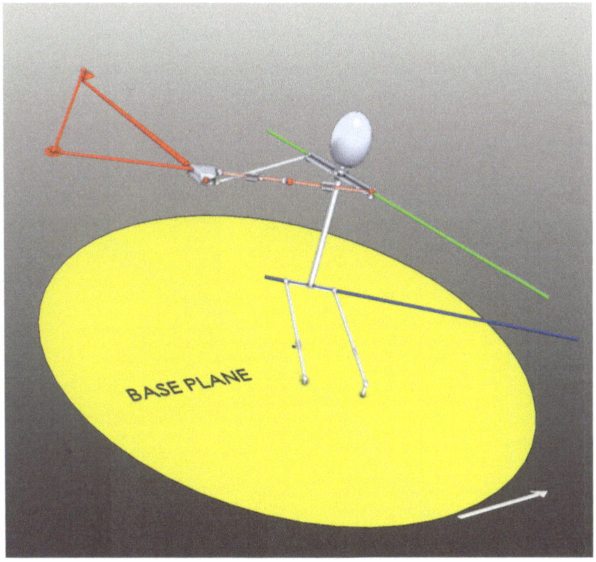

Figure 113: Full Rotation to Top of Swing

The right leg is still retaining the same relative position from address with the knee pointing slightly inward. This restrains the hip rotation as the shoulders rotate to the top of the backswing. The left leg rotates slightly inward to allow the upper body to rotate around the primary axis.

The torso should stay relatively centered, and the hips should rotate and not slide during the backswing. The slide is a lateral movement of the body off center, which results in what is commonly referred to as the reverse pivot.

There will be increased pressure on the back foot and leg, and some weight will shift to the back leg. This is the result of the backswing rotation and not the result of lateral motion or spine tilt.

Maintain a flat left wrist (FLW) and straight leading arm (SLA) throughout the backswing.

Step 5: Top of Backswing

Primary Rotation (green): from –85 to –90 degrees
Secondary Rotation (yellow): –90 degrees
Hip Rotation (blue): from –40 to –45 degrees
Clubface Location: from eleven thirty to twelve o'clock

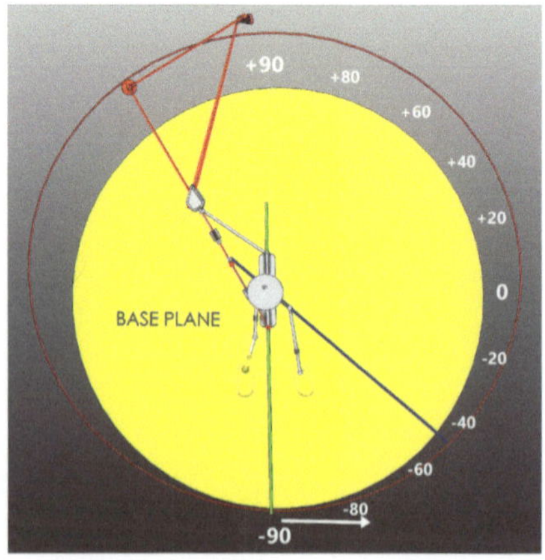

Figure 114: Step 5/Top of Backswing

At the top of the swing, there should be a brief pause of the shoulders (and club) as you drive off the right foot and begin to shift weight and pressure from the back leg to the front leg with a corresponding rotation of the hips counterclockwise in the opposite direction of the shoulder and club movement.

Revelation #15

One element of tempo is the pause at the top of the backswing; this allows the club to slow down and change direction. This creates the proper lag between the leading forearm and the club shaft as the momentum of the backswing rotates the arms and club clockwise while the shoulders and club stop and reverse direction.

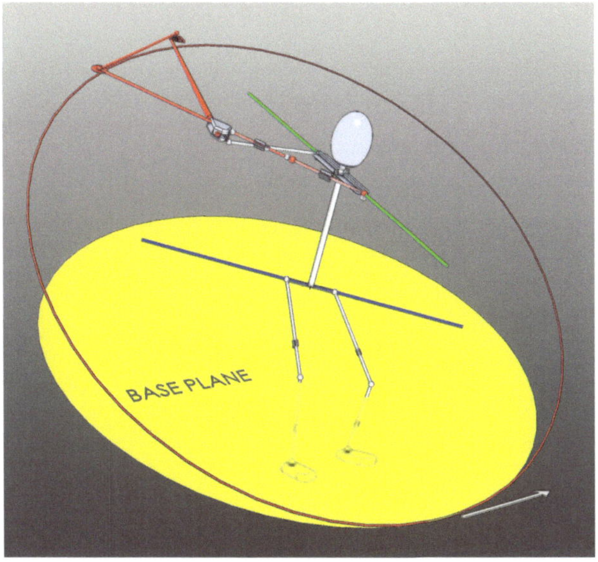

Figure 115: Top of Backswing

This counterclockwise rotation of the hips will force the shoulders to reverse direction and start the counterclockwise rotation of the shoulders, which, in turn, initiates the rotation of the straight leading arm back around the body (primary axis). The right elbow is still against the side, and the clubface is tangent to the swing path.

The elbow will lift away from the side at the top of the swing to allow the club momentum to stop and change direction as the chest and shoulders change direction and move in the counterclockwise direction. Once the club reverses direction and is also moving counterclockwise, you pull the elbow back in against your side during the initial downswing.

For beginners, it's a good idea to keep the upper arm and elbow against your side during the backswing. As you get more advanced with your technique, you can allow the elbow to lift some at the top of the swing.

Step 6: Initial Downswing (Primary Rotation CCW)

Primary Rotation (green): from –90 to –20 degrees
Secondary Rotation (yellow): –90 degrees
Hip Rotation (green): from –30 to +5 degrees
Clubface Location: from twelve o'clock to eight o'clock

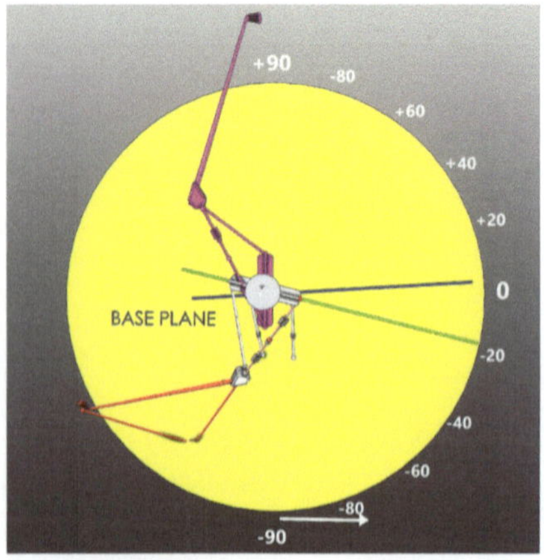

Figure 116: Step 6/Initial Downswing

The elbow remains against the side as the shoulders rotate counterclockwise (primary rotation counterclockwise) from approximately –90 degrees to approximately –30 degrees. Secondary rotation remains at –90 degrees during the initial downswing.

Continue pushing off the back leg to drive the hips, which rotates the shoulders counterclockwise, and the shoulder should be pulling the straight leading arm. This, in turn, pulls the club and clubhead onto the swing plane, which is the natural swing path for the clubhead. Again, this is the result of driving the downswing rotation and not the result of lateral motion or spine tilt.

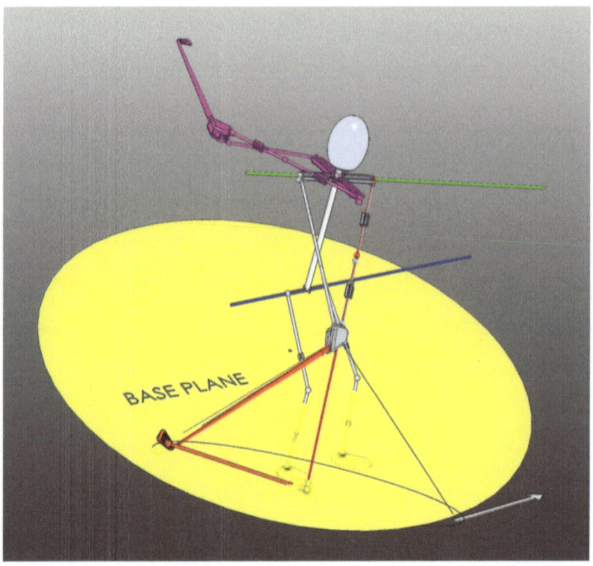

Figure 117: Initial Downswing

Step 7: The Release (Primary Rotation CCW and Secondary Rotation CCW)

Primary Rotation (green): from –20 to +5 degrees
Secondary Rotation (yellow): from –90 to 0 degrees
Hip Rotation (blue): from +5 to +20 degrees
Clubface Location: from eight thirty to six o'clock

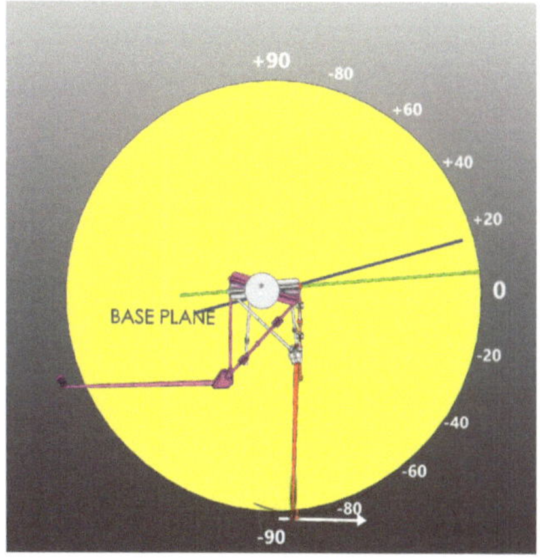

Figure 118: Step 7/The Release

As the shoulders continue to rotate counterclockwise in the downswing, the bent right elbow will need to lift away from the right side as the right arm straightens during the release, which will, in turn, cause the straight leading arm (secondary axis) to rotate counterclockwise from –90 degrees to 0 degrees at impact.

Revelation #16

Another element of tempo is the timing of the release so that the clubface angle of the secondary rotation coincides with the clubface angle of the primary rotation to yield the desired combined clubface angle.

The release involves the straightening of the trailing elbow and wrist, which allows the secondary rotation to occur. Timing of the release during the downswing determines speed of the secondary rotation and therefore distance.

The timing for straightening the right arm by extending the elbow from the side is what allows the clubface to rotate (left arm rotation) from open (with respect to the swing path) to neutral (perpendicular to the target line) at impact. The clubface will continue to rotate closed on the follow-through.

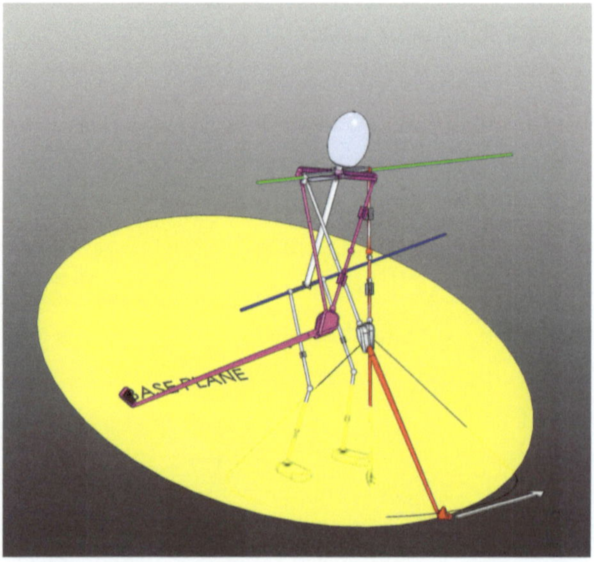

Figure 119: The Release

Step 8: Impact

Primary Rotation (green): +5 degrees
Secondary Rotation (yellow): 0 degrees
Hip Rotation (blue): +20 degrees
Clubface Location: six o'clock

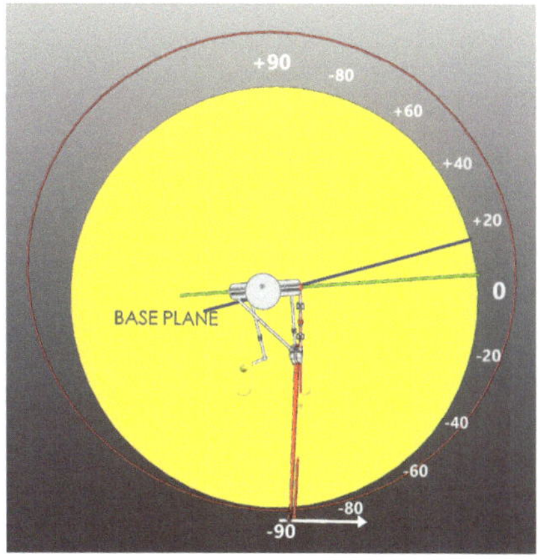

Figure 120: Step 8/Impact

The hips and shoulders have rotated back past the neutral position during impact. The secondary axis (straight left arm) has rotated from –90 degrees at the start of the release to 0 degrees at impact.

The weight and pressure from the back leg has shifted to the front leg as momentum from the downswing transfers energy from the golf clubhead to the golf ball.

When the clubface makes contact with the ball, the shoulder will be slightly past parallel, both arms will be straight, the flat left wrist will be facing the target, and the clubface will be almost square to the ball (perpendicular to the target line) as the clubface rotates from the open position into the neutral position (on impact) on the way to the closed position during the follow-through.

There's a lot happening in a very, very short amount of time as all the pieces of the swing come into play.

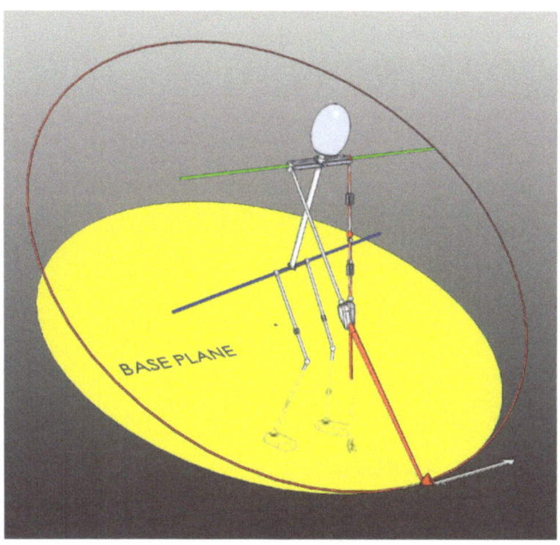

Figure 121: Impact

Step 9: The Follow-Through (Primary Rotation CCW and Secondary Rotation CCW)

Primary Rotation (green): from +5 to +75 degrees
Secondary Rotation (yellow): from 0 to 45 degrees
Hip Rotation (blue): from +25 to +40 degrees
Clubface Location: from six o'clock to three o'clock

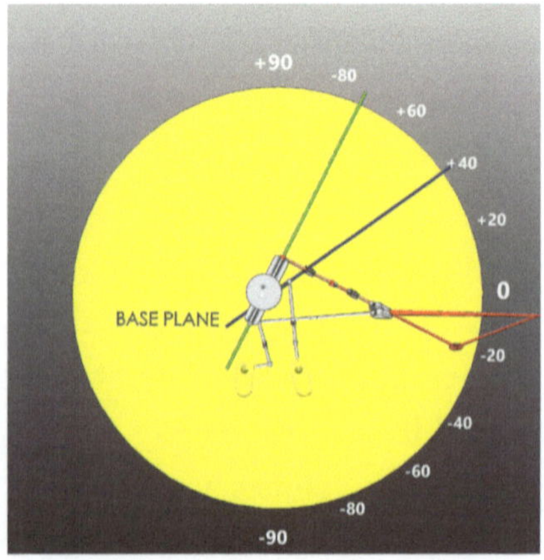

Figure 122: Step 9/The Follow-Through

After impact, the shoulders continue to rotate counterclockwise past the neutral position around the body (the primary axis). This, in turn, rotates the arms that are connected to the club, which is also rotating around the body.

Up to this point, the exercises have been focused on being centered as you rotate on the backswing to the top of the swing and then rotate on the downswing to impact. After impact, your weight must now shift forward toward the target on the follow-through as you rotate to the finish.

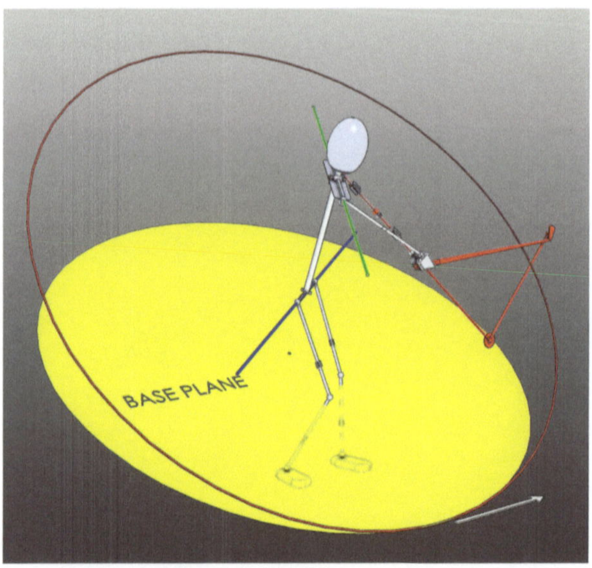

Figure 123: The Follow-Through

As the club and the arms rotate counterclockwise around the body in the follow-through, the straight right arm (with the flat right wrist) will continue to rotate counterclockwise. The trailing arm (right arm) remains straight as the left elbow begins to bend into the left side.

You can gauge a swing somewhat by the quality of the follow-through. Golfers who stop their swing after impact will likely not get the desired result. The goal is to deliver the maximum momentum and energy during the downswing to impact and then take the foot off the gas and allow the swing to coast to a stop.

Step 10: The Finish

Primary Rotation (green): +90 degrees
Secondary Rotation (yellow): 90 degrees
Hip Rotation (green): 90 degrees
Clubface Location: past twelve o'clock

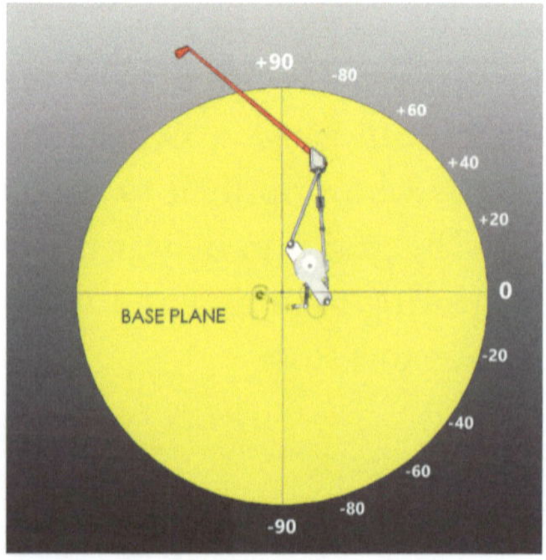

Figure 124: Step 10/The Finish

This motion will continue until the elbow is against the left side (at approximately 45 degrees of rotation) and the golfer has straightened from inclined to a vertical position. The shoulders will continue to rotate to full rotation (approximately 90 degrees) to the top of the follow-through.

The momentum from the rotation will carry the upper body and primary axis forward off the midplane in the direction of the target. Most, if not all, the weight has transferred to the front leg. Remember, if nothing else, it should look pretty!

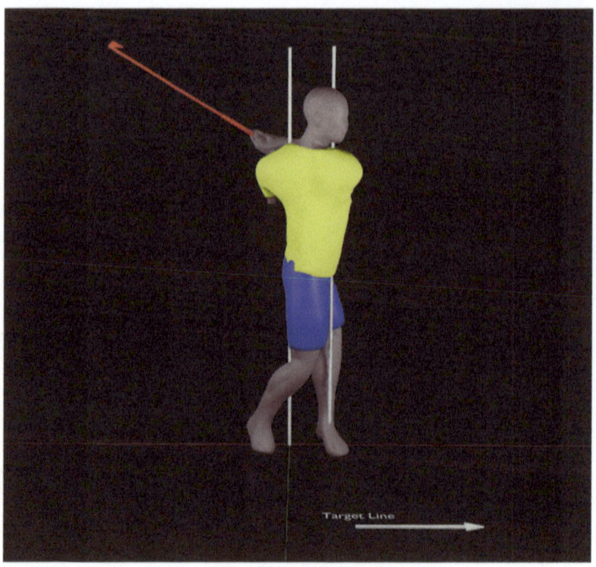

Figure 125: The Finish

The Follow-Through and the Finish: Completing the Swing

After impact, your weight must now shift forward toward the target on the follow-through as you rotate to the finish.

This chapter started with the premise that it would be easier to explain and understand the golf swing by breaking it down into smaller pieces. The same approach can be followed as well when it comes time to apply that knowledge to training the body.

The following chapters focus on step-by-step training exercises. Their purpose is to train the body to perform the individual motions necessary to hit a golf ball properly.

These exercises are divided into four categories:

1. **Primary Rotation:** Training the shoulders (Chapter 9)
2. **Secondary Rotation:** Training the straight left arm (Chapter 10)
3. **Tertiary Motion:** Training the right arm to tie primary and secondary together (Chapter 11)
4. **Putting It All Together:** Combining primary, secondary, and tertiary with a good follow-through and finish for the full swing (Chapter 12)

Takeaways:

So what did we learn in Chapter 8?

1. There are three distinct motions involved with the full swing:
    a. Primary rotation of the shoulders from address (0 degrees) to the top of the swing with the shoulders at 90 degrees clockwise at the top of the swing. With primary rotation, only the clubface travels along the base plane.
    b. Motion 2: Secondary rotation of the left arm 90 degrees, which is the result of the right elbow bending into the right side of the upper body. With the addition of secondary rotation, the clubface is lifted from the base plane to the midplane.
    c. Motion 3: Tertiary motion is done by rotating the left arm across the chest by bending the right elbow and folding the right upper arm to your side. Remember that the right upper arm should be against the right side of the body during most of the backswing.
2. The full swing can be divided into ten distinct steps that involve primary, secondary, and tertiary motion:
    a. Step 1: Address Position
    b. Step 2: Initial Takeaway (Primary Rotation CW)
    c. Step 3: Takeaway (Primary Rotation Clockwise and Secondary Rotation CW)
    d. Step 4: Full Rotation to Top of Swing (Primary Rotation CW and Secondary Rotation CW)
    e. Step 5: Top of Backswing
    f. Step 6: Initial Downswing (Primary Rotation CCW)
    g. Step 7: Release (Primary Rotation and Secondary Rotation CCW)
    h. Step 8: Impact
    i. Step 9: Follow-Through (Primary Rotation and Secondary Rotation CCW)
    j. Step 10: Finish Position

CHAPTER 9

Practicing with Purpose: Primary Rotation

When we look at living creatures from an outward point of view, one of the first things that strikes us is that they are bundles of habits. The more of the details of our daily life we can hand over to the effortless custody of automatism, the more our higher powers of mind will be set free for their own proper work.

—William James, The Principles of Psychology (1890)

The first eight chapters have provided a lot of information and hopefully insight into the golf swing, but don't run to the driving range and expect miracles. You now have extra knowledge for developing and improving your golf swing. It's time to put that knowledge into practice by not only training the mind, but also training the body.

First, a quick discussion about how your body learns to move.

The Neuromuscular System

The neuromuscular system includes all the muscles in the body and the nerves serving them.

Every movement the body makes requires communication between the brain and the muscles. The nervous system provides the link between thoughts and actions by relaying messages from the brain to other parts of the body.

Nerves and muscles, working together as the neuromuscular system, make the body move in a desired way.

Revelation #18

To be able to strike a ball properly, you need to develop the required neuromuscular connections for all the motions involved. This comes in part by practice and repetition of the *correct* motions.

How Does It Work?

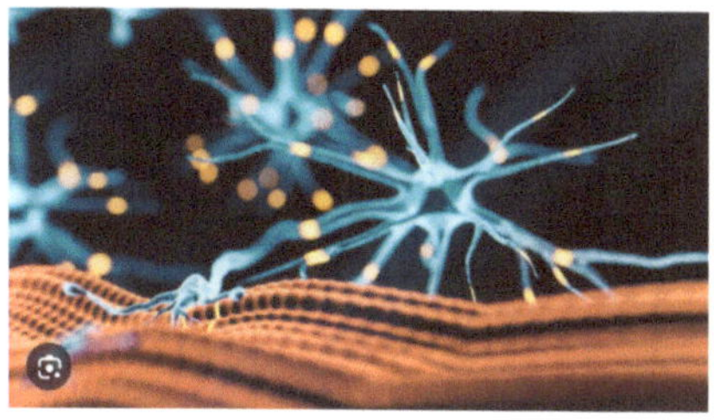

Figure 126: The Neuromuscular System

Nerves have cells called neurons. Neurons carry messages from the brain via the spinal cord. The neurons that carry these messages to the muscles are called motor neurons.

Each motor neuron ending sits very close to a muscle fiber. This is called a neuromuscular junction. The motor neurons release a chemical, which is picked up by muscle fiber, and this tells the muscle fiber to contract, which makes the muscles move.

So what does this have to do with the golf swing? Valid question. Please indulge me another short-story example.

You go to the range for a lesson. The instructor hands you an iron and tells you to take a swing. You address the ball with every intention of hitting a beautiful draw up the middle and out to the flag. Instead, the ball goes wildly to the right and fifty yards short of the intended target. What went wrong?

Well, for one, it's hard to strike a ball properly when someone's watching you. But more importantly, it's nearly impossible to properly strike the ball if you haven't developed the neuromuscular connections necessary to perform all the motions required to properly swing the golf club.

Revelation #19

Taking a stepwise approach to learning the swing involves training individual motions and muscle groups through repetition and exercise. Once these individual skills are mastered, they can be combined into an effective full swing.

There are many ways to practice the golf swing depending on your available time and goals. Swing practice often involves getting a bucket of balls and hitting them until the bucket is empty. But too often, we're mindlessly reinforcing bad habits rather than building good ones.

If practicing good habits reinforces good behavior, what does practicing bad habits reinforce?

The following are exercises that develop specific skills—practicing with a purpose.

Chapters 1 through 8 have attempted to lay a step-by-step approach for understanding all the parts of the golf swing. Mastering the swing should likewise be built in a stepwise manner, mastering each prerequisite motion before proceeding to the full swing.

The three important aspects for effective practicing are:

1. Adopt a stepwise approach to learning the swing.
2. Practice the right stuff.
3. Practice on a regular basis.

Each category contains a series of exercises that have a specific purpose. The series starts with exercises in the vertical world (standing erect) and then graduates to the inclined world (at the inclined address position).

The series of exercises follows this progression:

1. Motions that don't require any equipment and can be completed at home
2. The same exercises again with a golf club to study the same motion with the effects of gravity (e.g., the weight of a golf club)
3. The same exercises one last time but with a golf club and a golf ball

You'll notice that the first two progressions listed above don't involve hitting a golf ball and can be done at home. You do not need to go to the driving range to do many of the exercises in this chapter.

Speed is not the focus with these exercises. The emphasis should be on observation of the club path and clubhead orientation. These chapters are all about training muscle memory. Everything in golf practice revolves around repetition of the correct motions until muscle memory takes over. When that happens, the motion will be smooth (i.e., have the proper timing), be consistent, and will feel natural, i.e., you can do the motion without really thinking about it.

Chapter 9 Exercises—Primary Rotation (V to V to V)

Full shoulder rotation forms the foundation of a good swing. There is a strong connection between our brains and our arms and hands. However, our shoulders, though closer to the brain, are not used as much for everyday activities. That is, until you take up a sport like golf.

If you watch a professional strike the ball, a common element of all low handicap golfers is the ability to fully rotate the shoulders on the backswing and follow-through. Conversely, most high handicap golfers use way too much arm swinging and way too little shoulder rotation.

One of the best ways to improve your ball-striking ability is to improve your primary rotation, which, as we saw in Chapter 4, is the use of the upper body and shoulders.

These are progressive exercises, and all except the last exercise can be completed at home on a regular basis. The final exercise uses a golf ball and requires open-field practice at the driving range or somewhere similar.

Vertical position refers to standing erect, while inclined position means bent (at the hips) in a normal setup position.

And finally, the golf club for training should typically be a short iron, such as an 8 iron.

Variations on a Theme

Each of the following exercises are a variation of the above theme, with some comments and suggestions intended to help guide you through.

Progressive Exercises (V to V to V)

9	Address	Equipment	Primary Rotation only
9.1	Vertical	none	Arm Horizontal
9.2	Vertical	none	Upper Arms Lowered (tight to chest)
9.3	Vertical	with club	Arm Horizontal
9.4	Vertical	with club	Upper Arms Lowered (tight to chest)
9.5	Inclined	none	Upper Arms Lowered (tight to chest)
9.6	Inclined	with club	Upper Arms Lowered (tight to chest)
9.7	Inclined	with club (OHR)	Upper Arms Lowered (tight to chest)
9.8	Inclined	with club and ball	Upper Arms Lowered (tight to chest)

The operative words here are patience and persistence.

Exercise 9.1—Vertical Position Without Equipment and Arms Straight Out

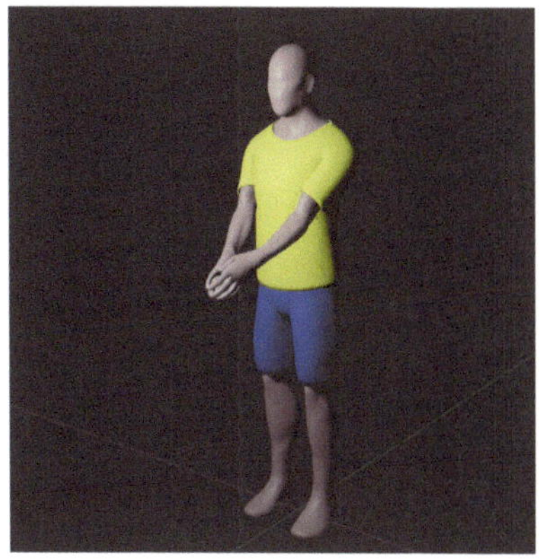

Figure 127: Exercise 9.1 Address

Arms are straight out in front and horizontal to the ground; your hands are in the prayer position. Your head remains steady and looking forward.

This is a good exercise to do in front of a mirror. Maintain good posture and make sure to keep the lower body quiet—don't twist your legs. This is also a good exercise to do while seated, which encourages your lower body to remain inactive and forces you to turn your upper body.

Rotation should be a full 180 degrees—90 degrees counterclockwise (backswing) and 90 degrees clockwise (follow-through) from the neutral position (facing forward).

Why is this exercise important?

Demonstrates the primary axis of rotation
Trains your brain to use your shoulders and not your arms
Reinforces the importance of keeping your head still and facing forward
Trains your mind on how to keep your body centered around the primary axis while rotating your upper body

Note that as you rotate, your hands remain in the vertical position during the entire rotation.

1. Stand erect with good posture (back straight and shoulders square). Refer to Chapter 4 if you'd like a refresher on proper posture.

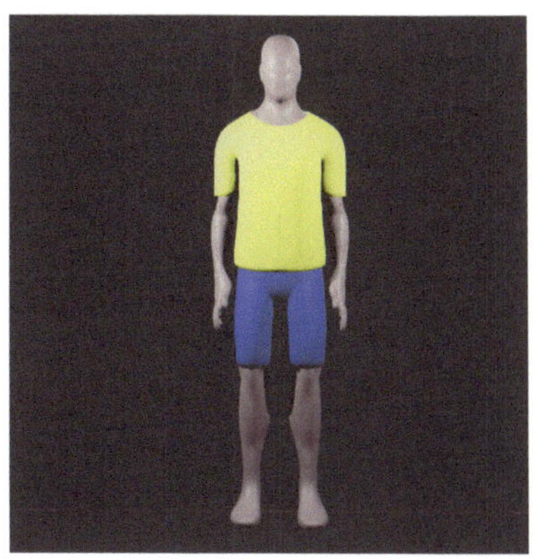

2. Extend your arms straight out in front of you with your hands flat and together, forming a V. This forms a triangle with your shoulders as the base of the triangle. This is the neutral position. Keep your arms as **close together** as possible and try to keep the inside of your elbows facing upward.

3. *Slowly* rotate the shoulders about 45 degrees clockwise while keeping your head facing forward. Do *not* allow the arms to take over. Make sure the movement is done with your *shoulders only*. If you turn correctly using your shoulders, you'll maintain the V as you turn. Do not bend your elbows.

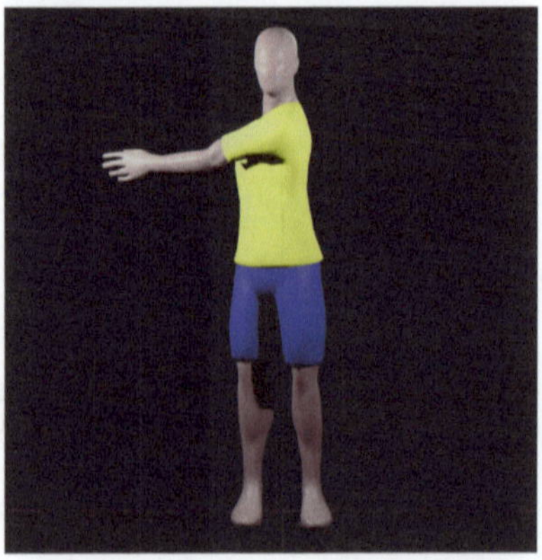

4. Slowly return to the neutral position.

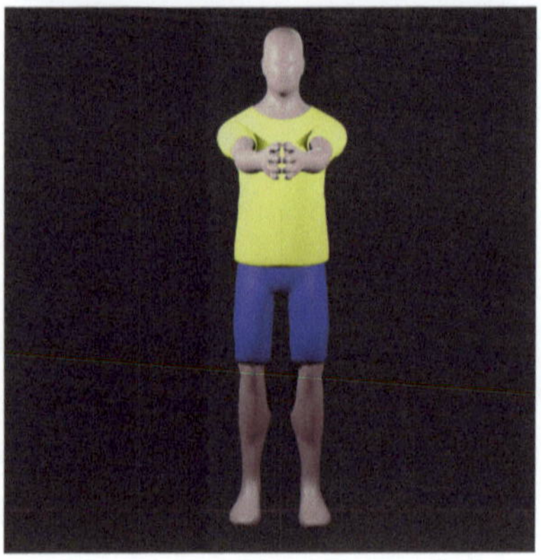

5. *Slowly* rotate your shoulders about 45 degrees counterclockwise while keeping your head facing forward. Don't allow your arms to take over. Make sure the movement is done with your *shoulders only*. If you turn correctly using the shoulders, you'll maintain the V as you turn. Do not bend either elbow.

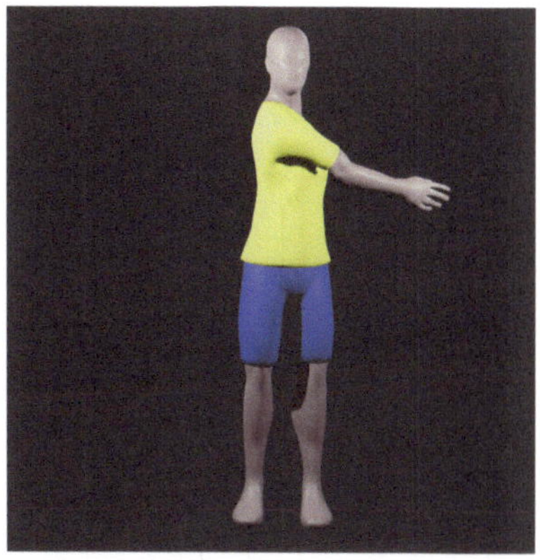

6. Slowly return to the neutral position. Repeat this exercise and gradually work your way up to 90-degree rotation of the shoulders or up to the maximum you can do.

Exercise 9.2—Vertical Position Without Equipment and Arms Lowered

Now repeat the previous exercise, but for the starting position, lower your arms from straight out in front of you until your upper arms are supported by your chest. This should feel comfortable since you no longer need to hold your arms out straight. Your upper arms should be resting tightly against your chest.

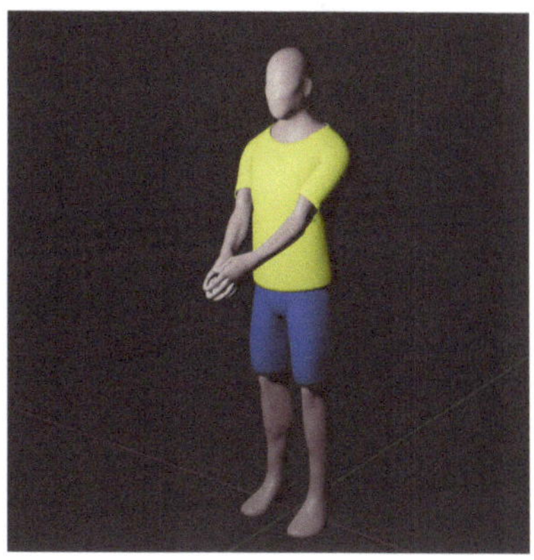

Figure 128: Exercise 9.2 Address

Keep your arms as close together as possible. Your upper arms must be tight against the body. You should be rotating the club with your chest and shoulders (and not your arms).

Try doing this with a hand towel tucked under each armpit. As you rotate, the towels should remain in place. This may seem easy now, but watch what happens as we advance through the exercises. This is also a good exercise to do with your eyes closed.

Why is this exercise important?

Demonstrates the primary axis of rotation

Trains your brain to use your shoulders and not your arms

Reinforces the importance of keeping your head still and facing forward

Trains your mind on how to keep your body centered around the primary axis while rotating your upper body

Trains you to rotate your arms with your chest

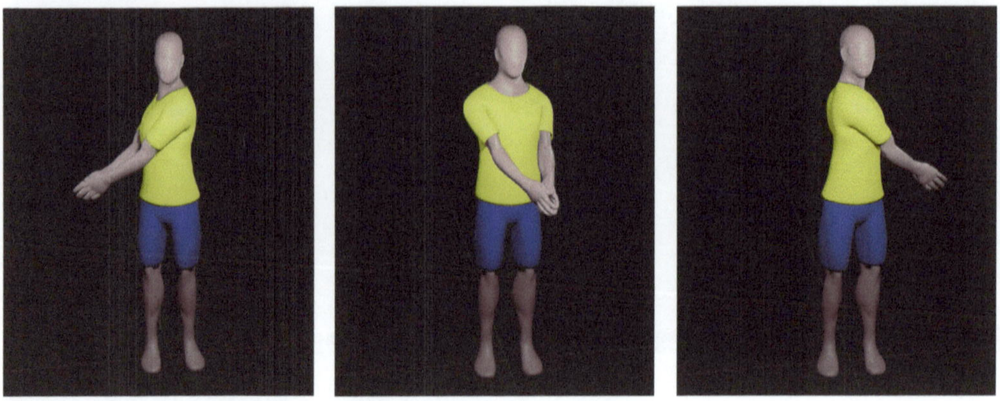

Figure 129: Exercise 9.2 Sequence

Exercise 9.3—Vertical Position with Golf Club and Arms Horizontal

Repeat Exercise 9.2 but with a golf club. Make sure to have a proper grip with the clubhead facing straight up (vertical) in front of you.

Why is this exercise important?

Demonstrates the primary axis of rotation
Trains your brain to use your shoulders and not your arms
Reinforces the importance of keeping your head still and facing forward
Trains your mind on how to keep your body centered around the primary axis while rotating your upper body
Gives you a visual for rotating an object (the club) around your body and feeling the effects of gravity

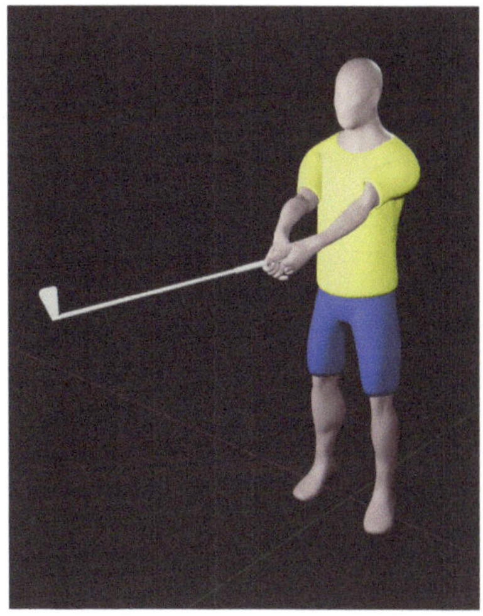

Figure 130: Exercise 9.3 Address

Again, you can do this in front of a mirror. Observe the position of the golf club and clubface as you complete the rotation. When your arms are straight out in front of you, the golf club should remain horizontal to the ground, and the clubface should remain vertical throughout the rotation.

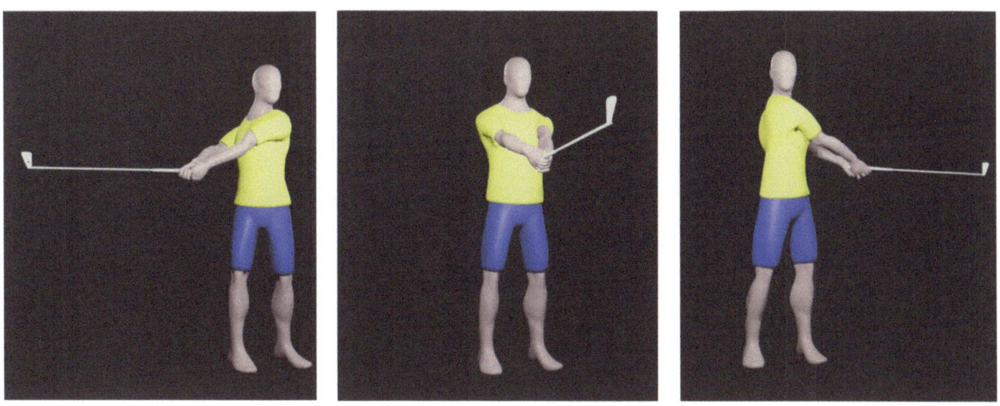

Figure 131: Exercise 9.3 Sequence

When you complete this exercise with your arms lowered and with hand towels under your armpits, the end of the clubhead should trace a semicircle around your body and remain the same distance from the ground. The clubface should remain vertical to the club path throughout the rotation.

Exercise 9.4—Vertical Position with Golf Club and Arms Lowered

Now repeat the previous exercise but lower your arms from straight out in front of you until your upper arms are supported by your chest. This should feel comfortable since you no longer need to hold your arms out straight. Your upper arms should be resting tightly against your chest.

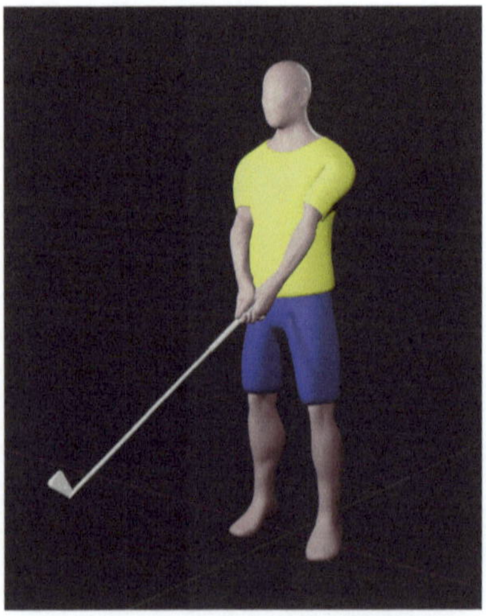

Figure 132: Exercise 9.4 Address

Try doing this with a hand towel tucked under each armpit. As you rotate, the towels should remain in place. This is also a good exercise to do with your eyes closed.

Note that as you rotate, the golf club is no longer horizontal and parallel to the ground (and to the base plane) during the rotation. However, the clubhead still traces a semicircle around the primary axis (your torso).

Why is this exercise important?

Demonstrates the primary axis of rotation

Trains your brain to use your shoulders and not your arms

Reinforces the importance of keeping your head still and facing forward

Trains your mind on how to keep your body centered around the primary axis while rotating your upper body

Gives you a visual for rotating a heavier object around your body and feeling the effects of gravity

Trains you to rotate the club with your chest and not your arms

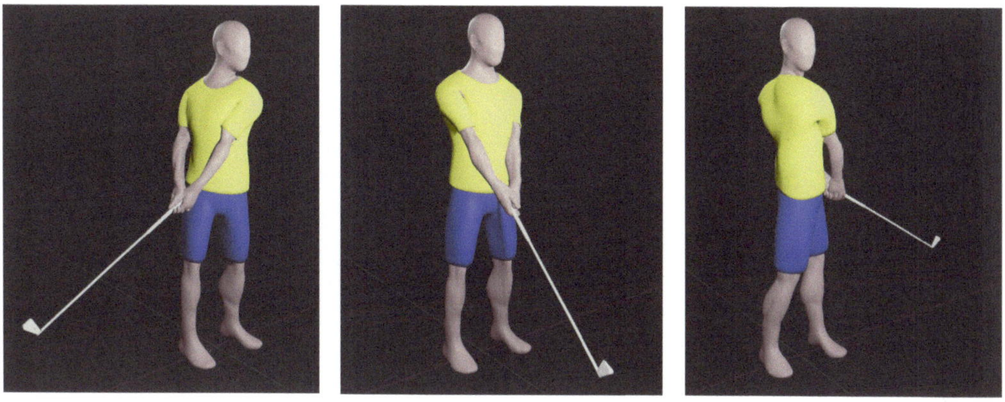

Figure 133: Exercise 9.4 Sequence

Exercise 9.5—Inclined Position Without Equipment

Repeat Exercise 9.4 without equipment and in the inclined position. Make sure that you have good posture and are tilting at the hips with your back straight. Don't bend your spine. You won't be able to do this exercise sitting down, but you will be able to do this exercise with your arms lowered and with hand towels under your armpits.

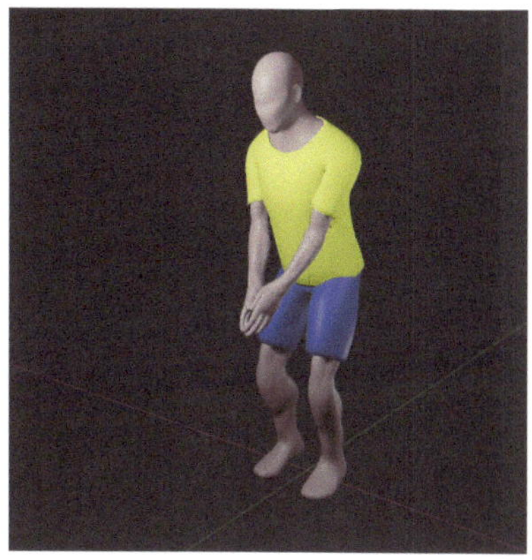

Figure 134: Exercise 9.5 Address

Why is this exercise important?

Demonstrates the primary axis of rotation
Trains your brain to use your shoulders and not your arms
Reinforces the importance of keeping your head still and facing forward
Trains your mind on how to keep your body centered around the primary axis while rotating your upper body with both arms straight
Teaches you how differently the rotation feels when you go from the vertical world to the inclined world (address position)

Again, you can do this in front of a mirror. As you rotate, your hands will trace a semicircle around the primary axis (your torso) but will rise above the ground at both ends by an amount proportional to the angle of inclination (spine tilt).

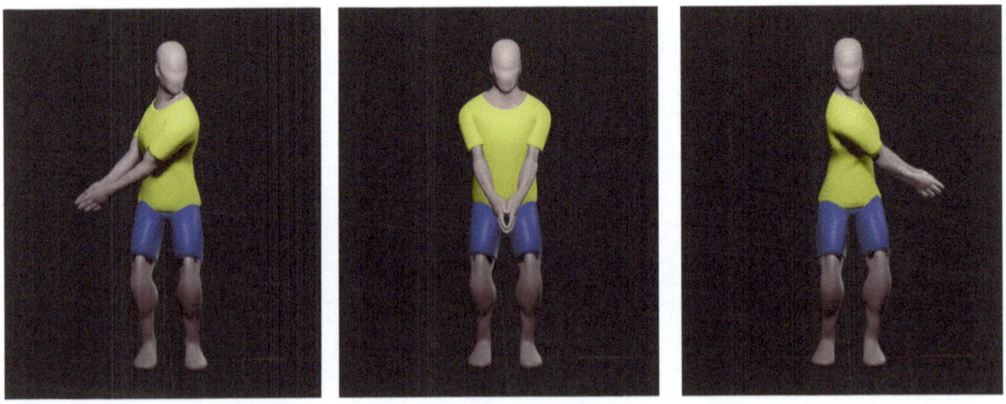

Figure 135: Exercise 9.5 Sequence

This is also a good exercise to do with your eyes closed, which will give you a better idea for what the motion feels like. Make sure you keep your head steady and face forward.

Exercise 9.6—Inclined Position with Golf Club

Repeat Exercise 9.5 but with a golf club in the inclined position. Make sure you have good grip and posture and are tilting at the hips with your back straight.

Keep your head steady and continue looking forward. Don't bend your spine. You won't be able to do this exercise sitting down, but you will be able to do this exercise with your arms lowered and with hand towels under your armpits.

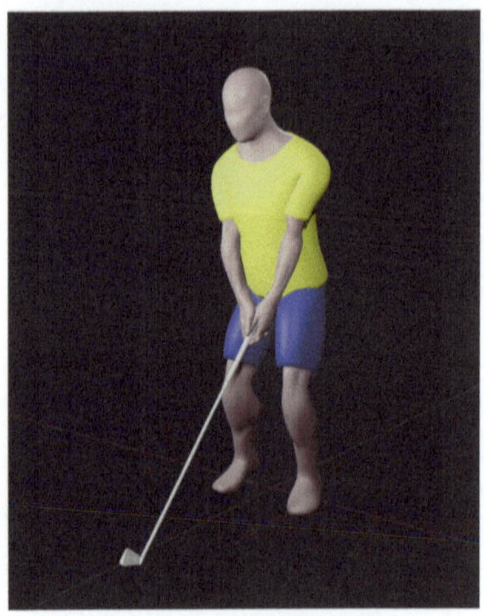

Figure 136: Exercise 9.6 Address

Why is this exercise important?

Demonstrates the primary axis of rotation

Trains your brain to use your shoulders and not your arms

Reinforces the importance of keeping your head still and facing forward

Trains your mind on how to keep your body centered around the primary axis while rotating your upper body with both arms straight

Gives you a visual for rotating a heavier object around your body and feeling the effects of gravity
Teaches you how differently the rotation feels when you go from the vertical world to the inclined world (address position)

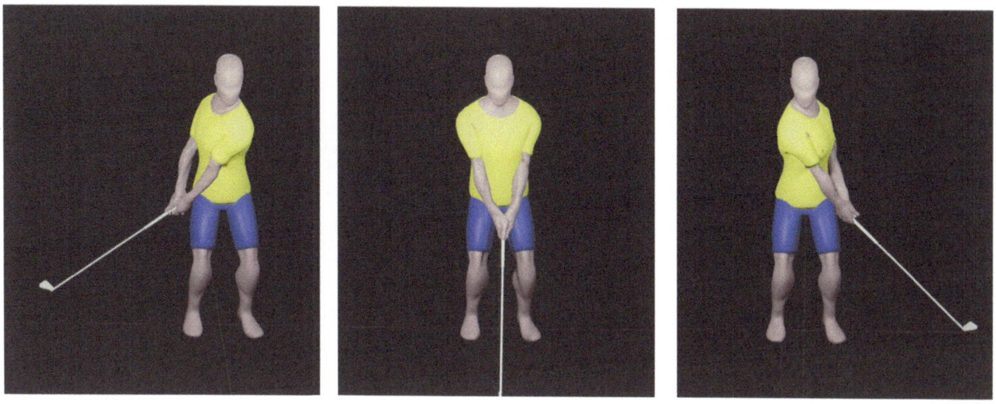

Figure 137: Exercise 9.6 Sequence

Observe the position of the golf club shaft and clubface as you complete the rotation. As you rotate, the clubhead will trace a semicircle around the primary axis (your torso) but will rise above the ground at both ends by an amount proportional to the angle of inclination (spine tilt). The clubface will remain perpendicular to the club path throughout the rotation.

From Chapter 3, we know that the feet should be about shoulder width apart, slightly wider for longer clubs and slightly closer for shorter clubs. Try the exercise with your eyes closed and your feet closer together. You can even do the exercise with your feet touching each other.

With a wide stance, you will be tempted to shift your weight from side to side. A narrower stance will force you to keep your weight centered, which promotes rotation. This is an excellent exercise for learning the importance of the balance necessary for a good rotation during the golf swing.

If you complete this motion in a cyclical fashion, moving back and forth (preferably on carpet or grass), you should be able to repeatably brush the ground. Repeat the motion until it is consistent and feels comfortable.

Holding the towel under your upper arms during the rotation trains your arms to stay tight to your torso during the swing. As you'll see later, when doing primary rotation properly, you'll feel like you're rotating the club with your chest (and not swinging your arms).

Exercise 9.7—Inclined Position with Golf Club and One-Hand Release (OHR)

Repeat Exercise 9.6 in the inclined position and with a golf club. Make sure that you have good grip and posture and are tilting at the hips with your back straight. Keep your head steady and looking forward. As you start the downswing, let go of the club with your right hand. We will refer to this as one-hand release, or OHR.

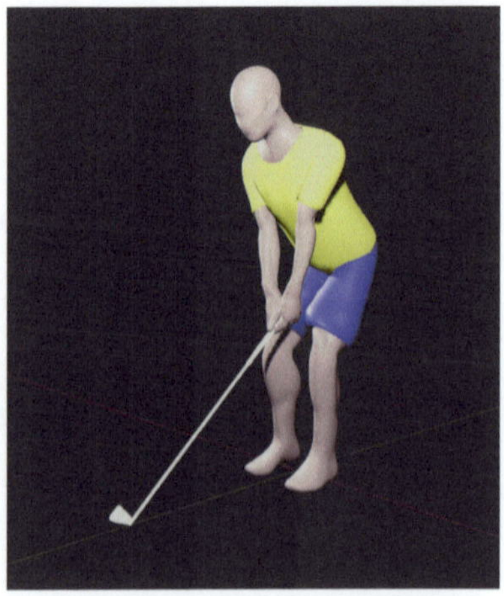

Figure 138: Exercise 9.7 Address

Why is this exercise important?

Demonstrates the primary axis of rotation
Trains the brain to use the shoulders and not the arms
Reinforces the importance of keeping the head still and facing forward
Trains the mind on how to keep the body centered around the primary axis while rotating your upper body
Gives you a visual for rotating the golf club around your body and feeling the effects of gravity and centripetal force
Teaches you how to time the downswing so that you're pulling the club with your left shoulder

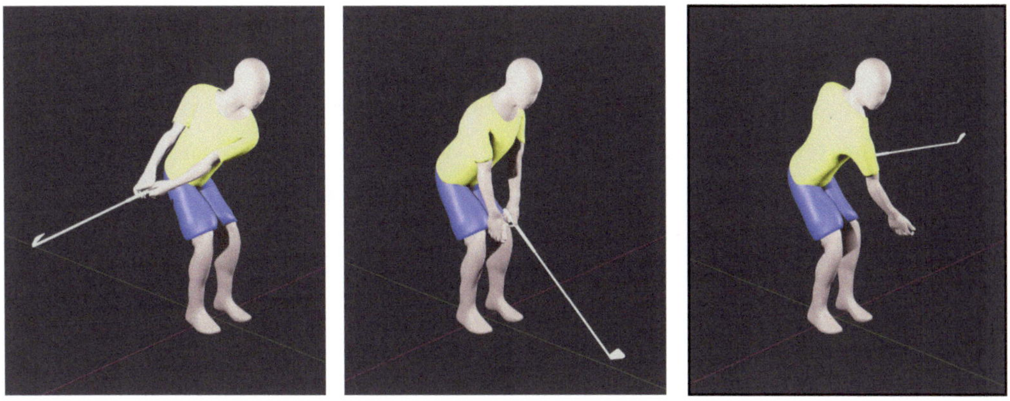

Figure 139: Exercise 9.7 Sequence

When you start the downswing, your left shoulder rotates counterclockwise and *pulls* your left arm, which, in turn, *pulls* the golf club back along the swing plane. When your shoulder is pulling your left arm (which holds the club), the club will follow a natural path back along the swing plane.

Often, golfers will start the downswing by trying to get the golf club back to the ball by steering it with their hands and arms.

As with a wagon example in Chapter 7, there's a big difference between pulling the club with your shoulder versus steering the club with your arms and hands. When you use your shoulder to pull your left arm and golf club, the club can find the natural swing path. This results in greater speed and accuracy.

This exercise is important for developing the timing and control required to pull the club with your left shoulder into the natural swing plane.

Your left hand and arm are connecting the club to your left shoulder (leading shoulder), which will pull the club. If your left arm, left hand, and the club are in the swing plane, the club will follow the natural path back to the bottom of the rotation and through the impact position into the follow-through.

Keep both arms straight for this exercise. Don't bend the right arm yet. We will be doing a variation of this later that will include secondary rotation, but for now, keep the V to V to V—both arms straight.

Try this exercise with your eyes closed. This is an excellent exercise for learning the importance of the balance necessary for a good golf swing.

If you do this motion in a cyclical fashion, moving back and forth (preferably on carpet or grass), you should be able to repeatably brush the ground.

This exercise is one of the *best* exercises for training your body on both the geometry and tempo of the proper swing. At this point, we're only using primary rotation, but you'll be surprised at how much distance you can achieve with shoulder rotation if you fully rotate, get the proper geometry (i.e., stay in the swing plane), and pull with your shoulder.

Exercise 9.8—Inclined Position with Golf Club and a Golf Ball

If you feel comfortable doing all the above exercises, it's now time to put a golf ball into motion. Repeat the previous exercise but with a golf ball.

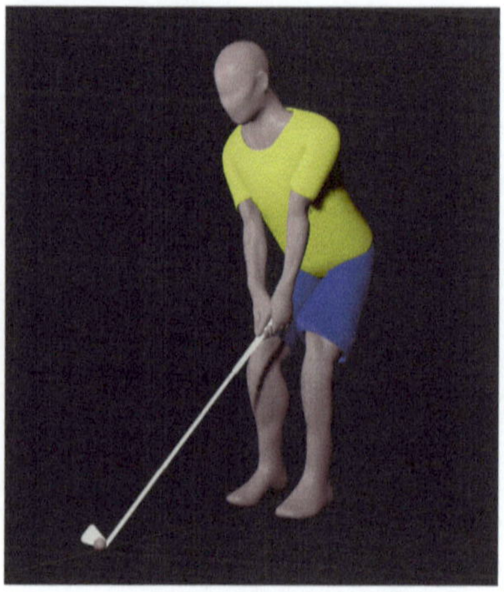

Figure 140: Exercise 9.8 Address

Remember: slow, slow, slow. There is nothing in these exercises that requires speed. Primary rotation is all about power and control. Start with limited rotation, say, maybe 30 degrees backswing and 30 degrees follow-through. Work your way up to full 90 degree primary rotation only. Don't attempt to complete the full swing using secondary rotation just yet. Take a pause every few minutes during practice and step back, shake it off, and then continue.

Finally, as your rotation gets longer and longer, make sure to have a brief pause at both ends of the stroke. Remember that the clubhead needs a bit of time to slow down and then reverse direction as you go from backswing and into downswing. We'll refer to this as latency at the top of the swing, and it will be important to remember when we discuss tempo.

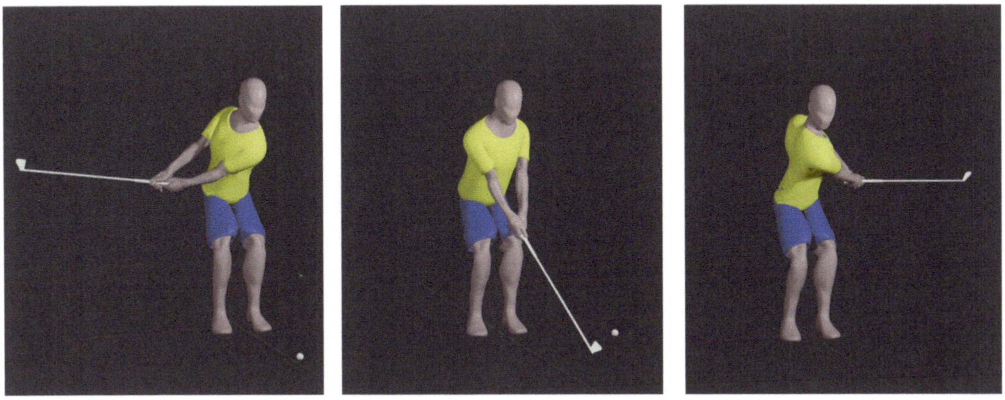

Figure 141: Exercise 9.8 Sequence

Whether you're a newbie golfer or an experienced professional, the above exercises for developing good primary rotation and maintaining it are important. Remember, primary rotation is the key to power and control.

Note: This limited swing with just primary rotation (shoulders) should feel a lot like putting or chipping (more on that in Chapter 13).

You are now ready to move onto the next chapter.

Takeaways:

So what did we learn in Chapter 9?

1. To be able to properly strike a golf ball, you need to develop the neuromuscular connections, commonly called hand-eye coordination, necessary to perform the proper motions to swing a golf club. Repetition of the correct motions forms these neuromuscular connections.
2. Primary rotation is the foundation of a good swing. Learning to rotate the shoulders and upper body through repeated exercises will improve both your ability to properly strike a ball and your understanding of how to properly swing a golf club.
3. Learning to control the shoulders (primary rotation) can take a lot of patient practice and repetition. If you get good control over your shoulders, the rest of the swing is that much easier.

CHAPTER 10

Practicing with Purpose: Secondary Rotation

Regret for wasted time is more wasted time.

—Mason Cooley

Chapters 1 through 8 laid out the model for the kinematics of the golf swing. Chapter 9 started to put into practice the prerequisite neuromuscular training necessary for primary rotation, which is the foundation of the golf swing. And we know that if primary rotation—rotation of the upper body and shoulders—provides power and control, secondary rotation provides speed, which equates to distance.

Mastering the swing should be completed step-by-step—learn and practice each prerequisite motion before proceeding to the full swing. With primary rotation as a backdrop, you now need to understand and put into practice secondary rotation, which is the rotation of your leading arm. In the case of right-handed golfers, this would be the straight left arm (SLA).

It's no mistake that I always use the term "straight left arm" in lieu of "left arm." This is intentional—it emphasizes the importance of keeping your leading arm straight during the backswing.

The exercises in this chapter focus on the motion the straight left arm makes during the swing. It is no accident that your trailing arm, the right arm for right-handed golfers, isn't used at all in these exercises.

Three important aspects for effective practice are: adopt a stepwise approach to learning the swing; practice the right stuff; and practice on a regular basis.

The rest of this chapter focuses on step-by-step training exercises. Their purpose is to train your body to perform the individual motions necessary to hit a golf ball properly.

Each category contains a series of exercises that have a specific purpose. The series starts with exercises in the vertical world (standing erect) and then graduates to the inclined world (at the inclined address position).

The series of exercises follows this progression:

1. Motions that do not require any equipment and can be completed at home
2. The same exercises again with a golf club only to study the same motion with the effects of gravity (e.g., the weight of a golf club)
3. The same exercises one last time but with a golf club and a golf ball

You can do many of these exercises at home. Remember, this chapter is all about training muscle memory. Speed is not the focus with these exercises. The emphasis is on repetition until each exercise is smooth and consistent and feels natural.

Secondary Rotation—Training the Straight Left Arm

If the foundation of a good swing is full shoulder rotation, the key to distance is secondary rotation. Remember that secondary rotation is the rotation of the straight leading arm and club around an axis that runs through the leading arm (left arm for RH golfers).

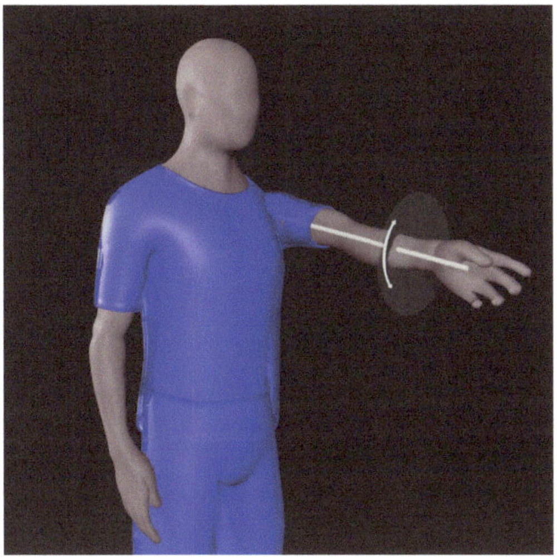

Figure 142: Secondary Rotation

If you watch a professional strike the ball, it's amazing to see how far they hit the ball with seemingly minimal effort. This is in large part due to the timing of the release during the downswing. But to get the timing right, you need to train your body and brain to rotate your leading arm properly. It doesn't necessarily come naturally.

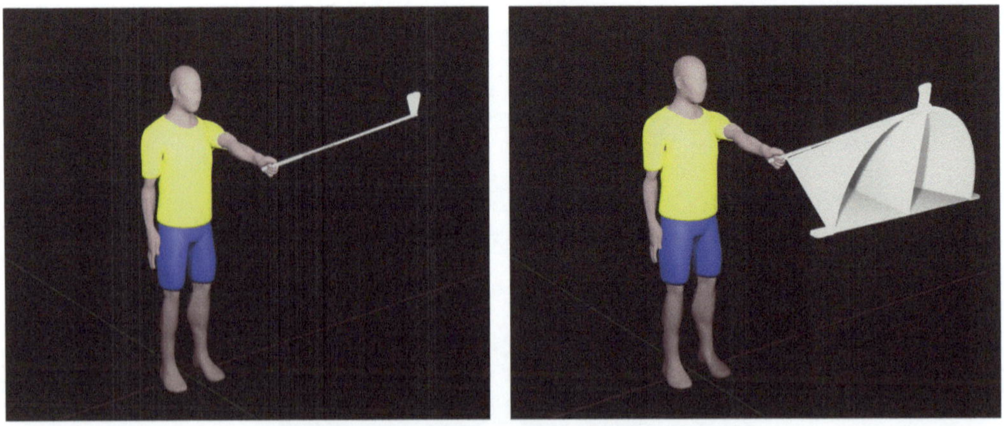

Figure 143: Secondary Rotation and the Club Path

The exercises in this chapter can be used to develop and maintain good secondary rotation. These are progressive exercises, and all except the last one can be completed at home on a regular basis. The final exercise uses a golf ball and requires open-field practice at the driving range or somewhere similar.

Vertical position refers to standing erect, while inclined position means bent (at the hips) in normal setup position. And finally, the golf club would typically be a short iron like an 8 iron.

Chapter 10 Exercises—Secondary Rotation (The SLA)

Variations on a Theme

This basic motion will be used in each of the following exercises as we build a correct secondary rotation. You will repeat this exercise using each of the setups listed below. Remember to hold the club with the proper grip. The clubface should be perpendicular to the club path during the entire exercise.

10	Straight Left Arm Rotation	V to E to V (partial)	Secondary Rotation Only
10.1	Vertical	none	Arm Horizontal
10.2	Vertical	with club	Arm Horizontal
10.3	Vertical	with club	Upper Arm Lowered (tight to chest)
10.4	Inclined	with club	Upper Arm Lowered (tight to chest)
10.5	Inclined	with club and ball	Upper Arm Lowered (tight to chest)

Each of the above exercises use some variation of secondary rotation of the straight left arm as outlined above. Note that most of the exercises are completed in both the vertical and inclined position. The exercise starts with no equipment and progresses to a golf club and finally to a golf club and a ball.

Exercise 10.1—Vertical Position Without Equipment

We are going to start the progression by repeating an exercise from Chapter 5 which was provided so you could understand secondary rotation. Remember, that is the rotation of your leading arm a full 180 degrees, 90 degrees counter-clockwise (backswing), and 90 degrees clockwise (follow-through) from the neutral position (facing forward).

We will start secondary rotation of exercises in the vertical position without equipment. The emphasis is on observation and not speed. Repeat this exercise and observe the position of the flat leading wrist. Repeat each exercise until the motion is smooth and feels natural.

1. Stand facing a wall about arm's length distance away with good posture (back straight and shoulders square).

2. Extend your left arm straight out in front of you at shoulder height. Close your left hand as if you were gripping the golf club. Point to the wall with the tip of your left thumb. It's imperative that you have a flat left wrist. It should be facing to the left.

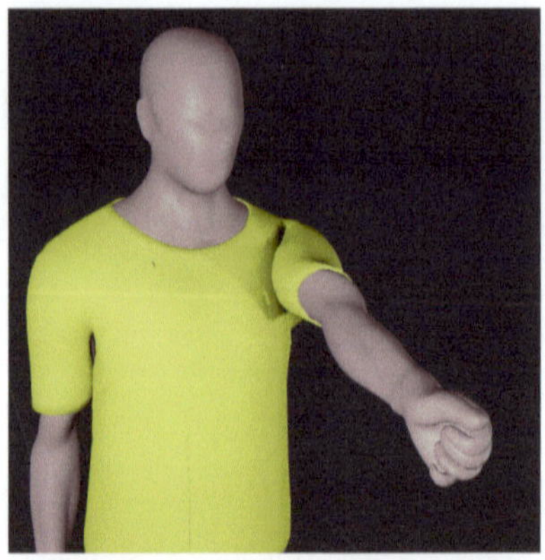

3. While touching the wall lightly with your left thumb, *slowly* rotate the arm about 90 degrees clockwise (as if you were locking a door with a key). Don't allow the wrist to hinge or cock. Make sure you keep a flat left wrist. This movement should finish with the left hand in the pronate position facing the ground (your flat left wrist facing up).

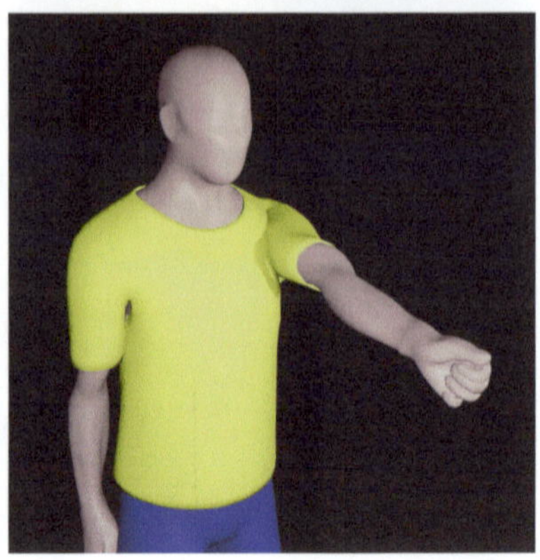

4. Slowly return counterclockwise to the neutral position (flat left wrist facing left).

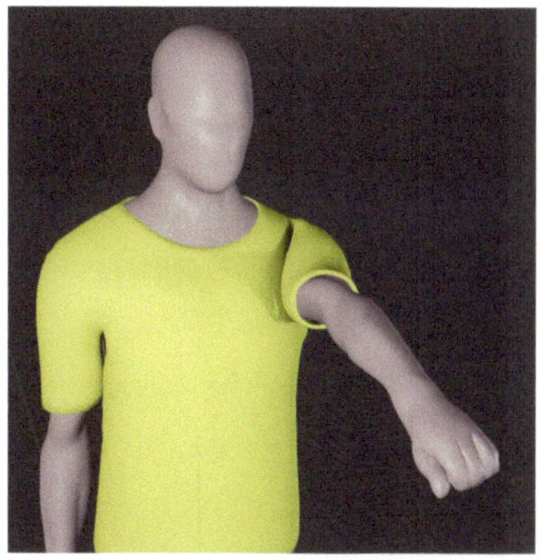

5. Continue touching the wall lightly with your left thumb and *slowly* rotate the arm about 90 degrees counterclockwise (as if you were unlocking a door with a key). Don't allow the wrist to hinge or cock. Make sure that you keep a flat left wrist. The movement should finish with the left hand in the supinate position facing straight up to the sky (your flat left wrist facing the ground).

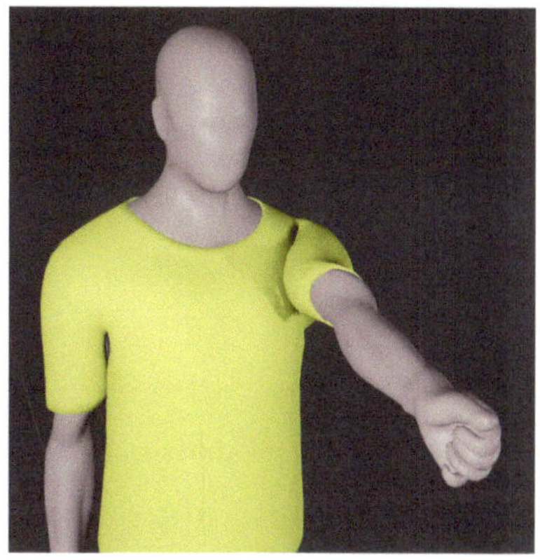

6. Slowly return to the neutral position.

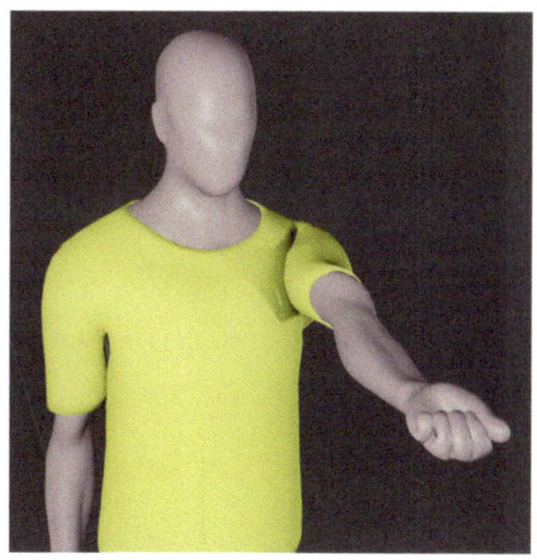

Why is this exercise important?

Demonstrates secondary rotation
Trains the brain to rotate the leading arm (straight left arm) a full 180 degrees.
Reinforces the importance of keeping the arm straight and the left wrist flat and fully pronated (hyperextended)

Remember, the wrist joint is an ellipsoidal joint and does not rotate. Ellipsoidal joints enable multidirectional movements but not rotational motion. The wrist can provide extension, flexion, abduction, adduction, or circumduction movement. When you hear someone say, "Use more wrist," what they really mean is, "Rotate the leading arm."

Exercise 10.2—Vertical Position with Golf Club

This exercise builds on Exercise 10.1 but with a golf club. Make sure to have a proper grip with the clubhead facing straight up (vertical) in front of you. Rotate the leading arm (straight left arm) a full 180 degrees (90 degrees clockwise from neutral on the backswing and 90 degrees counterclockwise after impact).

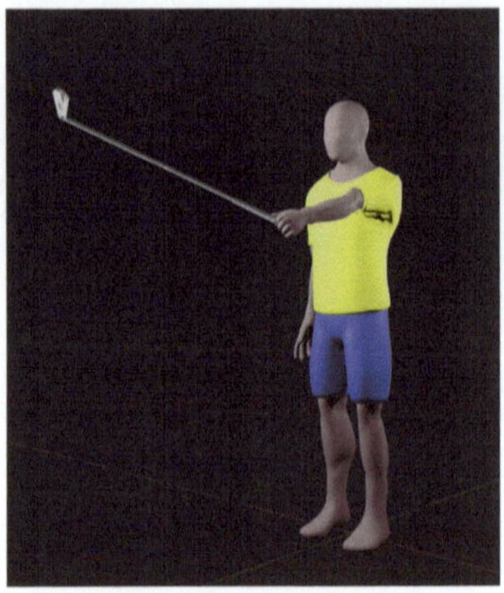

Figure 144: Exercise 10.2 Address

Why is this exercise important?

Demonstrates secondary rotation
Trains the brain to rotate the leading arm (straight left arm) a full 180 degrees
Reinforces the importance of keeping the arm straight and the left wrist flat and fully pronated (hyperextended)
Provides a visual for rotating a club with your straight left arm while feeling the effects of gravity

Observe the position of the golf club and clubface as you complete the rotation. When your arm is straight out in front of you, the golf club should rotate around the secondary axis. The rotation of the club forms a cone, the clubhead tracing a semicircle at the base of the cone. The clubface should remain perpendicular to the path formed by this rotation throughout the 180 degree rotation.

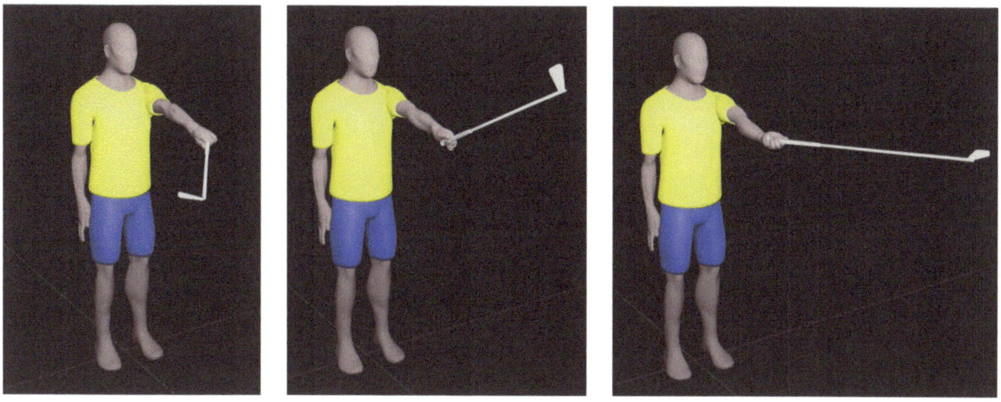

Figure 145: Exercise 10.2 Sequence

Note that doing this motion holding a golf club is a bit tricky due to gravity and the weight of the club. If you remember from Chapter 7, gravity is always present and always pulling the club down. The leading arm can only supply limited applied force but can do so quickly under the right circumstances. Additionally, the leading arm is hard to control without some help. The next exercise demonstrates the importance of lowering the arm against the side of the chest, which helps with control.

Exercise 10.3—Vertical Position with Golf Club and Arm Lowered

This exercise builds on Exercise 10.2 but with the arm lowered against your chest. Make sure to have a proper grip with the right hand and put the clubhead facing straight up (vertical) in front of you in the neutral position.

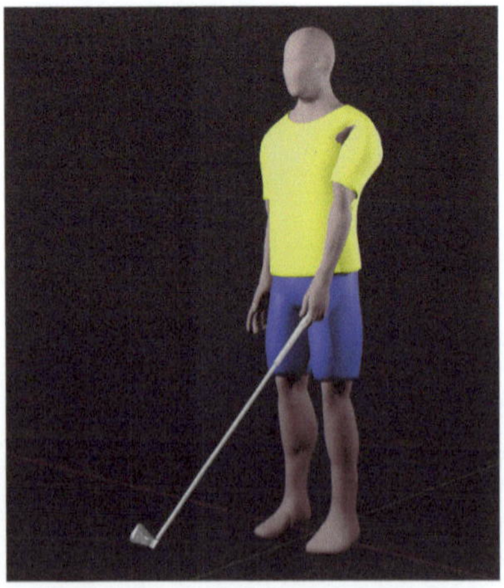

Figure 146: Exercise 10.3 Address

Why is this exercise important?

Demonstrates secondary rotation

Trains the brain to rotate the leading arm (straight left arm) a full 180 degrees

Reinforces the importance of keeping the arm straight and the left wrist flat and fully pronated (hyperextended)

Provides a visual for rotating a club with your straight left arm while feeling the effects of gravity

Demonstrates importance of keeping the upper arm against the chest for control

Observe the position of the golf club and clubface as you complete the rotation. When your arm is lowered, the golf club still rotates around the secondary axis, and the clubface remains perpendicular to the semicircular path formed by this rotation throughout the full rotation.

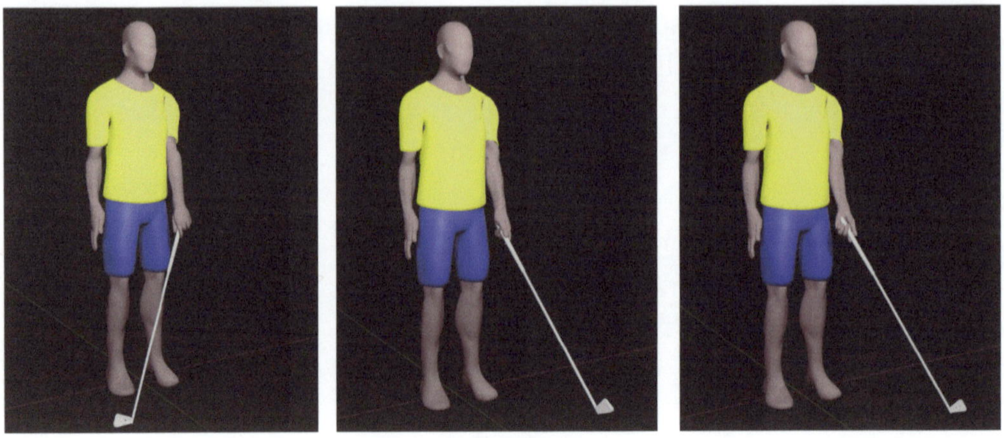

Figure 147: Exercise 10.3 Sequence

Now let's repeat the exercise, but tilt at the hips into the inclined position with some shoulder rotation to see the effects of geometry and motion on control of the leading arm.

Exercise 10.4—Inclined Position with Golf Club and Arm Lowered

This exercise builds on Exercise 10.3 but with a golf club in the inclined position and some shoulder rotation. Make sure to have a proper grip and put the clubhead facing the target line (vertical) in front of you at address.

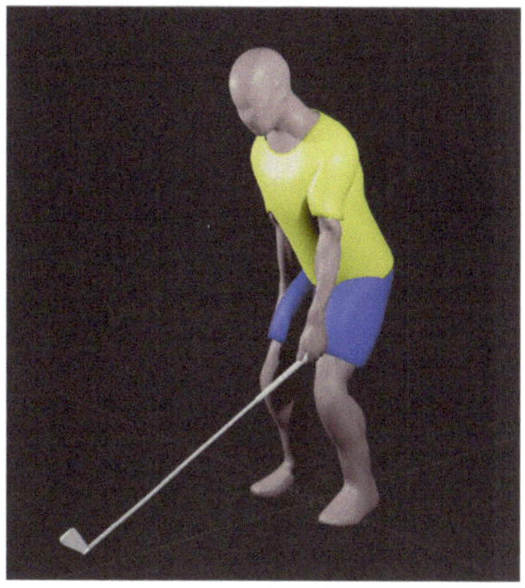

Figure 148: Exercise 10.4 Address

Why is this exercise important?

Demonstrates the secondary axis of rotation
Trains the brain to rotate the leading arm (straight left arm) a full 180 degrees
Reinforces the importance of keeping the left wrist flat and fully pronated (hyperextended)
Demonstrates the importance of keeping your arm tight against your chest during the backswing rotation
Provides a visual for rotating a light object around your leading arm while feeling the effects of gravity and centripetal force
Teaches you how differently the rotation feels when you go from the vertical world to the inclined world (address position)

If you complete this motion in a cyclical fashion, moving back and forth (preferably on carpet or grass), you should be able to repeatedly brush the ground.

Again, this is also a good exercise to do with your eyes closed, which will give you a better idea of what the motion feels like.

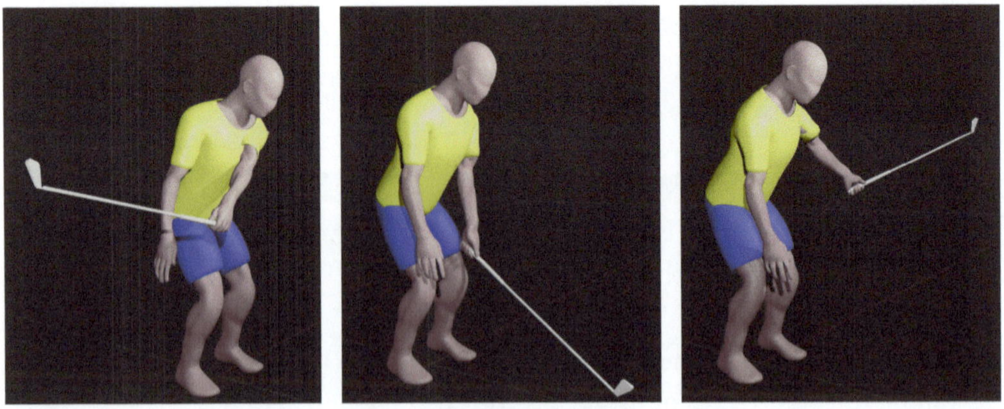

Figure 149: Exercise 10.4 Sequence

This is an important exercise that helps train the brain for timing, tempo, and feel of the club for both geometry (kinematics) and energy (kinetic effects). Remember that tempo is the timing of each part of the swing. For example, the backswing and downswing may have a count of three. The backswing is on count one and count two and then the downswing to impact is on count three.

Let's see what happens when we try hitting a ball using only the leading arm.

Exercise 10.5—Inclined Position with Golf Club and Ball

This exercise builds on Exercise 10.4 but adds a golf club and a ball. Make sure you have good posture and are tilting at the hips with your back straight. Your head should be steady and looking forward.

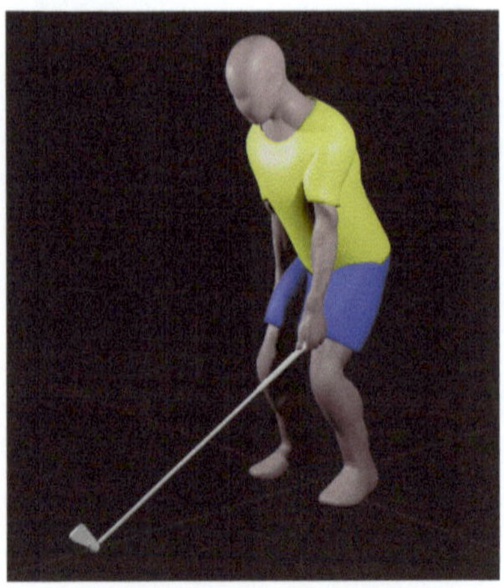

Figure 150: Exercise 10.5 Address

For this exercise, you should only be using your straight left arm (SLA) and not your trailing arm. You may find this difficult, but it's a fascinating exercise and worth mastering. It brings into play the effects of some of the physics from Chapter 7, namely the effect of gravity due to the weight of the club and centripetal force due to the rotation of the club. During the swing, you must balance these two forces: gravity pulling down and centripetal force pulling out.

Why is this exercise important?

Demonstrates the secondary axis of rotation

Trains the brain to rotate the leading arm (straight left arm) a full 180 degrees

Reinforces the importance of keeping the left wrist flat and fully pronated (hyperextended)

Teaches you how differently the rotation feels when you go from the vertical world to the inclined world (address position)

Provides a visual for rotating a light object around your leading arm while feeling the effects of gravity and centripetal force

Demonstrates the importance of keeping your arm tight against your chest during the backswing rotation

Demonstrates the importance of lag (a brief pause) at the top of the backswing

Highlights the importance of pulling the straight left arm and club with the left shoulder during the downswing (notice that the club will find its natural path because there's no interference from the trailing right arm)

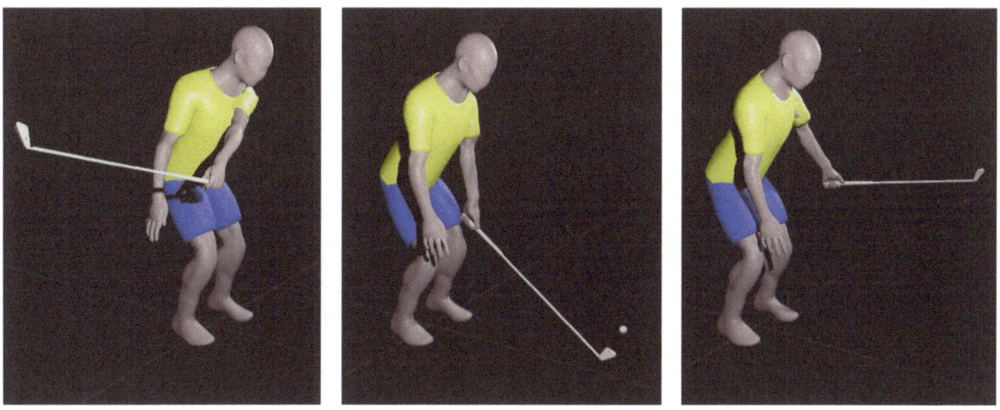

Figure 151: Exercise 10.5 Sequence

It's important to keep the upper left arm tight against your chest during the backswing and the downswing. You should be rotating your arm with your chest during the backswing. If your arm isn't kept tight to your chest, your arm is free-floating in space, making it difficult to hit the ball using one arm.

Your upper arm remains tight against your chest during the backswing and downswing, but after impact, your right arm should separate from the chest due to the momentum of the rotation.

Repeat this exercise with your eyes closed, which will give you a better idea of what the motion feels like. When you complete this exercise with your eyes closed, keep your feet tightly together. Once you get good at this exercise, it's possible to hit the ball one-handed with your eyes closed.

Moving Forward with Confidence

Developing good secondary rotation is key to developing speed and distance in the full swing. The last exercise demonstrates the difficulty controlling the leading arm (secondary rotation) without some guidance. That guidance is provided by the trailing arm and tertiary motion.

As I noted in the beginning of this chapter, one of the aspects of effective practice is to practice often. I recommend completing these exercises often. When you've mastered both primary and secondary rotation, it's time to see what happens when you combine power, control, and speed together in the next set of exercises. Speed is not the focus with these exercises. The emphasis should be on observation of the club path and clubhead orientation. Repeat the exercise until each exercise is consistent, smooth, and feels natural.

Takeaways:

So what did we learn in Chapter 10?

1. To be able to properly strike a golf ball, you need to develop the neuromuscular connections, commonly referred to as hand-eye coordination, necessary to perform the motions required to swing a golf club properly. Repetition of the correct motions form these neuromuscular connections.
2. Learning to rotate the leading arm (straight left arm for right-handed golfers and straight right arm for left-handed golfers) through repeated exercises will improve both your ability to properly strike a ball and your understanding of how to properly swing a golf club.

CHAPTER 11

Practicing with Purpose: Tertiary Motion

The eight laws of learning are explanation, demonstration, imitation, repetition, repetition, repetition, repetition, repetition.

—John Wooden

Chapters 1 through 8 laid out the model for the kinematics of the golf swing. In Chapter 9, we started to put into practice the prerequisite neuromuscular training necessary for primary rotation, which is the foundation of the golf swing. Chapter 10 focused on training the body to perform secondary rotation, which provides speed that equates to distance.

The emphasis in this chapter is the use of the trailing arm (right arm for RH golfers) to tie primary rotation and secondary rotation together. Tertiary motion uses the right arm to connect primary rotation and secondary rotation together into the coordinated motion necessary to get the golf clubhead into the swing plane and the clubface into the proper orientation.

Three important aspects for effective practice are: practice the right stuff and practice it often; adopt a stepwise approach to learning the swing; and practice on a regular basis.

The rest of this chapter focuses on step-by-step training exercises. The purpose of these exercises is to use the trailing arm (right arm) to connect the primary rotation (shoulders and upper body) to the secondary rotation (the straight left arm) to perform the motions necessary to hit a golf ball properly.

Each exercise has a specific purpose. The series starts with exercises in the vertical world (standing erect) and then graduates to the inclined world (in the address position).

Each series follows the following progression:

- Starts with exercises with motions that do not require any equipment and can be completed at home
- Repeats the exercises with a golf club to study the same motion with the effects of gravity (e.g., the weight of a golf club)
- Finally, repeats the exercises with a golf club and a golf ball

You can do many of these exercises at home. Remember, this chapter is all about training muscle memory. Speed is not the focus with these exercises. The emphasis is on repetition until each exercise is smooth, consistent, and feels natural.

Tertiary Motion—How to Use the Trailing Arm During the Golf Swing

We have seen that shoulder rotation (primary rotation) is the foundation for power and control and that rotation of the left arm (secondary rotation) is the key to speed and distance. But these two rotations are of limited value when used independently. When we tie them together, the result is powerful.

Tertiary motion guides the straight left arm across the chest during the backswing. This is done by shortening the distance between the wrists and the right shoulder during the backswing by bending the right elbow and placing the upper right arm against the torso. The bending of the right elbow causes the left arm to move across the chest while it rotates (secondary rotation) in a controlled fashion. **This movement moves the clubhead from the base plane and into the swing plane**.

Note that bending the right elbow against the right side accomplishes three things:

- It allows the left arm to rotate clockwise around the secondary axis that runs through the straight left arm.
- It stabilizes the left arm, which allows for better control.
- It shortens the right side of the V formed by the two arms and allows some room for the straight left arm to move across the chest (shoulders) on the backswing, which lifts the clubhead into the swing plane.

The following are progressive exercises to help develop the motion and timing required to synchronize primary and secondary rotation using tertiary motion. The final exercise uses a golf ball and requires open-field practice at the driving range or somewhere similar.

Chapter 11 Exercises—Tertiary Motion V to E to V (Full)

Variations on a Theme

Tertiary motion will be used in each of the following exercises. You will repeat each exercise using the setups listed below. Remember to hold the club with the proper grip.

11	Tertiary Motion	V to E to V (Full)	Secondary Rotation Only
11.1	Vertical	w/o equip-ment	Arm Horizontal
11.2	Vertical	w/o equip-ment	Upper Arms Lowered (tight to chest)
11.3	Vertical	with club	Upper Arms Lowered (tight to chest)
11.4	Inclined	with club	Upper Arms Lowered (tight to chest)
11.5	Inclined	with club (OHR)	Upper Arms Lowered (tight to chest)
11.6	Inclined	with club and ball	Upper Arms Lowered (tight to chest)

Note that most of the exercises are done in both the vertical position and in the inclined position. The exercise starts with no equipment and then is repeated with an exercise stick, which progresses to a golf club and finally to a golf club and a ball.

Tertiary Motion Exercises

Exercise 11.1—Vertical Position Without Equipment and Arms Straight Out

Put your arms straight out in front of you and horizontal to the ground with your hands in the prayer position. Keep your feet close together and make sure your head remains steady and looking forward. A narrow stance promotes good balance around the center of the body. Maintain good posture and make sure to keep the lower body quiet. Do not twist your legs.

Why is this exercise important?

Demonstrates the importance of tertiary motion (right arm) for connecting primary rotation (shoulder rotation) to secondary rotation (rotation of the straight left arm)

Trains your trailing arm (right arm) and elbow to bend and shorten the distance between your right wrist and right shoulder while keeping your right upper arm tight against your side

1. Stand erect with good posture and remain in the vertical position (back straight and shoulders square). Your flat left wrist (FLW) should be facing to the left and toward the target line.

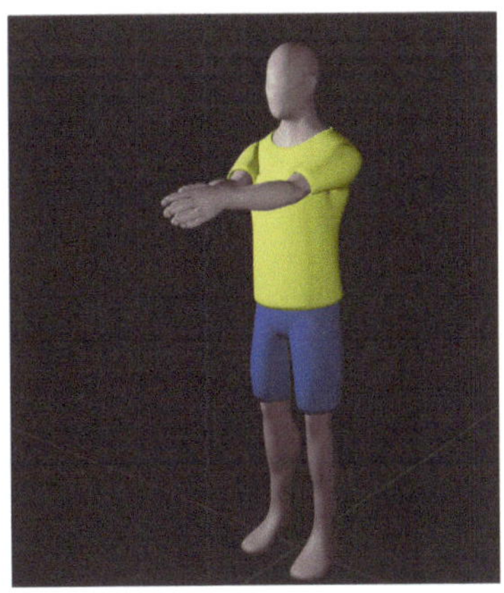

2. As you rotate clockwise for the backswing, your right elbow is bending against the right side of your upper body.

   Notice how your hands rotate from a vertical position (facing the target line) to a horizontal position (facing the sky).

   Your arms have gone from the V position to the Y position and will stay in this position as your shoulders continue to turn to a full 90 degrees.

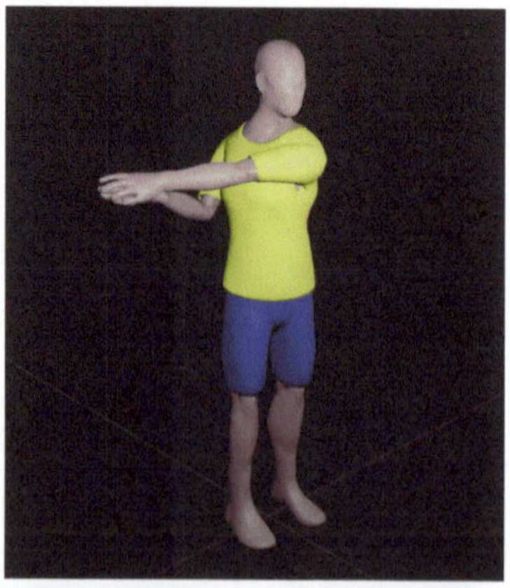

3. As you reverse direction, you maintain the Y position of the arms and your shoulders until you have returned to about the 45 degree mark, at which point you start to straighten the right arm. This is the release in the golf swing.

   As you return to the neutral position (0 degrees), both arms should again be straight (in the V position), and the flat left wrist should be vertical and facing the target line.

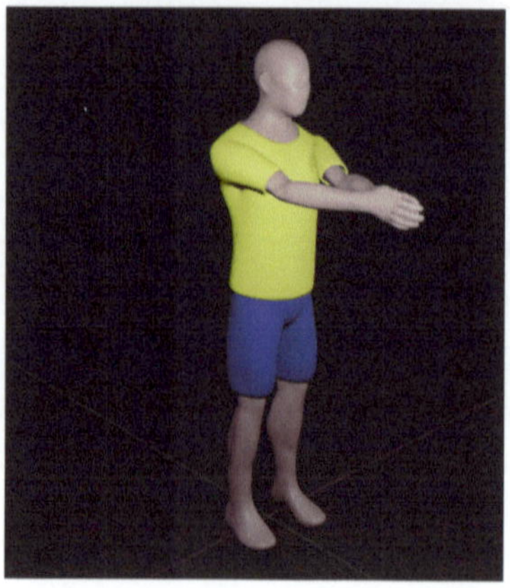

4. Continue to slowly rotate your arm 90 degrees counterclockwise. Keep both arms straight and don't allow your wrist to hinge or cock. Make sure you keep a flat left wrist.

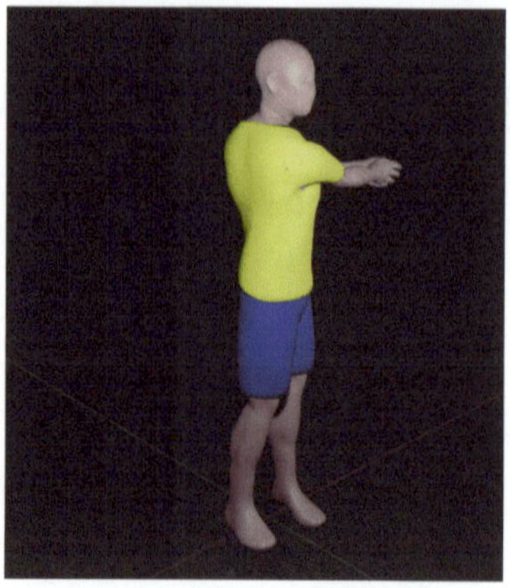

5. Slowly return to the neutral position.

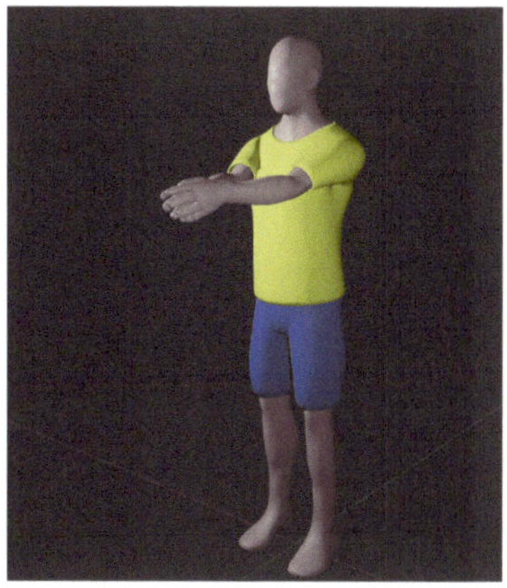

Exercise 11.2—Vertical Position Without Equipment and Arms Lowered

Now repeat the previous exercise but allow your arms to lower from straight out in front of you until your upper arms are supported by your chest. This should feel comfortable since you no longer need to hold your arms out straight. Your upper arms should be resting tightly against your chest.

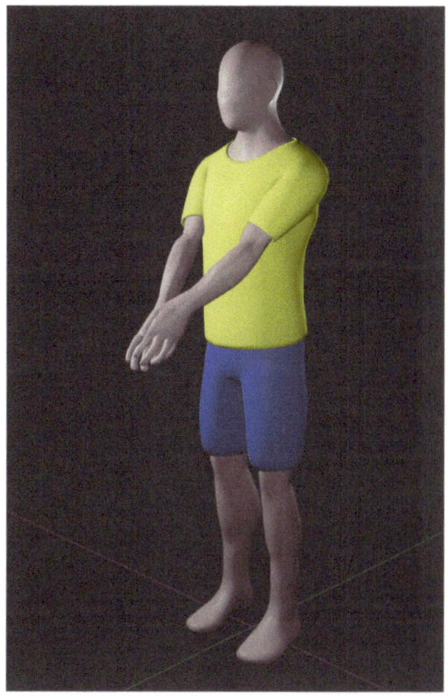

Figure 152: Exercise 11.2 Address

Why is this exercise important?

Demonstrates the importance of tertiary motion (right arm) for connecting primary rotation (shoulder rotation) to secondary rotation (rotation of the straight left arm)

Trains your trailing arm (right arm) and elbow to bend and shorten the distance between your right wrist and right shoulder while keeping your right upper arm tight against your side

Demonstrates importance of keeping the upper arms against the chest for control

Keep your arms as close together as possible, and your upper arms must be tight against your chest. You should be rotating the club with your chest and shoulders and not your arms.

As you rotate clockwise (backswing), your right elbow is bending against the right side of your upper body.

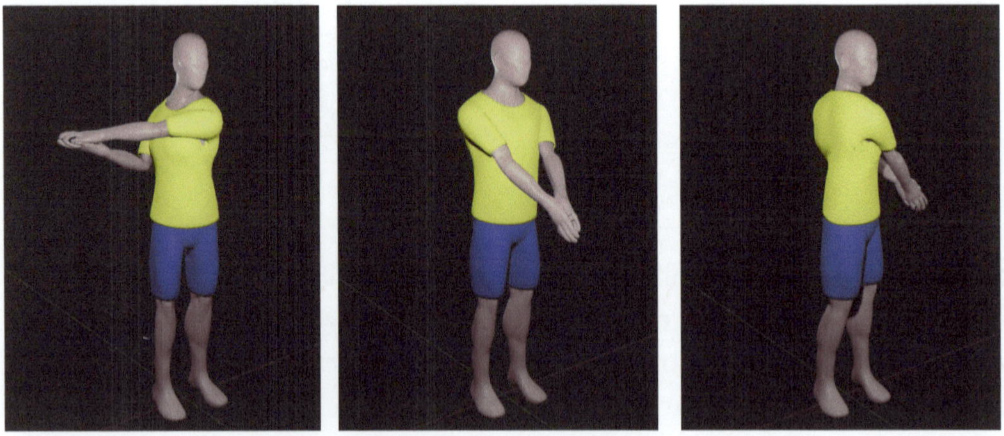

Figure 153: Exercise 11.2 Sequence

Notice how your left hand rotates from a vertical position (facing the target line) to a horizontal position (facing the sky). As your shoulders reach approximately 45 degrees, your right elbow and upper arm should be against your right side, and the straight left arm has rotated a full 90 degrees. Your flat left wrist is facing skyward and is slightly below the shoulder plane now. Your arms have gone from the V position to the Y position and will stay in this position as your shoulders continue to turn to a full 90 degrees.

As you reverse direction and rotate counterclockwise, you maintain the Y position of the arms and your shoulders until you have returned to about the 45 degree mark, at which point you start to straighten the right arm. As you return to the neutral position (0 degrees), both arms should again be straight (in the V position), and the flat left wrist should be vertical and facing the target line.

Continue to rotate past neutral position 90 degrees counterclockwise. Both arms remain straight and lowered against your chest on the follow-through.

Now let us repeat this exercise but with a golf club.

Exercise 11.3—Vertical Position with Club and Arms Lowered

Repeat Exercise 11.2 but with a golf club. Make sure to have a proper grip with the clubhead facing straight up (vertical) in front of you.

Keep your arms as close together as possible, and your upper arms must be tight against the body. Your upper arms should be resting tightly against your chest. You should be rotating the club with your chest and shoulders and not your arms.

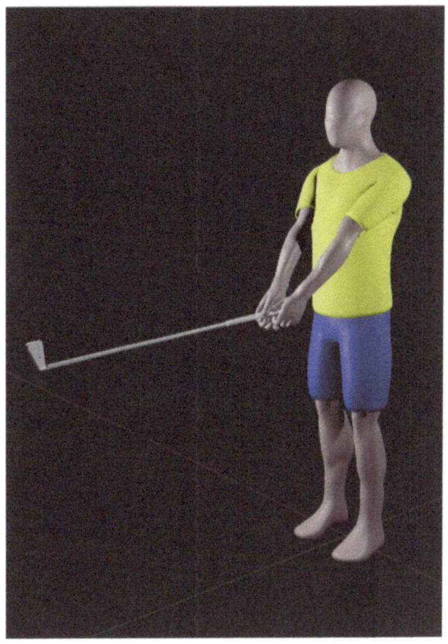

Figure 154: Exercise 11.3 Address

Why is this exercise important?

Demonstrates the importance of tertiary motion (the right arm) for connecting primary rotation (shoulder rotation) to secondary rotation (rotation of the straight left arm)

Trains your trailing arm (right arm) and elbow to bend and shorten the distance between your right wrist and right shoulder while keeping the right upper arm tight against your side

Gives you a visual for rotating a club with weight around your leading arm (straight left arm) while feeling the effects of gravity

As you rotate counterclockwise (backswing), your right elbow is bending against the right side of your upper body. This is the takeaway in the golf swing.

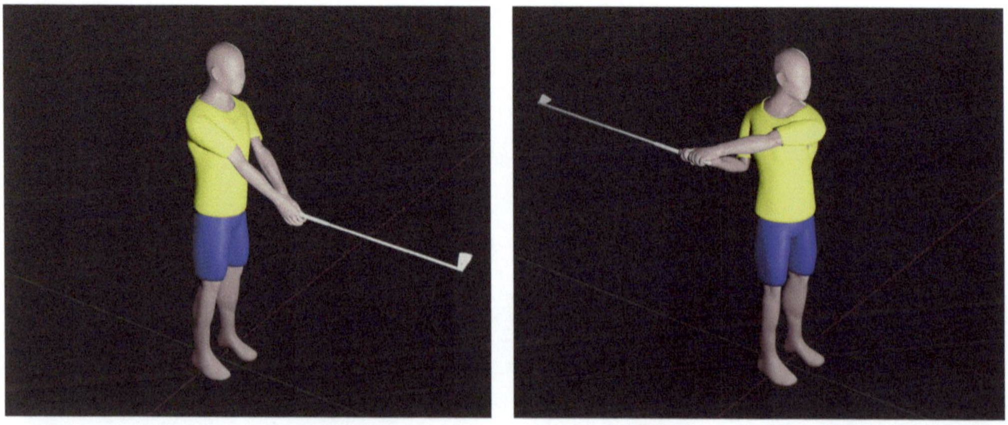

Figure 155: Exercise 11.3 Backswing Sequence

As you reverse direction, you maintain the Y position of the arms and your shoulders until you have returned to about the 45 degree mark, at which point you start to straighten the right arm. This is the release in the golf swing.

As you return to the neutral position (0 degrees), both arms should again be straight (in the V position), and the flat left wrist should be vertical and facing the target line. The arms remain straight for much of the follow-through as your weight shifts to the front foot.

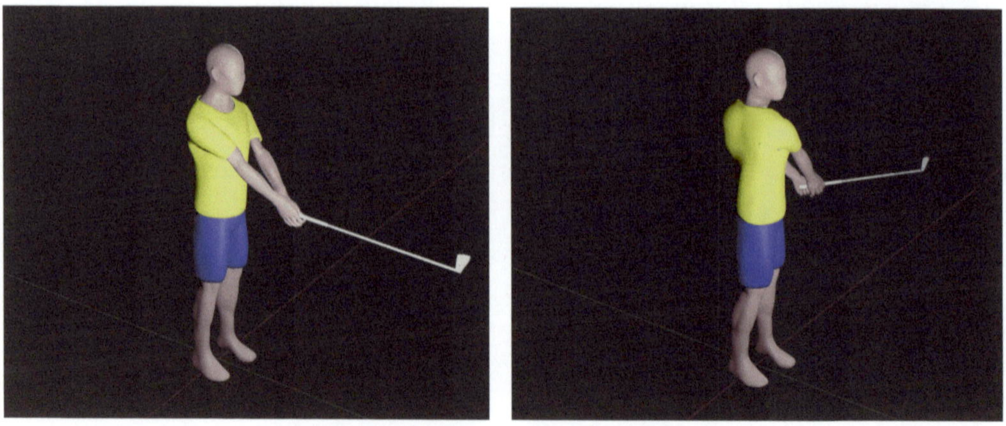

Figure 156: Exercise 11.3 Follow-Through Sequence

Again, you can do this in front of a mirror. Observe the position of the golf club and clubface as you complete the rotation. When your arm is straight out in front of you, the golf club should rotate around the secondary axis, and the clubface should remain perpendicular to the path formed by this rotation throughout the full rotation. The clubface should start perpendicular to the club path created by this rotation and be tangent to the club path at the top of the backswing.

We are going to repeat Exercises 11.2 through 11.3, but instead of standing erect, we're going to complete the exercise in the address position.

Exercise 11.4—Inclined Position with Club

Repeat Exercise 11.3 in the inclined position and with a golf club. Make sure you have good grip and posture and are tilting at the hips with your back straight. Keep your head steady and look forward. Don't bend your spine.

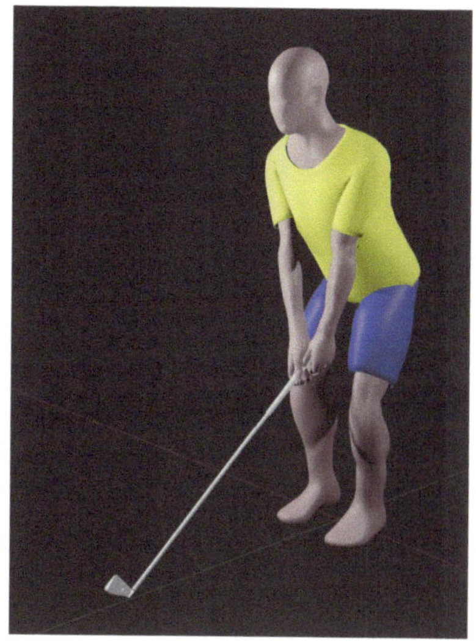

Figure 157: Exercise 11.4 Address

Why is this exercise important?

Demonstrates the importance of tertiary motion (the right arm) for connecting primary rotation (shoulder rotation) to secondary rotation (rotation of the straight left arm)

Trains the trailing arm (right arm) and elbow to bend and shorten the distance between your right wrist and right shoulder while keeping the right upper arm tight against your side

Gives you a visual for rotating a club with weight around your leading arm (straight left arm) while feeling the effects of gravity

Teaches you how differently the rotation feels when you go from the vertical world to the inclined world (address position)

As your shoulders reach 90 degrees, your right elbow and upper arm should be against your right side, and the straight left arm has rotated a full 90 degrees.

Your left arm has rotated from a vertical position (facing the target line) to a horizontal position (facing the sky). The *right* wrist should bend (hinge extension) sufficiently to maintain a flat left wrist (FLW) during the backswing.

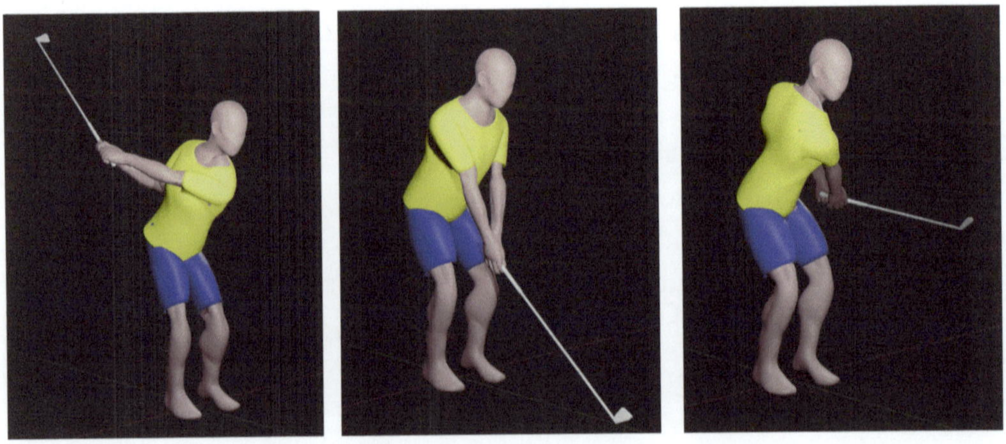

Figure 158: Exercise 11.4 Sequence

As you return to the neutral position (0 degrees), both arms should again be straight (in the V position), and the flat left wrist should be vertical and facing the target line. The momentum of the rotation will carry the arms and the club into the follow-through.

From Chapter 3, we know that the feet should be about shoulder width apart, slightly wider for longer clubs and slightly closer for shorter clubs. Try the exercise with your eyes closed and your feet closer together. You can even do the exercise with your feet touching each other.

With a wide stance, you will be tempted to shift your weight from side to side. A narrower stance will force you to keep your weight centered, which promotes rotation. This is an excellent exercise for learning the importance of the balance necessary for a good rotation during the golf swing.

If you do this motion in a cyclical fashion, moving back and forth (preferably on carpet or grass), you should be able to repeatably brush the ground. Repeat the motion until it is consistent and feels comfortable.

Exercise 11.5—Inclined Position with Golf Club and One-Hand Release (OHR)

Repeat Exercise 11.4 in the inclined position and with a golf club. Make sure you have good grip and posture and are tilting at the hips with your back straight. Keep your head steady and looking forward. As you start the downswing (in step 6), let go of the club with your right hand. Your left hand and arm are connecting the club to the left shoulder (leading shoulder), which will pull the club. If your left arm, left hand, and club are in the swing plane, the club will follow the natural path back to the bottom of the rotation and through the impact position into the follow-through.

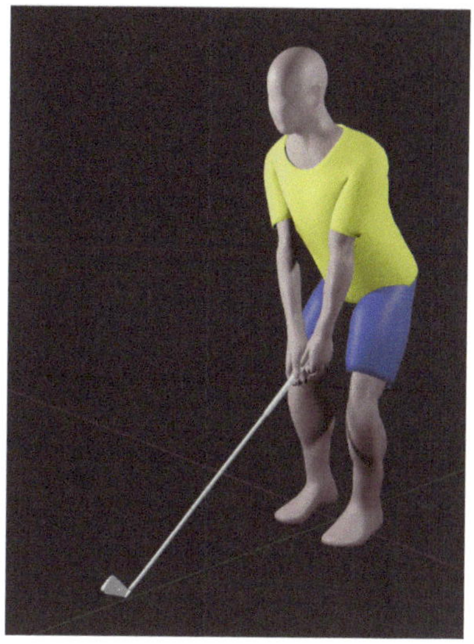

Figure 159: Exercise 11.5 Address

Why is this exercise important?

Demonstrates the importance of tertiary motion (the right arm) for connecting primary rotation (shoulder rotation) to secondary rotation (rotation of the straight left arm)

Trains the trailing arm (right arm) and elbow to bend and shorten the distance between your right wrist and right shoulder while keeping your right upper arm tight against your side

Gives you a visual for rotating a heavier object around your body and feeling the effects of gravity and centripetal force

Teaches you how to time the downswing so that you're pulling the club with your left shoulder

When you start the downswing, your left shoulder rotates counterclockwise and *pulls* your left arm, which, in turn, *pulls* the golf club back along the swing plane. When your shoulder is pulling your left arm (which holds the club), the club will follow a natural path back along the swing plane.

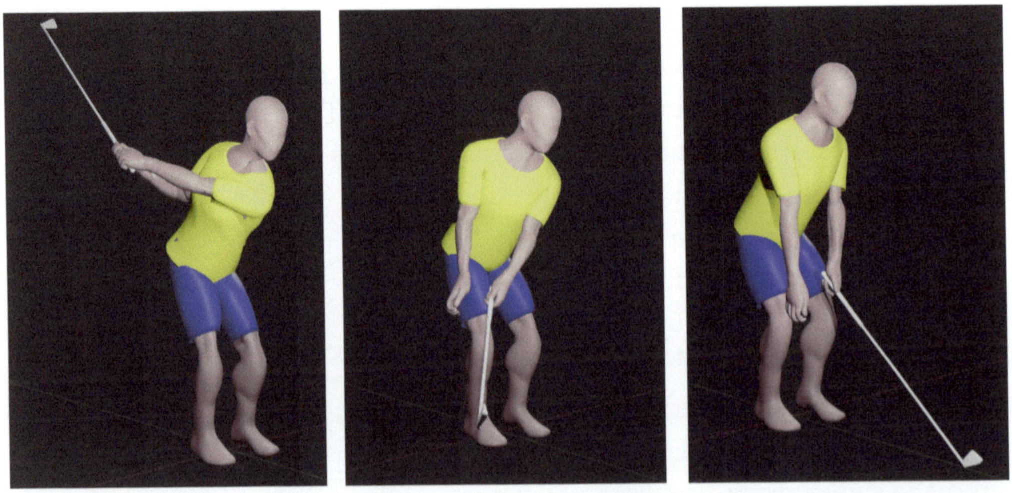

Figure 160: Exercise 11.5 Sequence

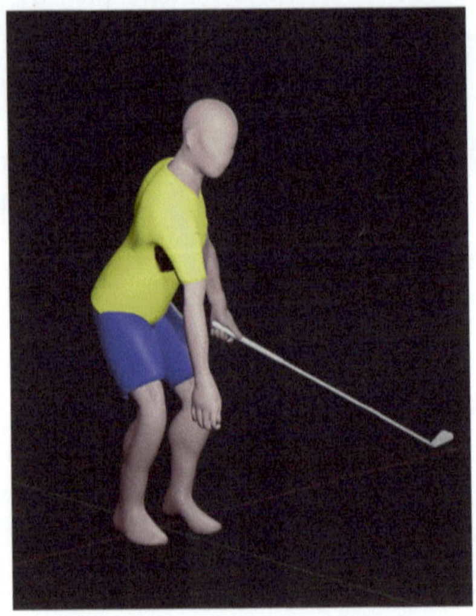

Figure 161: Exercise 11.5 Follow-Through

Often, golfers will start the downswing by trying to get the golf club back to the ball by steering it with their hands and arms.

As with a wagon example in Chapter 7, there is a big difference between pulling the club with your shoulder versus steering the club with your arms and hands. When you use the shoulder to pull the left arm and golf club, the club can find the natural swing path. This results in greater speed and accuracy.

This exercise is very important for developing the timing and control to develop the motion, which pulls the club with your left shoulder into the natural swing plane.

When you do this exercise with your eyes closed, keep your stance narrow. This is an excellent exercise for learning the importance of the balance necessary for a good golf swing. With a wide stance, you will be tempted to shift your weight from side to side, and with a narrower stance, you will need to keep your weight centered, which promotes rotation.

This exercise is one of the best exercises for training the body on both the geometry and timing of the proper swing. At this point, we're using both primary and secondary rotation only, but you'll be surprised at how much distance you can get with shoulder rotation if you fully rotate, achieve the proper geometry (i.e., stay in the swing plane), and pull with your shoulder.

Exercise 11.6—Inclined Position with Club and Golf Ball

If you can do the above exercise consistently and smoothly, it is now time to put a golf ball into motion. Repeat Exercise 11.5 but with a golf ball.

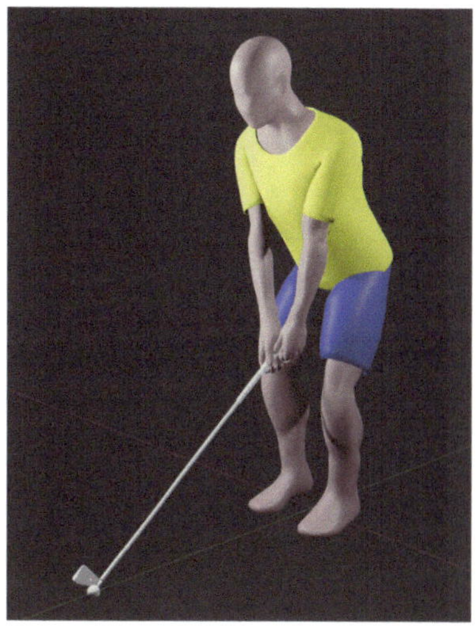

Figure 162: Exercise 11.6 Address

Remember: slow, slow, slow. There is nothing in these exercises that requires speed. Primary rotation is all about power and control. Start with limited rotation, say, maybe 30 degrees backswing and 30 degrees follow-through. Work your way up to a full 180 degree primary rotation only. Take a pause every few minutes during practice and step back, shake it off, and then continue.

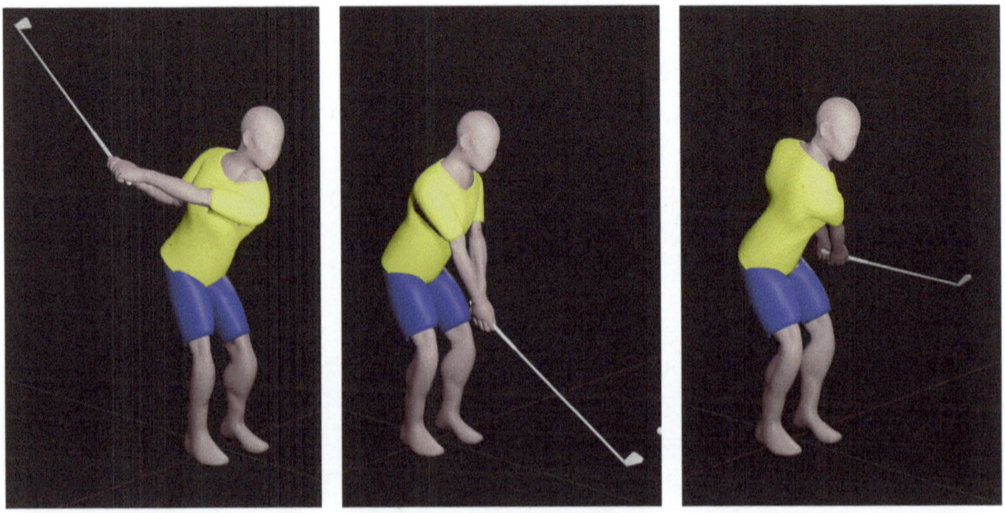

Figure 163: Exercise 11.6 Sequence

Finally, as your rotation gets longer and longer, make sure to have a brief pause at both ends of the stroke. Remember that the clubhead needs a bit of time to slow down and then reverse direction as you go from backswing and into downswing. We will refer to this as latency at the top of the swing, and it's important when we discuss tempo.

Remember that the exercises in Chapters 9, 10, and 11 are all about muscle training. You'll want to repeat these exercise often as you carefully train your shoulders, leading arm (straight right arm), and trailing arm in the motions necessary to swing a golf club correctly.

As you get better and better at these exercises, you'll find that practicing with a bucket of balls at the range becomes much more meaningful and productive.

Takeaways:

So what did we learn in Chapter 11?

1. To be able to properly strike a golf ball, you need to develop the neuromuscular connections, commonly referred to as hand-eye coordination, necessary to perform the motions required to swing a golf club properly. Repetition of the correct motions form these neuromuscular connections.
2. You use tertiary motion to coordinate primary and secondary rotations. Training the trailing arm and elbow (right arm/elbow for right-handed golfers and left arm/elbow for left-handed golfers) through repeated exercises will improve both your ability to properly strike a ball and your understanding of how to properly swing a golf club.

CHAPTER 12

Practicing with Purpose: Putting It All Together

Don't start something that you cannot finish.

—Justin Somper

Chapters 1 through 8 laid out the model for the kinematics of the golf swing. In Chapter 9, we started to put into practice the prerequisite neuromuscular training necessary for primary rotation, which is the foundation of the golf swing. Chapter 10 focused on training the body to perform secondary rotation, which provides speed that equates to distance. Chapter 11 focused on tertiary motion with the geometry and timing needed to coordinate primary and secondary.

The emphasis in this chapter is on what happens after impact, specifically the follow-through and the finish. After impact, the momentum from the rotation of the swing will carry the upper body and primary axis forward off the midplane in the direction of the target. Most, if not all, the weight is transferred to the front leg.

Three important aspects for effective practice are: practice the right stuff and practice it often; adopt a stepwise approach to learning the swing; and practice on a regular basis.

Each exercise has a specific purpose. The series starts with exercises in the vertical world (standing erect) and then graduates to the inclined world (in the address position).

Each series follows the following progression:

- Starts with exercises with motions that do not require hitting a ball and can be completed at home
- Repeats the exercise with a golf club to study the same motion with the effects of gravity (e.g., the weight of a golf club)
- Finally, repeats the exercise with a golf club and a golf ball

You can do many of these exercises at home. Remember, this chapter is all about training muscle memory. Speed is not the focus with these exercises. The emphasis is on repetition until each exercise is smooth, consistent and feels natural.

The Follow-Through and the Finish—Completing the Swing

Learning the proper motions and balance after impact are key to a good swing. The following exercises help develop a sense for the follow-through and finish. Up to this point, the exercises have been focused on being centered as you rotate on the backswing to the top of the swing and then rotate on the downswing to impact. After impact, your weight must now shift forward toward the target on the follow-through as you rotate to the finish.

Revelation #17

A good swing needs a good follow-through and a good finish.

Exercise 12.1—Follow-Through and Finish in the Vertical World

This is a simple exercise in the vertical position with both arms in front holding a club for weight and balance. Stand erect with good posture and remain in the vertical position (back straight and shoulders square) on the follow-through and finish.

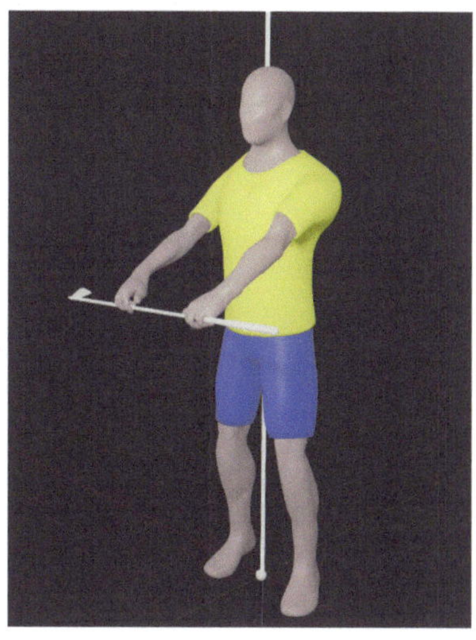

Figure 164: Exercise 12.1 Address

Keep your feet about shoulder width apart and make sure your head remains steady and looking forward. You can repeat this exercise and vary the distance, but the feet don't go much further than shoulder width. A narrow stance promotes good balance around the center of the body.

Why is this exercise important?

Demonstrates the importance of the follow-through and finish for the golf swing

Trains you to shift your weight forward over the front leg after impact

As you rotate through the backswing, your center of gravity should remain centered over both feet. There should be increased pressure on the back leg (right leg for RH golfers) as you resist leg sway on the backswing. Leg sway is when you rotate your upper body by twisting your legs instead of rotating your torso.

After a brief pause at the top of the rotation, the hips and shoulders reverse direction as you rotate counterclockwise back to the neutral position. Your weight remains centered over both feet as you push off the back foot to drive the hips and shoulders back around the primary axis.

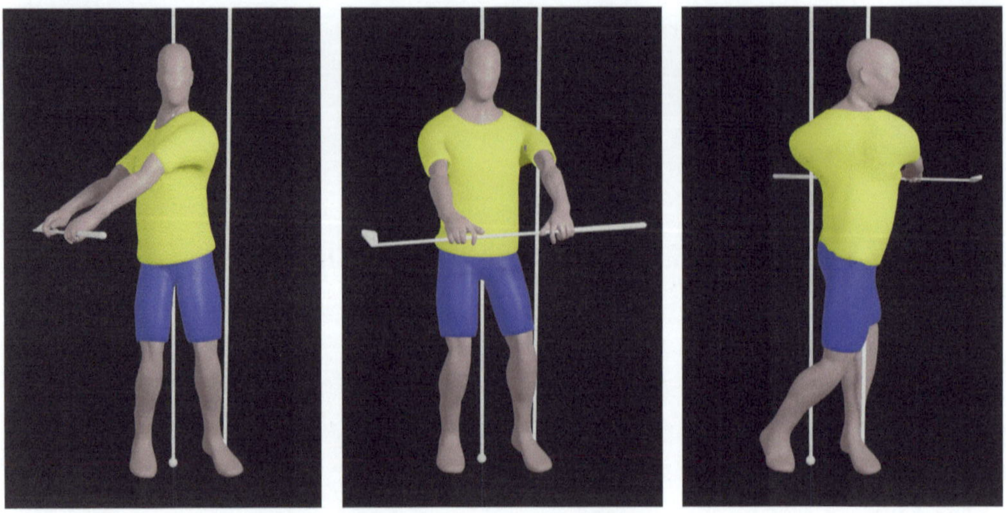

Figure 165: Exercise 12.1 Sequence

As you return to the neutral position, the hips rotate past the midplane, and the shoulders and club are parallel to the target line. As you continue to rotate past the impact position (neutral), the upper body will start to shift forward as your weight shifts to the front leg. Your center of gravity, which has centered over both feet up to this point, will start to shift forward (toward the target).

Unlike many of the other exercises, the focus of this exercise is really on your torso, i.e., your core, and not so much on your arms and shoulders. Your core has been the pillar of stability for many of the exercises associated with the backswing, downswing, and impact. Your torso has remained relatively centered up to impact but must now shift forward to get the best transfer of energy from the clubhead and to the ball. At impact, the remaining rotational energy must be allowed to dissipate smoothly through a good finish. It's kind of like easing up on the gas pedal of a race car as you cross the finish line, but not a second sooner. You then need to give the car a chance to coast to a stop before you run out of track.

At the finish, your shoulders and hips have rotated 90 degrees (or more) past the impact position. You should be standing upright and facing the target. Your center of gravity is over the front leg and foot. You should be able to tap your back foot on the ground since it is no longer supporting weight.

Exercise 12.2—Follow-Through and Finish from the Inclined Address Position

Repeat the above exercise but in the inclined (address) position. Keep your stance narrow and make sure your head remains steady and looking forward. A narrow stance promotes good balance around the center of the body.

You are really just holding a club for balance. You can actually do the exercise with or without a club. As you rotate through the backswing, your center of gravity should remain centered over both feet. There should be increased pressure on the back leg (right leg for RH golfers) as you resist leg swaying on the backswing.

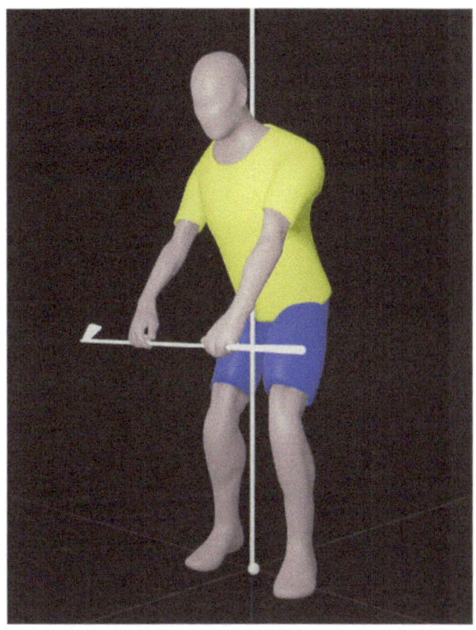

Figure 166: Exercise 12.2 Address

Why is this exercise important?

Demonstrates the importance of the follow-through and finish for the golf swing
Trains you to shift your weight forward over the front leg after impact
Teaches you how differently the rotation feels when you go from the vertical world to the inclined world (address position)

After a brief pause at the top of the swing, the hips and shoulders reverse direction as you rotate counterclockwise back to the neutral position. Your weight remains centered over both feet as you push off the back foot to drive the hips and shoulders back around the primary axis.

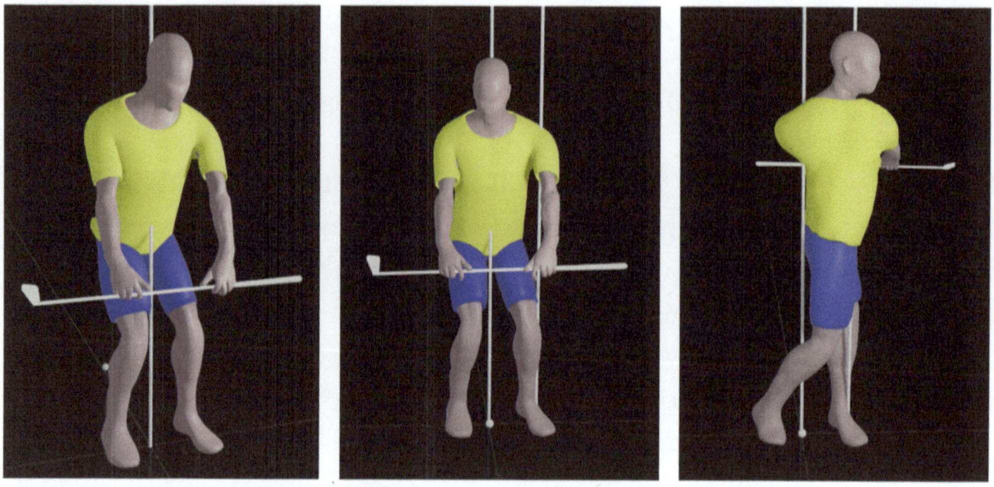

Figure 167: Exercise 12.2 Sequence

As you return to the neutral position, the hips rotate past the midplane, and the shoulders and club are parallel with the target line. As you continue to rotate past the impact position (neutral), the upper body will start to shift forward as your weight shifts to the front leg. Your center of gravity, which has been centered over both feet up to this point, will start to shift forward (toward the target), and you will go from the inclined position to the vertical position.

At the finish, your shoulders and hips have rotated 90 degrees (or more) past the impact position. You should be standing upright and facing the target. Your center of gravity is over the front leg and foot. You should be able to tap your back foot on the ground since it is no longer supporting any weight.

Exercise 12.3—Follow-Through and Finish: The Full Swing

This exercise builds on Exercise 12.1 and 12.2 but with a golf club and a ball. Make sure to have a proper grip with the clubhead facing straight up (vertical) in front of you in the neutral position.

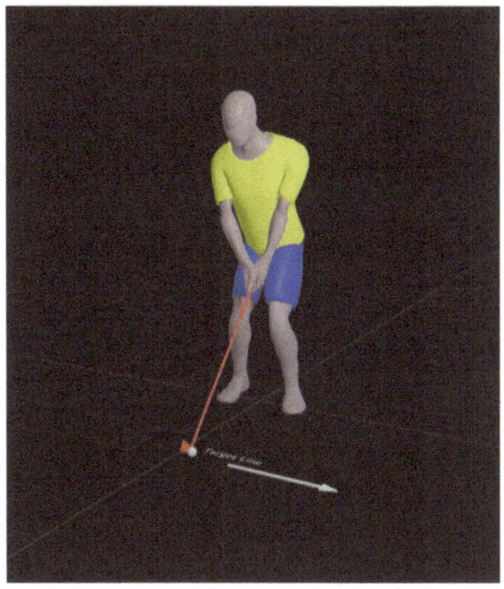

Figure 168: Exercise 12.3 Address

First practice the full swing, including follow-through and finish, without a ball. Make sure to complete the swing with weight shift and follow through. When this feels comfortable, add a golf ball.

Perform the exercise starting from the inclined (address) position with a golf club and a ball. Keep your stance relatively narrow and make sure your head remains steady and looking forward. A narrow stance promotes good balance and rotation around the center of the body.

Why is this exercise important?

Demonstrates the importance of the follow-through and finish for the golf swing-
Trains you to shift your weight forward over the front leg after impact
Reinforces the importance of proper weight shift during the follow-through and finish of the full swing

As you rotate through the backswing, your center of gravity should remain centered over both feet. There should be increased pressure on the back leg (right leg for RH golfers) as you resist leg swaying on the backswing.

After a brief pause at the top of the swing, the hips and shoulders reverse direction as you rotate counterclockwise back to the neutral position. Your weight remains centered over both feet as you push off the back foot to drive the hips and shoulders back around the primary axis.

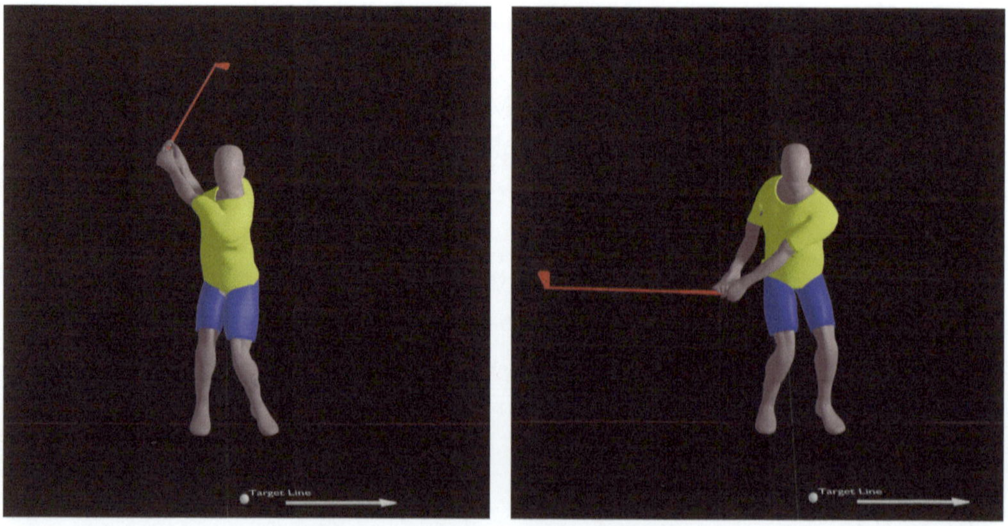

Figure 169: Exercise 12.3 Backswing Sequence

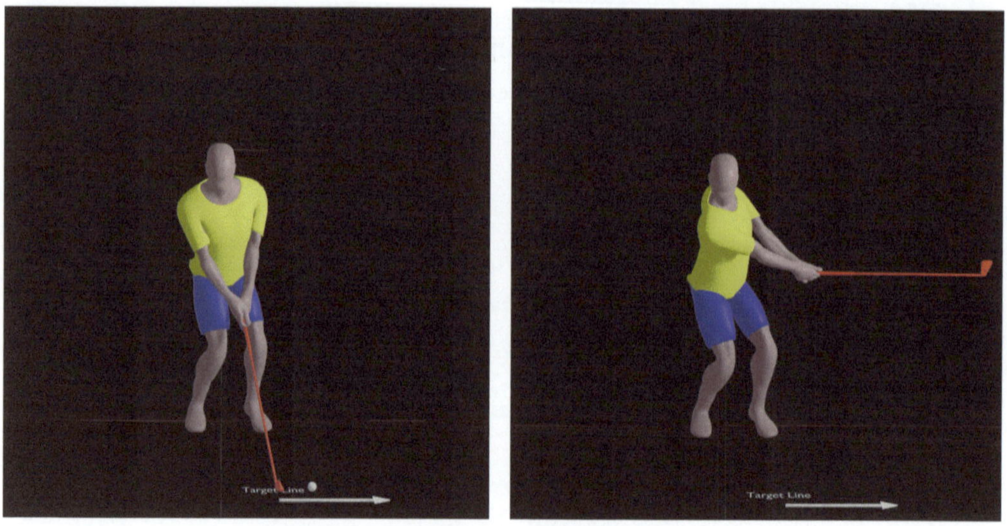

Figure 170: Exercise 12.3 Impact and Follow-Through

As you return to the neutral position, the hips have rotated past the mid-plane, and the shoulders and club are parallel with the target line. As you continue to rotate past the impact position (neutral), the upper body will start to shift forward as your weight shifts to the front leg. Your center of gravity, which has been centered over both feet up to this point, will start to shift forward (toward the target), and you will go from the inclined position to the vertical world.

At the finish, your shoulders and hips have rotated 90 degrees (or more) past the impact position. You should be standing upright and facing the target. Your weight should be over the front leg and foot. You should be able to tap your back foot on the ground since it is no longer supporting any weight.

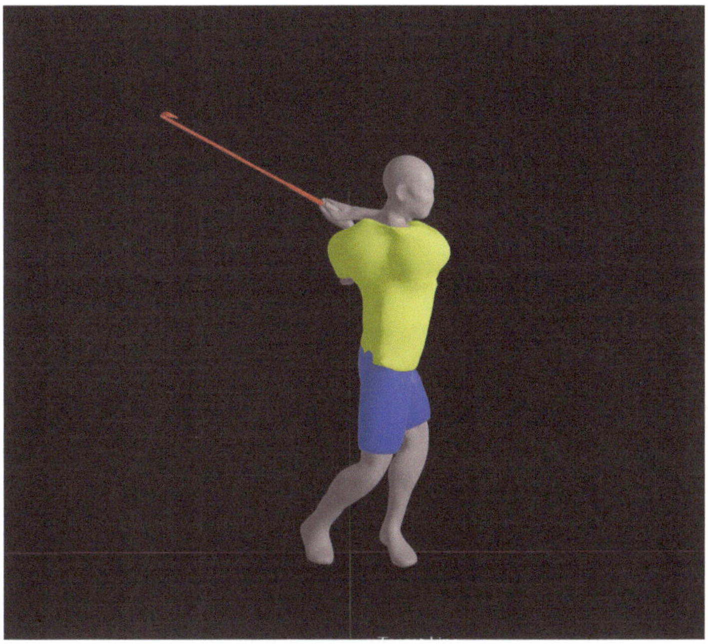

Figure 171: Exercise 12.3 The Finish

Hopefully Chapters 1 through 8 provided useful *knowledge* about the golf swing. The exercises in Chapters 9 through 12 helped establish the neuromuscular connections needed to use that knowledge. The next chapter puts all of that knowledge and practice to use for each of the clubs in the bag, starting with the putter and ending with the driver.

Takeaways:

So what did we learn in Chapter 12?

1. To be able to properly strike a golf ball, you need to develop the neuromuscular connections, commonly referred to as hand-eye coordination, necessary to perform the motions required to swing a golf club properly. Repetition of the correct motions form these neuromuscular connections.
2. A good follow-through and finish are key to an effective golf swing. Learning to shift your weight properly from impact to the finish through repeated exercises will improve both your ability to properly strike a ball and your understanding of how to properly swing a golf club.

CHAPTER 13

Putting, Chipping, Pitching, and the Full Swing

The whole is more than the sum of its parts.

—Aristotle

Developing a good golf swing requires developing all the proper body movements necessary to execute a swing. Shoulder rotation is the foundation of a good swing, second only to a good grip in order of importance. Rotation of the straight left arm is critical for speed and distance. Tertiary motion ties these two rotations together.

If you've mastered the exercises in Chapters 9, 10, 11, and 12, you're ready to put that hard work into practice.

Learning Each Club

Getting to know you,
Getting to know all about you.
Getting to like you,
Getting to hope you like me.

—Rodgers and Hammerstein, The King and I

Please indulge me once more for a short story.

You go to the range for a lesson, and while you're waiting, you look around and notice that the most common clubs in people's hands are their drivers and irons. There's an abundance of golfers on the mats practicing the long shots while the putting green and chipping area are practically empty. When your instructor arrives, he/she asks you to pull out a midiron and take some swings. Rarely does the instructor have you start by pulling out the putter.

This is ironic when you stop to consider that the average golfer uses the putter forty putts per round. That same golfer will use their midiron or hybrid maybe ten to fifteen shots per round. The short game shots comprise more than half the game, but the average golfer unwittingly spends most of their practice time on the full shot.

This book covered all of the motions for the full swing. This chapter focuses on how to apply these motions to execute swing types associated with *all* the clubs in the bag.

In Chapter 8, the full swing was divided into ten discrete steps:

Step 1: Address
Step 2: Initial Takeaway (Primary Rotation CW)
Step 3: Takeaway (Primary Rotation Clockwise and Secondary Rotation CW)
Step 4: Full Rotation to end of Backswing (Primary Rotation CW)
Step 5: End of Backswing
Step 6: Downswing (Primary Rotation CCW)
Step 7: Release (Primary Rotation Counterclockwise and Secondary Rotation CCW)
Step 8: Impact
Step 9: Follow-Through (Primary Rotation and Secondary Rotation CCW)
Step 10: Finish (Primary Rotation CCW)

These steps can be applied to all the swing types, namely putting, chipping, pitching, the partial swing, and the full swing. Entire books have been written about each of these swing types. The goal of this chapter is not to present an exhaustive examination of any one of these but to simply demonstrate how the fundamentals of kinematics apply to each.

Revelation #20

There are five specific club types: the putter, wedges, irons, fairway woods, and, of course, the driver. Each of these club types uses primary rotation and may use some degree of secondary rotation.

The game is played from the tee box to the hole. For example, you usually start with the driver to get onto the fairway. You then go to the fairway wood or iron to get on or close to the green. A good wedge shot puts you on the green before you finally pull out the putter. However, when learning golf, it's more effective to reverse the order and start with the putter and work your way back through the clubs in the bag.

Start with the putter, which requires good grip, setup, and primary rotation. Then, switch a wedge for the putter and practice chipping, which, like putting, is about control and uses a good grip, setup, and primary rotation. Add a little secondary rotation, i.e., practice pitching at varying distances, and as you get better and better, add some more distance and progress into the partial swing. Finally, practice the full swing, which requires good grip, good setup, full primary rotation, full secondary rotation, and a good finish.

The swing model provided in Chapters 2 through 6 can now be understood in context with each swing type. The payoff for the muscle training in Chapters 9, 10, 11, and 12 can be applied for each swing type using each club in the bag.

The distinction between chipping, pitching, partial, and full swing no longer needs to be defined in nebulous terms but can be understood in accurate and specific terms using the concepts of primary rotation and secondary rotation and specific kinematic positions.

Putting

Drive for show and putt for dough.

—Bobby Locke

This famous maxim, familiar to all golfers and golf enthusiasts, was coined by Bobby Locke, a legendary PGA golfer and the first South African to win a major.

Putting involves relatively short distances, typically from several inches to several yards, which is interesting because the putter has the largest percentage range of any club in the bag. In comparison, the median driving distance is 219.55 yards. There are other club distances of note: the median 3 wood goes 186.89 yards, the 7 iron clocks in at 133.48 yards, and the pitching wedge averages a distance of 73.97 yards.

There's another interesting side note regarding the putter. Statistics from the United States Golf Association (USGA) state the average male golfer shoots a 95 to 99 and has at least 40 putts per round, or 2.2 putts per hole. Most recreational and amateur golfers are well above this number, while professional golfers average about 32 putts per round and 1.8 putts per hole.[10]

The putter has the distinction of having the largest *percentage* range of any club in the bag as well as being the most used club in the bag.

[8] 18Birdies. (n.d.-a). *Putting by the numbers – part One.* 18Birdies Knowledge Base. https://help.18birdies.com/article/496-putting-by-the-numbers-part-one

Club	Typical Distance in Yards	Delta in Yards	Percentage Difference
Driver	200–260	60	30%
3 Wood	180–235	55	31%
5 Wood	170–210	40	24%
7 Wood	160–200	40	25%
3 Hybrid	163–205	42	26%
3 Iron	160–200	40	25%
4 Iron	150–180	30	20%
5 Iron	140–170	30	21%
6 Iron	130–160	30	23%
7 Iron	120–150	30	25%
8 Iron	110–140	30	27%
9 Iron	95–130	35	37%
Pitching Wedge	80–120	40	50%

Sand Wedge	60-100	40	67%
Lob Wedge	50-90	40	80%
Putter	0.5-24	23.5	4700%

Putting uses the following steps:

Step 1: Address
Step 2: Initial Takeaway (Primary Rotation CW)
Step 5: End of Backswing
Step 6: Downswing (Primary Rotation CCW)
Step 8: Impact
Step 9: Follow-Through

Putting is about distance and line, or, more precisely, exerting enough force to get the ball to roll the right distance along the right path. The average first putt distance for a handicap golfer is 18.5 feet. As a result, the swing path of the putter is relatively short.

The main emphasis for putting is control. Remember, primary rotation provides power and control, and secondary rotation provides speed. Therefore, it makes sense that putting uses primary rotation, because putting is all about control.

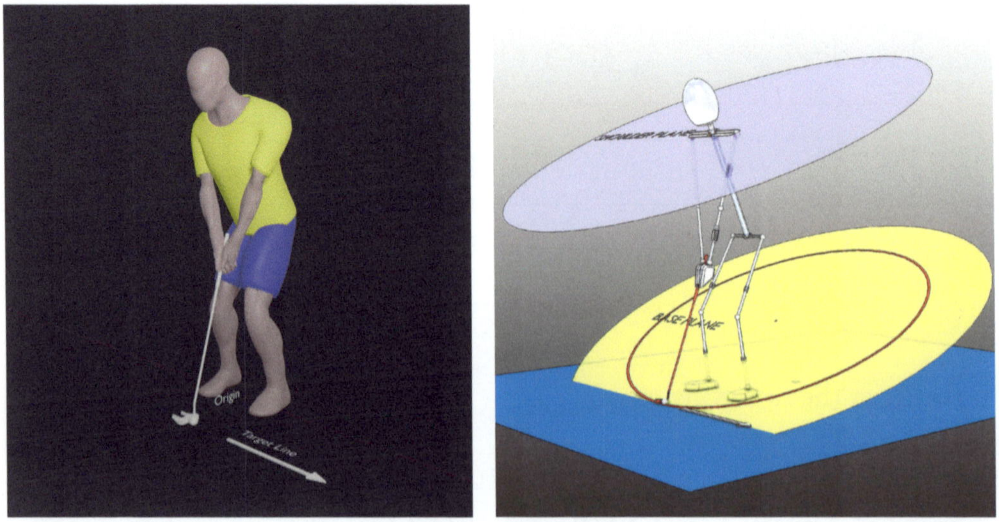

Figure 172: Putting Address Position

The kinematics of the putter are simple. The putter is typically the shortest club in the bag, which means that it has the steepest swing plane. The entirety of the putter swing (rotation) is on the base plane using only primary rotation.

There are no significant rotational forces (centripetal force), and the rules of physics that apply are more linear than rotational because of the slow rotation and short arc. During a full swing with a driver, the shoulders turn a full 180 degrees. Total rotation for putting is usually less than 20 degrees of shoulder rotation.

We've stressed in previous chapters the idea of clubface and club path. The putter clubface needs to contact the ball perpendicular to the target line.

The club path is a relatively short distance. The putter stroke is basically all shoulder rotation over a very short arc, and the clubface remains perpendicular to the club path over the entire stroke.

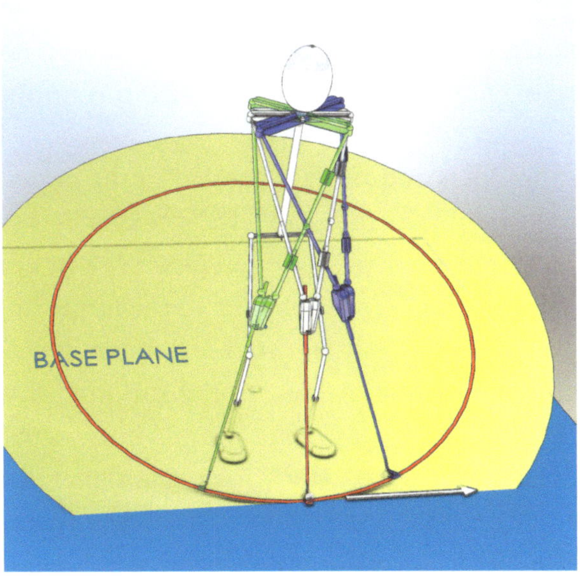

Figure 173: Putter Clubhead Path

The rotation of the club is accomplished using shoulder rotation, and the hands, arms, and lower body remain very quiet. The longer the distance, the more the shoulder rotation, and conversely, the shorter the distance, the smaller the shoulder rotation.

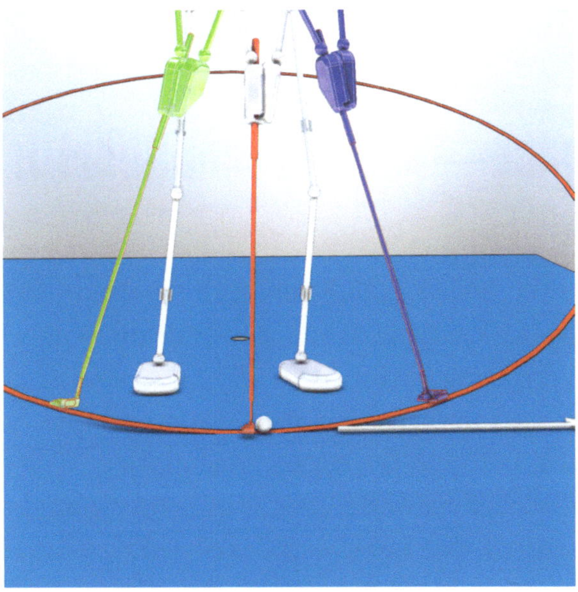

Figure 174: Putting Clubface Orientation

There are a couple of variations of the putter shot that are commonly used.

The stance is square with the feet, hips, and shoulders parallel to the target line at address. The biggest difference is in the arm positioning.

1. Straight Arm: Shoulders and feet are parallel to the target line. Both arms are extended and straight, forming a V. The stroke is completed by moving your shoulder counterclockwise and then clockwise in a steady motion.
2. Bent Arms: Shoulders and feet are parallel to the target line. Both arms are extended but bent at the elbow so that both upper arms are against your upper body. This provides some additional support to the arms so that they are less likely to take over during the putt; the arms are locked into the upper body and shoulders. The stroke is completed by moving your shoulders counterclockwise and then clockwise in a steady motion.

Points to note:

1. Good grip and proper stance are important.
2. Think primary rotation (shoulders, shoulders, shoulders). Remember, the putter stroke is all about primary rotation on the base plane.
3. Arms and hands need to be quiet during the stroke. Use the shoulders. Head, lower body, and hips remain still before, during, and after impact.

Chipping—Wedges and Short Irons

A chip shot is a short game shot used around the putting surface with a low trajectory. It generally travels mainly along the ground. Chipping is usually done with a wedge (for example, a gap wedge or pitching wedge) or a short iron (for example, an 8 or a 9 iron).

The technique used to hit a chip shot is quite simple. The stroke is like the putting stroke, a back-and-forth rotational motion, with the length of the stroke varying by the distance of the shot. Your wrists should not break during the stroke. Like putting, the chip shot relies on primary rotation, which is all about the shoulders.

A wide variety of clubs are used for chip shots. The less lofted club you use, the lower the ball will fly and the more it will roll without changing your backswing length. Of course, you can use a club with more loft, like a sand wedge or pitching wedge, but players often use a lower lofted club like an 8 or 9 iron on longer chips to get less loft and more roll. The best way to determine what each club produces and which you like best is to experiment on the practice green.

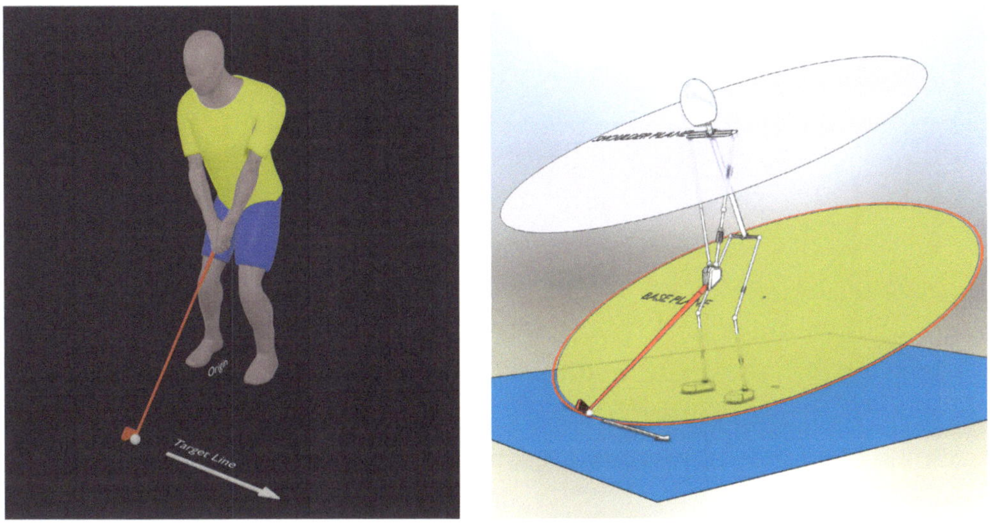

Figure 175: Chipping Address Position

Chipping uses the following steps:

Step 1: Address
Step 2: Initial Takeaway (Primary Rotation CW)
Step 5: End of Backswing
Step 6: Downswing (Primary Rotation CCW)
Step 8: Impact
Step 9: Follow-Through (Primary Rotation CCW)

There are a couple of variations of the chip shot.

Square Stance

Shoulders and feet are parallel to the target line. Both arms are extended and straight, forming a V. The stroke is completed by moving the shoulder counterclockwise and then clockwise in a steady motion and is primarily primary rotation and very little (if any) secondary rotation.

The following is the setup for chipping with a square (neutral) stance:

- Your back is straight, and you are bending at the hips with knees slightly bent.
- The upper body is symmetric with respect to the midplane.
- Maintain a neutral grip, both arms straight and tight to the upper body.
- Your shoulders, hips, and feet should be parallel to the target line.
- The ball just be just forward of center.

The initial backswing is a clockwise rotation of the shoulders (primary rotation). The amount of backswing depends on the distance required. The club path stays on the base plane, and the clubhead remains perpendicular to the club path. With longer chips, the right elbow can start to bend into the side but should be limited to minimize secondary rotation. The right arm remains straight.

Remember that chipping, like putting, is more about control and not distance. Primary rotation is all about control, and secondary rotation provides distance. Since chip shots are close to the green and require accuracy, limit the amount of secondary rotation.

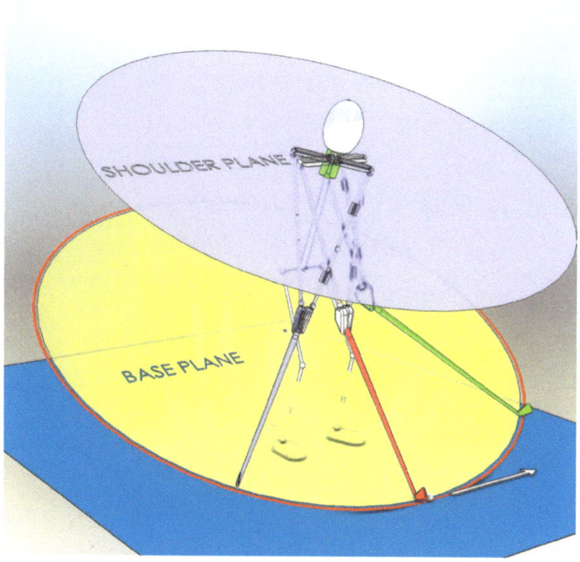

Figure 176: Chipping Clubhead Path

At the top of the stroke, the clubface is still perpendicular to the club path (which is open with respect to the target line). The shoulders reverse direction and rotate counterclockwise. The clubhead returns to the neutral position on the same club path created by the backswing.

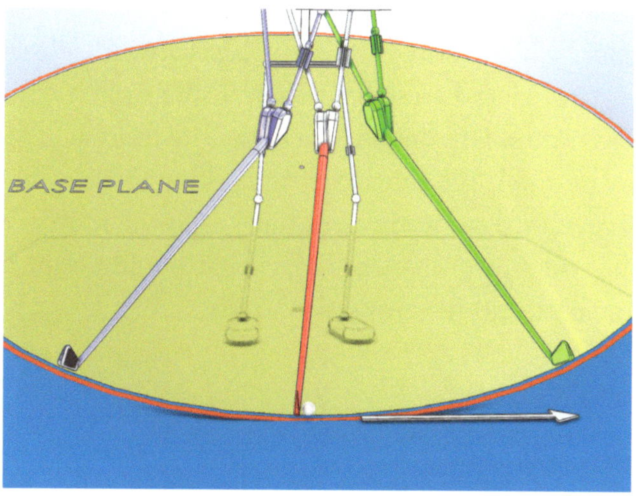

Figure 177: Chipping Clubface Orientation

At impact, the clubface is perpendicular to the club path and the target line as the clubhead continues counterclockwise along the same club path to the finish. At the finish, the clubhead is still on the base plane, and the clubface is perpendicular to the club path.

Advantages of a Square Stance

- Simple to understand and learn
- Uses neutral stance and grip
- Very symmetrical execution across the midplane
- Very limited amount of backspin and, if struck properly, little or no sidespin
- More roll

Disadvantages of a Square Stance—

- Requires a lot of discipline and practice to execute using only the shoulders while keeping the arms and hands quiet
- Typically limited to shorter shots

Open Stance

The body is turned at an angle into the target line with the right foot forward to open the stance, which moves the right hip forward (closer to the ball). The left arm is extended and straight; however, the right arm is slightly bent at the elbow to accommodate the open stance. The more you open the stance (turn into the target line), the more the right elbow bends. Don't overdo the open stance. You open the stance just enough to get the trailing elbow to bend against your side, which promotes primary rotation and reduces the temptation to use secondary rotation during the stroke.

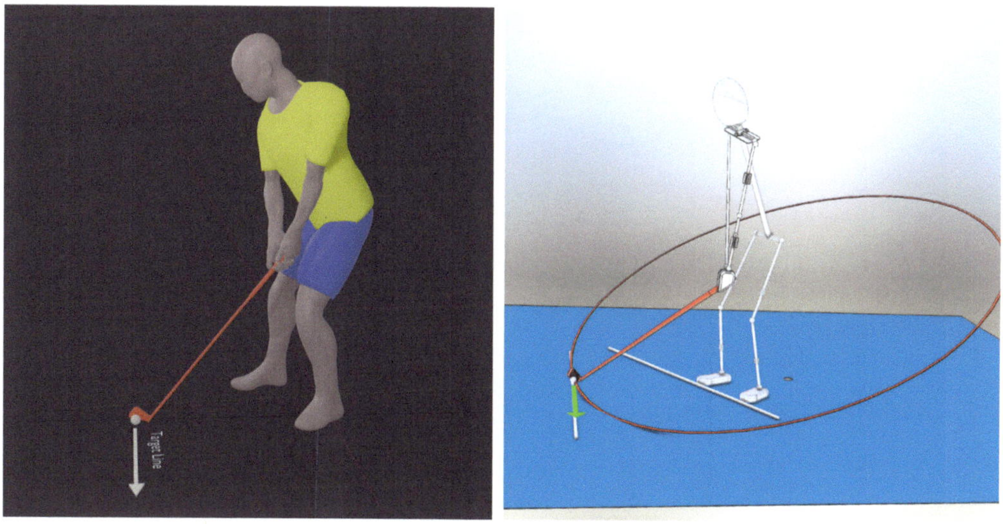

Figure 178: Chipping with Open Stance

The following is the setup for chipping with an open stance:

- Your back is straight, and you are bending at the hips with knees slightly bent.
- Rotate the body toward the target line by moving the right foot forward to open the stance, which, in turn, moves the right hip forward (closer to the ball).
- The leading arm (left arm) is straight, and the trailing arm (right arm) is bent at the elbow so that the upper right arm is against the right side of the torso.
- Your shoulders, hips, and feet are angled with respect to the target line.
- The ball is just forward of center.

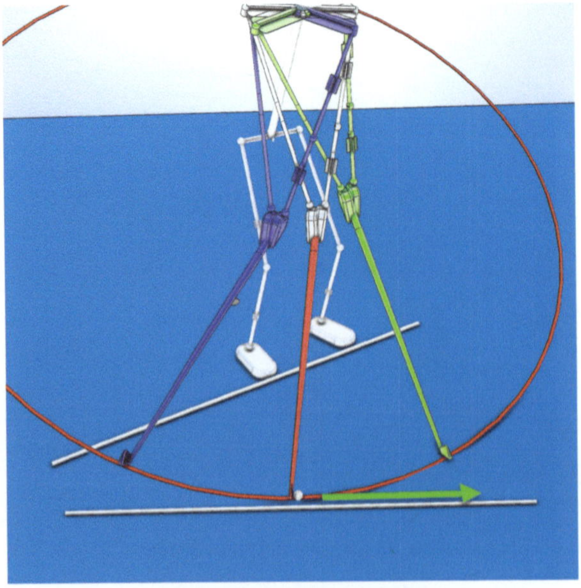

Figure 179: Open Stance Geometry

The initial backswing is a clockwise rotation of the shoulders (primary rotation). The amount of backswing depends on the distance required. The club path stays on the base plane, and the clubhead remains perpendicular to the club path.

At the top of the stroke, the clubface is still perpendicular to the club path (which is open with respect to the target line). The shoulders reverse direction and rotate counterclockwise. The clubhead returns to the neutral position on the same club path created by the backswing.

The leading arm (left arm) remains straight. At impact, the clubhead continues clockwise along the same club path to the finish. At the finish, the clubhead is still on the base plane, and the clubface is perpendicular to club path.

Advantages of an Open Stance

- Makes it easier to keep the right arm against the right side so that the arms turn in conjunction with the shoulders and upper body
- Makes it easier to keep the arms and hands quiet during the swing
- Adds some loft to the clubface because of the Out-to-In swing path

- Good for both shorter and slightly longer chip shots and is a natural lead to pitch shots
- More backspin and higher loft with less roll

Disadvantages of an Open Stance

- Requires a little more understanding and learning to set up and execute
- Adds some clockwise sidespin (left to right) because of the Out-to-In swing path

Whether using the square stance or the open stance, the execution is completed with your shoulders. The clubface remains perpendicular for the entire shoulder rotation, and the club path is a semicircle around the primary axis and on the base plane. The stroke is like a putt but typically with a longer swing arc (i.e., the shoulders rotate more than with a putt). Because a chip uses a lofted club (e.g., a wedge or an iron), the ball will have a lofted trajectory.

Pitching

A pitch shot is a short game shot with a higher trajectory and more spin, designed to keep the ball in the air longer as it travels to its target. Unlike chip shots that employ a straight back-and-forth motion, pitch shots require primary rotation and some secondary rotation. Pitching usually is done with a wedge (for example, a gap wedge or pitching wedge) or a short iron (for example, an 8 or a 9 iron).

When hitting a basic pitch shot, think about taking the club back to about waist level with some amount of secondary rotation. Start the swing by rotating your shoulders as if you were starting a full golf swing.

After the initial takeaway, add secondary rotation of the leading arm (straight left arm). At the end of a limited backswing, there should be a brief pause, then start rotating the shoulders counterclockwise back toward your target to strike the ball. The distance you're trying to carry the ball will impact how big of a backswing you take and how much secondary rotation you use. Like with chipping, you can hit a pitch shot with many different clubs.

Pitching uses the following steps.

Step 1: Address
Step 2: Initial Takeaway (Primary Rotation CW)
Step 3: Takeaway (Primary Rotation CW and Secondary Rotation CW)
Step 4: Limited (if Any) Rotation to End of Backswing (Primary Rotation CW)
Step 5: End of Backswing
Step 6: Downswing (Primary Rotation CCW)
Step 7: Release (Primary Rotation CCW and Secondary Rotation CCW)
Step 8: Impact
Step 9: Follow-Through (Primary Rotation CCW and Secondary Rotation CCW)

Note that the primary difference between a chip shot and a full swing is the limited primary and secondary rotation.

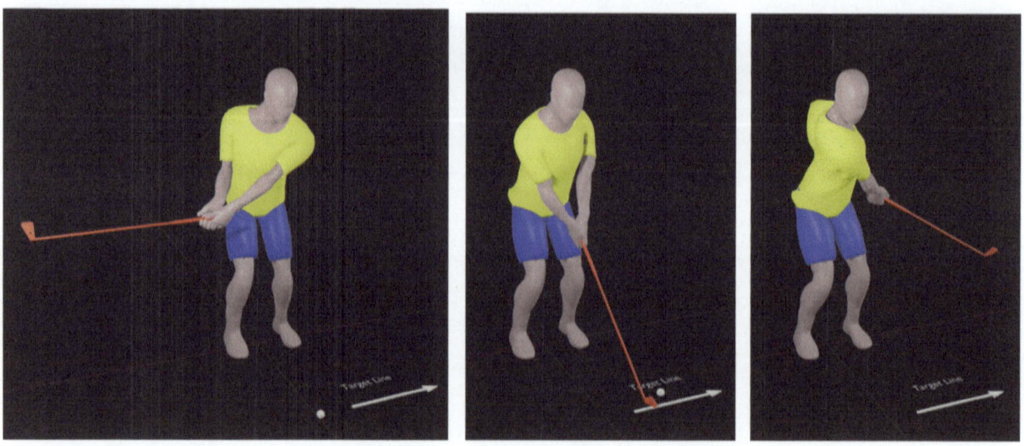

Figure 180: Pitching Address Square Stance Sequence

Like the chip shot, there are a couple of variations of the pitch shot. You can use a square stance, or you can open the stance slightly, and there are similar advantages and disadvantages.

Square Stance

Shoulders and feet are parallel to the target line. Both arms are extended and straight, forming a V. The stroke is completed by moving the shoulder counterclockwise and then clockwise in a steady motion, and it is largely primary rotation while using some degree of secondary rotation.

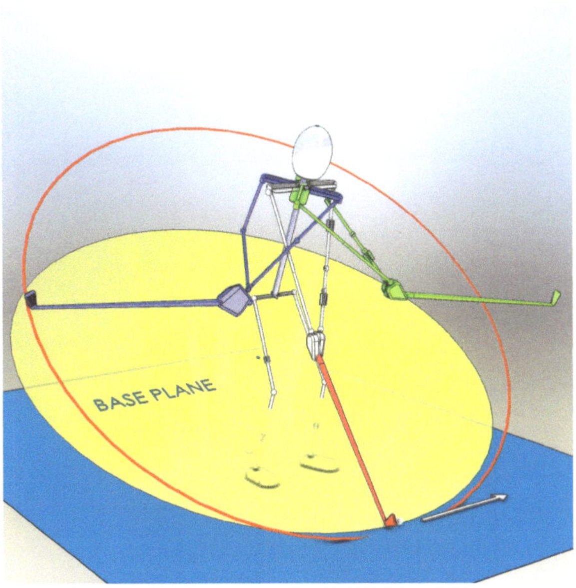

Figure 181: Pitching Geometry Square Stance

Open Stance

The body is turned at an angle into the target line (open stance) with the right foot forward to open the stance, which moves the right hip forward (closer to the ball). The left arm is extended and straight; however, the right arm is slightly bent at the elbow to accommodate the open stance. The more you open the stance (turn into the target line), the more the right elbow bends. The stroke is done by moving the shoulder counterclockwise and then clockwise in a steady motion while using some degree of secondary rotation.

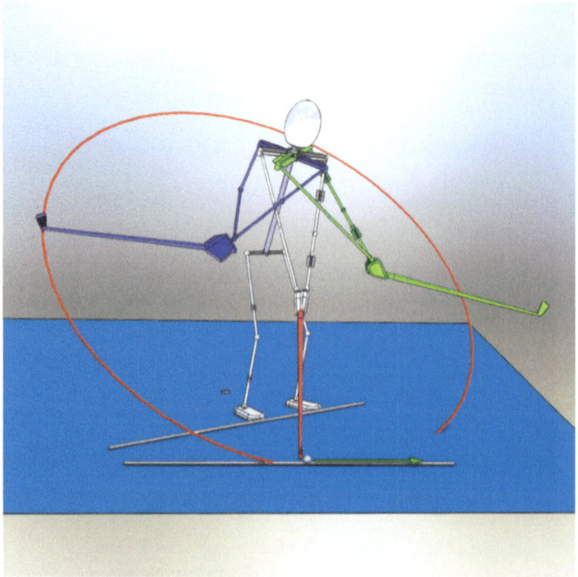

Figure 182: Pitching Geometry Open Stance

Whether using the neutral stance or the open stance, the execution is done with the primary rotation (shoulders) and some degree of secondary rotation (rotation around the straight left arm).

The clubface opens as the shoulders rotate on the backswing because the right arm/elbow continues to bend against the side to guide additional secondary rotation of the leading arm.

The stroke is like the full swing, which only uses the first three positions with limited, if any, rotation in step 4. Because a pitch uses a lofted club (e.g., a wedge or an iron), the ball will have a lofted trajectory.

The biggest difference of the chip shot versus the pitch shot is the degree of secondary rotation. The chip shot uses mostly primary rotation and minimal secondary rotation, because the distances are typically shorter and require more control and less speed.

A pitch shot uses both primary rotation and a significant amount of secondary rotation, because distances from the green are longer and require higher clubhead speeds.

The Partial Swing—Wedges, Short Irons, and Midirons

The partial swing is usually completed using a wedge or any iron when you want to get limited distance from a given club.

When hitting with a partial swing shot, think about taking the club back to about waist level with a slight amount of wrist hinge (tertiary motion). Rotate your shoulders as if you were starting a full golf swing along with the simultaneous secondary rotation of the leading arm (straight left arm).

At the end of the limited backswing, there should be a brief pause, then start rotating back toward your target to strike the ball. The distance you're trying to carry the ball will impact how big of a backswing you take and how much secondary rotation you use. Like with pitching, you can hit this type of swing with many different clubs.

The partial swing uses the following steps.

Step 1: Address
Step 2: Initial Takeaway (Primary Rotation CW)
Step 3: Takeaway (Primary Rotation Clockwise and Secondary Rotation CW)
Step 4: Limited Rotation to End of Backswing (Primary Rotation CW)
Step 5: End of Backswing
Step 6: Downswing (Primary Rotation CCW)
Step 7: Release (Primary Rotation CCW and Secondary Rotation CCW)
Step 8: Impact
Step 9: Follow-Through (Primary Rotation CCW and Secondary Rotation CCW)
Step 10: Finish (Primary Rotation CCW)

Note the primary difference between a pitch shot and a partial swing is that the pitch shot does not use as much primary rotation in step 4, whereas a partial shot can use considerably more.

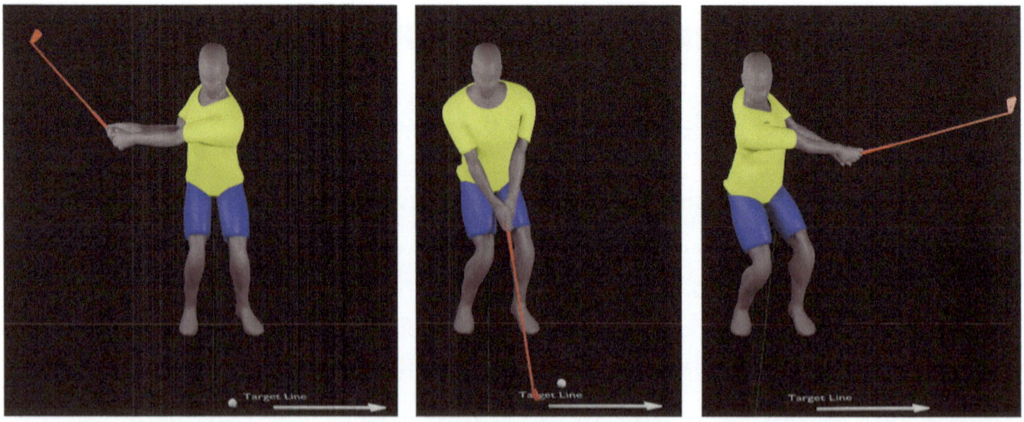

Figure 183: Partial Swing Sequence

The following is the setup for a partial shot:

1. Stance: Shoulders and feet are parallel to the target line. Both arms are extended and straight, forming a V. The stroke is completed by moving the shoulder counterclockwise and then clockwise in a steady motion and is primarily primary rotation while using some degree of secondary rotation.

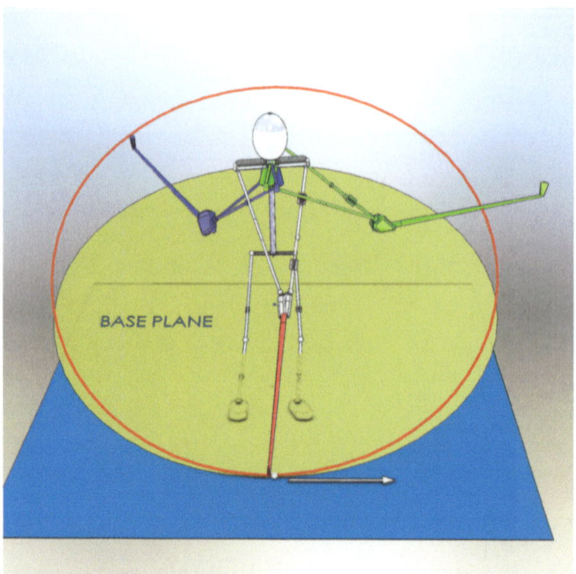

Figure 184: Partial Swing

The execution is completed with the primary rotation (shoulders) and secondary rotation (rotation around the straight left arm). The clubface opens as the shoulders rotate, because the right arm/elbow bends to guide some secondary rotation. The more lofted the club (e.g., a wedge or an iron), the more lofted the ball trajectory.

One of the biggest differences between the kinematics of the pitch shot and the partial swing is the degree of primary rotation. A pitch shot uses a significant amount of secondary rotation, because distances are shorter, and thus, there is usually a need for control and more backspin. A partial swing uses more primary rotation, because the distances are typically longer and require both control and speed.

The Full Swing—Everything But the Putter

The full swing is used to get maximum distance from a given club. The full swing is usually completed using everything in the bag except the putter.

When hitting with a full swing, think about taking the club back initially with all shoulder rotation, i.e., a one-piece takeaway. As you continue to rotate the shoulders clockwise, start to bend the trailing elbow and wrist (tertiary motion) as you lift the clubhead onto the swing plane. As you continue to rotate your shoulders back, there is additional secondary rotation of the leading arm (straight left arm) as it moves across the chest. You continue full shoulder rotation to the top of the backswing.

There should be a brief pause of the shoulders as the club slows down and stops, then you start rotating back toward your target to strike the ball. Hold the release to get the maximum distance for the selected club. Continue through impact, and complete the rotation with a good finish.

The full swing uses the following steps.

Step 1: Address
Step 2: Initial Takeaway (Primary Rotation CW)
Step 3: Takeaway (Primary Rotation CW and Secondary Rotation CW)
Step 4: Full Rotation to Top of Backswing (Primary Rotation CW)
Step 5: End of Backswing
Step 6: Downswing (Primary Rotation CCW)
Step 7: Release (Primary Rotation CCW and Secondary Rotation CCW)
Step 8: Impact
Step 9: Follow-Through (Primary Rotation CCW and Secondary Rotation CCW)
Step 10: Finish (Primary Rotation CCW)

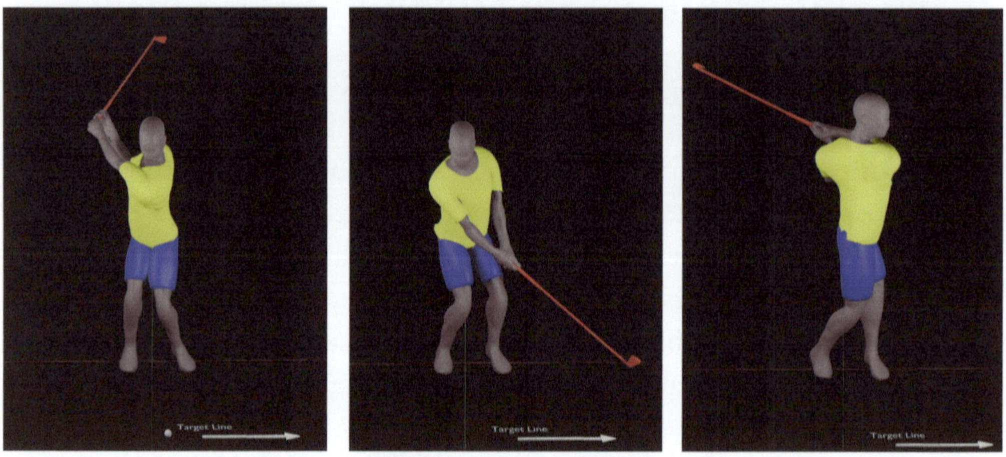

Figure 186: The Full Swing Sequence

The execution is completed with both primary rotation (shoulders) and secondary rotation (rotation around the straight left arm). The clubface opens as the shoulders rotate because the right arm/elbow bends to guide some secondary rotation. The more lofted the club (e.g., a wedge or an iron), the more lofted the ball trajectory.

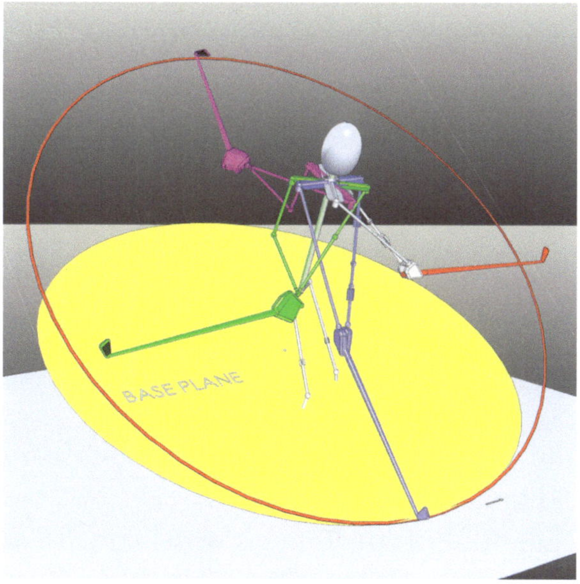

Figure 187: The Full Swing

Even though the kinematics are fundamentally the same for all clubs, the tempo varies, because each club has differences in length, mass stiffness, and many other small physical differences. Consequently, the golfer must train the brain to get the timing down for each club, and this can only be done by—you guessed it—practicing.

Takeaways:

So what did we learn in Chapter 12?

1) Primary rotation, secondary rotation, and tertiary motion apply in varying degrees to all the clubs in the golf bag. The degree of each depends on the club and swing type.
2) Swing types can be categorized by the degree of primary rotation and secondary rotation and the club type used for the swing:

  a) Putter—Limited Primary Rotation (usually less than 20 degrees)
  b) Chipping—Limited Primary Rotation
  c) Pitching—Limited Primary Rotation with Limited Secondary Rotation
  d) Partial Swing—Limited Primary Rotation with Full Secondary Rotation
  e) Full Swing—Full Primary Rotation with Full Secondary Rotation

CHAPTER 14

The Ten Demons: Swing Flaws

Sometimes you have to confront your demons and sometimes even let them loose to genuinely find a place where you can gain some understanding.

—Peter Mullan

In the game of golf (as in the game of life), there are the gods and the demons. Every golfer, whether amateur or professional, shares a special relationship with both. On a good day, we enjoy the attention of the golf gods and sink that thirty-foot putt. On a bad day, the demons rear their ugly heads, and we watch the ball hook wickedly to the left and make a big splash as it hits the water.

The demons in golf are often the result of a swing flaw or multiple swing flaws. Most of these flaws can be put into one of three main categories:

1. Improper setup issues (static geometry)
2. Swing (rotation) issues (dynamic geometry)
3. Tempo issues (timing issues)

To get a pure shot, the kinematics and the timing need to be precise. A small deviation in any part of the geometry of either the setup or the swing (rotation) can have a significant impact on where the ball will end up.

Revelation #21

Understanding the geometry of the golf swing goes a long way toward recognizing swing flaws as well as correcting them.

One could argue that improper grip ultimately leads to a majority of kinematic problems (i.e., problems with the geometry of the shot). I put the grip issues in a category of its own because of the importance of a good grip. If you don't get the grip right, the rest of the swing doesn't really matter.

You could fill a whole book on just the kinematics of swing flaws. However, this chapter focuses on ten of the most common swing flaws that every golfer contends with.

Professionals and low handicap golfers, through sheer athleticism and lots of hard work, have learned to control and even use these flaws to their advantage. The rest of us mere mortals struggle to control these flaws every time we step onto a golf course.

This is my rendition of the top ten flaws, which are arguably subjective. Nonetheless, they are what they are.

	Flaw	Cause	Result	How to Correct
1	**Grip Issues**	A strong grip (or weak grip) instead of a neutral grip	Strong grip will increase secondary rotational speed and distance but will adversely affect control and consistency.	Use a neutral grip with the wrist hyperextended and a straight left arm.
2	**Improper Setup:** Poor posture	Bending the spine instead of tilting the hips; too much spine tilt	A curved spine off the midplane tilts the shoulder plane and swing plane out of position, which can cause many other issues.	Address the ball by bending at the hips with the back straight. Keep the spine (primary axis) on the midplane.
3	**Improper Setup:** Excessive Spine Tilt.	Too much spine tilt away from the midplane	Spine tilt away from the midplane also tilts the shoulder plane and swing plane out of position, which causes many other issues.	Keep the spine (primary axis) on the midplane.

	Flaw	Cause	Result	How to Correct
4	**Primary Axis Rotation:** Arms out of sync with torso	Starting the backswing with the arms instead of the shoulders	The arms get out of sync with the torso. This is a result of too much arm and not enough shoulder.	Start the backswing with a one-piece rotation of the shoulders (OPR).
5	**Secondary Axis Geometry:** Bending the leading arm	Bent leading arm on backswing or downswing (left arm for RH golfers)	This kills the geometry of the secondary rotation, resulting in loss of speed and consistency.	Keep the leading arm straight on the backswing (SLA).
6	**Secondary Axis Geometry:** Allowing the wrist to cock during the backswing	Left wrist cocked instead of a flat left wrist	This kills the geometry of the secondary rotation, resulting in loss of speed and consistency.	Keep a flat left wrist (FLW).
7	**Secondary Axis Rotation:** Limited or no secondary rotation	Failing to complete secondary rotation on the backswing	There is a loss of speed (and therefore distance) generated by secondary rotation.	Make a full 90-degree clockwise rotation of the straight leading arm on the backswing.

	Flaw	Cause	Result	How to Correct
8	**Tempo:** Starting the downswing with the arms instead of the shoulders	Pushing the club rather than pulling the club with the shoulders (i.e., steering the club)	There is a loss of power, speed, and consistency.	Pull the club with the left shoulder on the downswing.
9	**Tempo:** Releasing secondary rotation too soon	Releasing the secondary rotation at the start of the downswing	This kills the speed of the club and therefore the distance the ball travels.	Hold the release of the secondary rotation to get speed.
10	**Tempo:** Follow-Through and Finish	Not completing the swing (rotation) after impact	There is a loss of distance.	Complete the swing to the finish with proper geometry and weight shifting.

1. Grip Issues—Grip is Too Strong (or Too Weak)

A good grip is one of the fundamental requirements of a good golf swing. If the grip is flawed, the rest of the swing is compromised. A strong grip can help a golfer achieve more clubhead speed and hence more distance, but it's usually at the expense of accuracy. A strong grip will promote a hooked shot that will often peel off to the left and into the woods.

Figure 191: Weak Grip

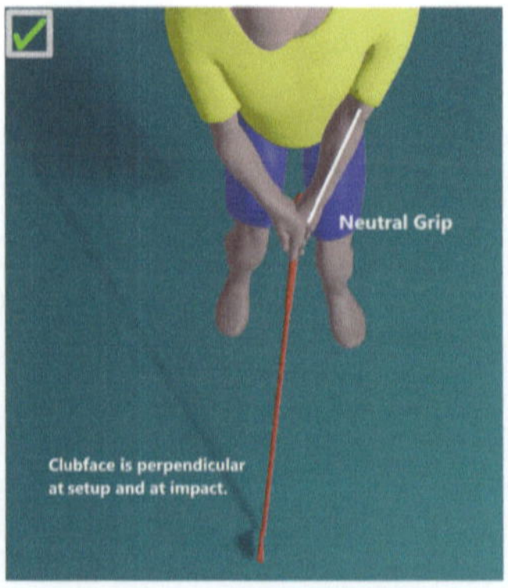

Figure 188: Neutral Grip

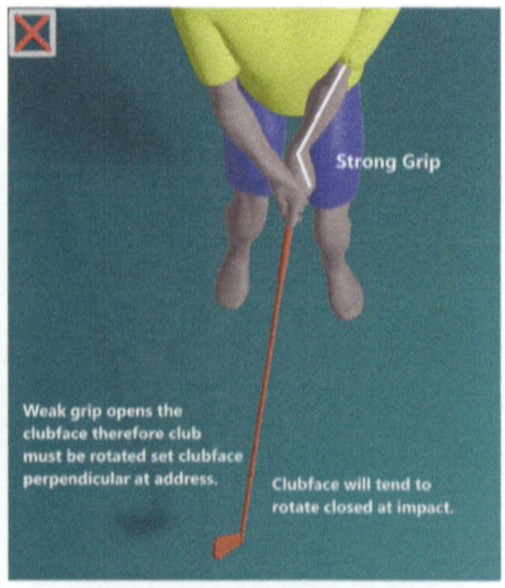

Figure 190: Strong Grip

Many low handicap golfers intentionally use a strong grip to get more distance, but they understand the potential issues with a strong grip and know how to tame the demon. Most of us either don't understand the issues resulting from a strong grip or don't have the time to hit five hundred balls a day. Adjustments to either tempo or geometry are needed to compensate for a strong (or weak) grip.

Suggestion: Maintain a *neutral* grip with a flat left wrist, especially if you are a beginner golfer or an intermediate-level golfer who suffers from inconsistency from shot to shot and who tends to pull shots to the left of the target line. A neutral grip typically starts with a slightly cupped left wrist, which gradually flattens throughout the swing.[11]

[11] Haney, H. (2009b, November 16). *Hank Haney: Keep your left wrist flat.* Golf Digest. https://www.golfdigest.com/story/hank_haney_flat_wrist

2. Improper Setup: Poor Posture

A good and consistent golf swing requires good geometry at setup. The upper body should be inclined by bending at the hips and not by bending the back.

High handicap golfers often assume the address position by bending their back. This affects many aspects of the swing including weight distribution, ability to rotate the hips and shoulders, and ability to keep the upper arms in sync with the upper body.

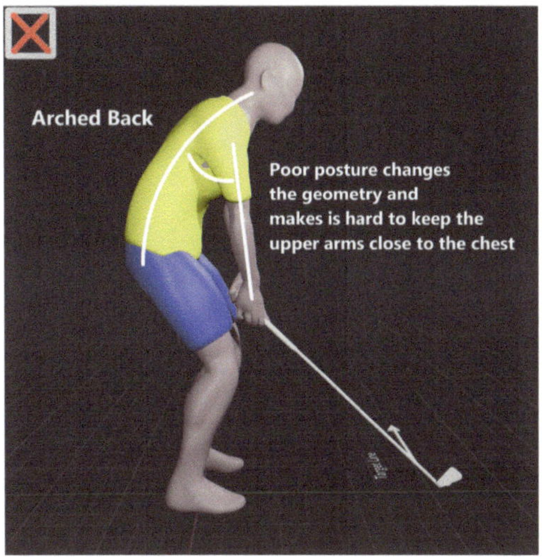

Figure 193: Poor Posture

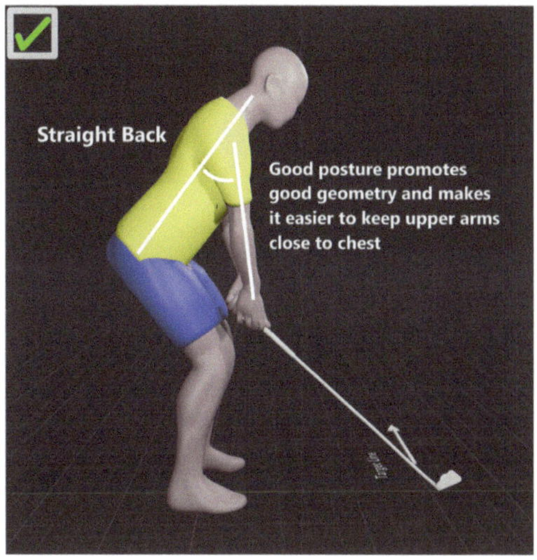

Figure 192: Good Posture

When the back is arched, the arms tend to hang away from the upper body. Keeping the back straight and pivoting at the hips allow the arms to stay closer to the chest. This makes it easier to rotate the arms with the shoulders and the upper body during the backswing and downswing.

Suggestion: Maintain good posture during setup. Keep the back straight and pivot at the hips during setup. Repeat exercise 3a and exercise 3b from Chapter 3.

3. Improper Setup: Excessive Spine Tilt

Primary rotation is the rotation of the torso, arms, and the golf club around the primary axis, which runs through the center of the torso. The primary axis needs to be on the midplane during setup and needs to stay centered during the backswing and downswing.

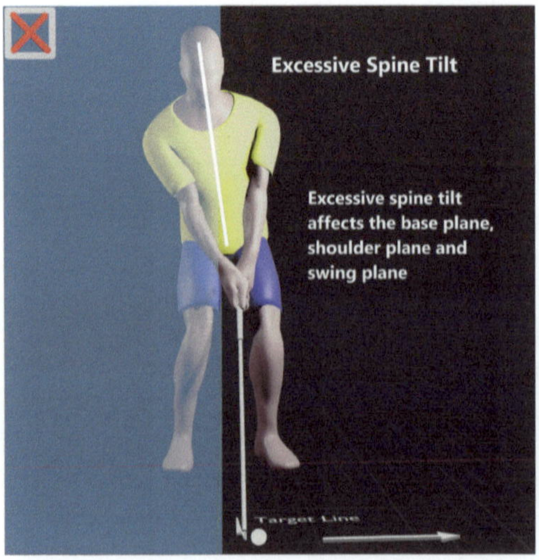

Figure 195: Excessive Spine Tilt

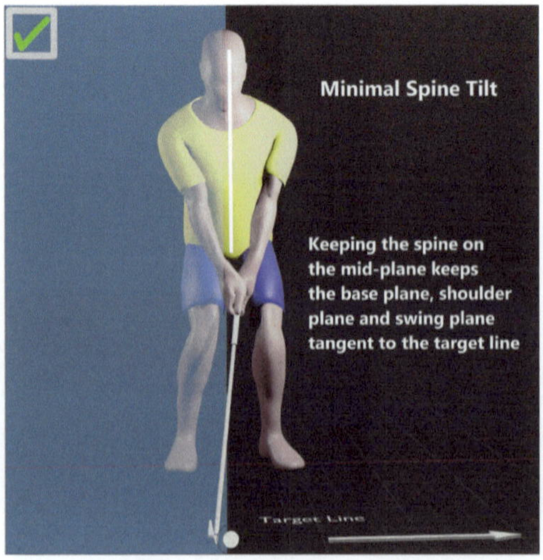

Figure 194: Minimal Spine Tilt

There are two big misconceptions that many golfers believe.

- **a.** They confuse shoulder tilt with spine tilt during setup, which causes the primary axis to wander off the midplane (static geometry problem).
- **b.** They slide the spine (primary axis) off the midplane during the backswing, which kills consistency (dynamic geometry problem).

Low handicap golfers do use a small amount of primary axis tilt (spine tilt), especially for the driver, but again, they hit hundreds of balls every day and understand how to use spine tilt correctly. The average weekend golfer needs to use the KISS (keep it simple, stupid) rule and just keep the primary axis near the midplane at address and centered for the backswing and downswing.

Suggestion: Keep the primary axis on the midplane—in other words, make sure the midplane runs right through the middle of the body during setup. Keep the primary axis (center of the torso) on the midplane through the entire backswing.

4. Primary Axis Rotation: Swinging with the Arms

Low handicap golfers rotate the club with their shoulders. High handicap golfers swing the club with their arms with minimum shoulder rotation. If you want to hit a ball consistently with power, you need to use your shoulders. It is really that simple. You can't hit a ball consistently with power if you're swinging the club with your arms. You must rotate the club with your shoulders.

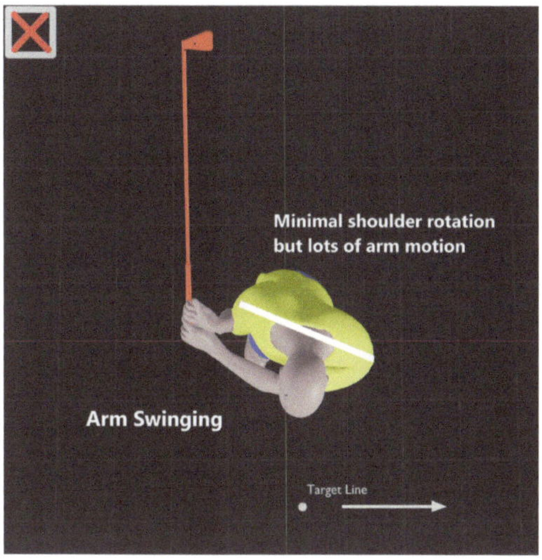

Figure 196: Minimal Shoulder Rotation

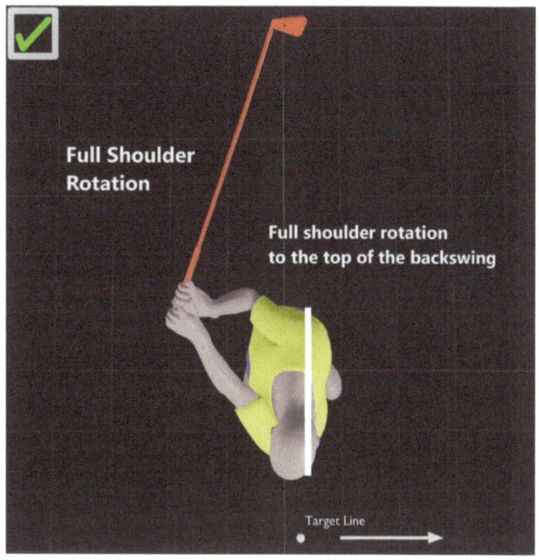

Figure 197: Full Shoulder Rotation

This is by far one of the most common issues with high handicap golfers and is perhaps the single biggest difference between high handicap golfers and low handicap golfers.

If you doubt me, go to the range on a nice summer weekend and watch people practice. Once you're aware of primary rotation (see Chapter 3), it becomes easy to spot the shoulder rotation golfers versus the arm swingers.

Suggestion: Rotate the club with your shoulders, and do not swing the club with your arms. Use your upper body (torso) to rotate the arms by keeping the upper arms close to your chest. Keep a straight left arm during the entire backswing. Repeat the exercises from Chapter 9.

5. Secondary Axis Geometry—Bending the Leading Arm

The leading arm (the straight left arm) must remain straight during the entirety of the backswing. This is a very common issue with high handicap golfers. Even if they start the swing with a straight left arm, they invariably bend the arm as they approach the top of the backswing.

As soon as the leading arm bends, the geometry required for secondary rotation is destroyed, and it becomes almost impossible to get the clubhead back onto the natural swing path. This simple motion takes the club out of the swing plane and dooms the rest of the swing.

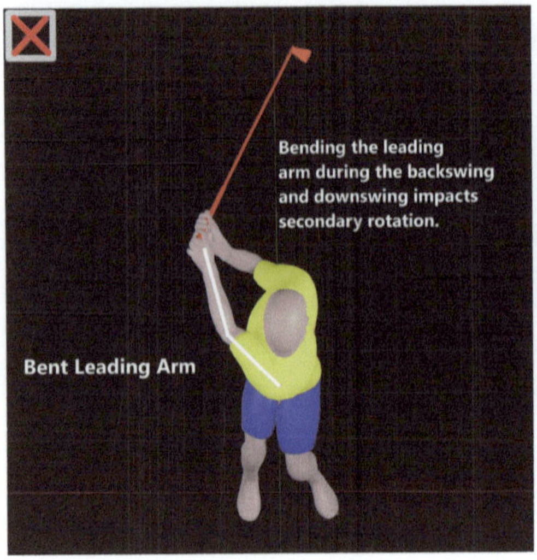

Figure 198: Bent Leading Arm

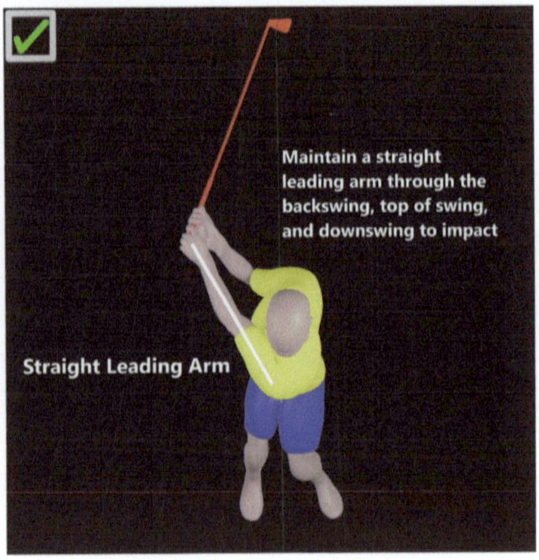

Figure 199: Straight Leading Arm

Suggestion: Start with straight arms as a good setup. During the initial takeaway, keep both arms straight. Consciously maintain a straight leading arm (left arm) to the top of the backswing and make sure that the leading arm remains straight as the left shoulders start the downswing by pulling the straight left arm back toward the impact zone.

6. Secondary Axis Geometry—Allowing the Wrist to Hinge During the Backswing

Not only must the leading arm (the straight left arm) remain straight during the entirety of the backswing, but the left wrist must also stay flat, and the wrist should be hyperextended (pronated). Cocking the left wrist during the backswing is another common problem with high handicap golfers. They may start the swing with a straight left arm and flat left wrist, but invariably, they hinge the wrist during the backswing.

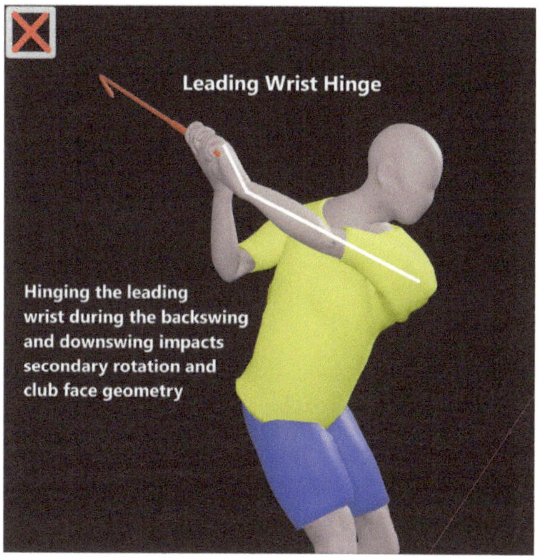

Figure 200: Cupped Leading Wrist

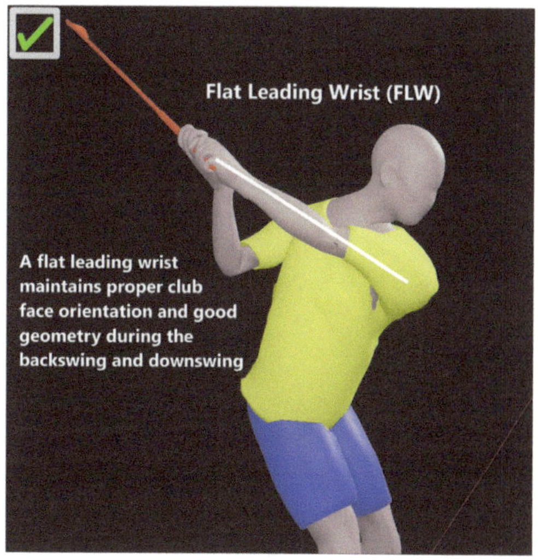

Figure 201: Flat Leading Wrist

As soon as the wrist moves, the geometry required for secondary rotation is destroyed. Hinging the wrist takes the club out of the swing plane and dooms the rest of the swing.

Suggestion: Start with straight arms as of a good setup, which includes a flat left wrist. Consciously maintain the flat left wrist to the top of the swing and through the downswing into the impact zone.

Some professional and low handicap golfers will manipulate their wrist hinge to gain extra yardage. For amateurs this will likely result in a poor shot. Focus on mastering to hit solid consistent shots with a flat leading wrist and stay away from trying to manipulate the leading wrist.

7. Secondary Axis Rotation—Limited Secondary Rotation

There's a good possibility that you didn't even know about secondary rotation until you read Chapter 4. Now, knowing that secondary rotation is the rotation of the club around the straight left arm, you also know that it is the secret to clubhead speed, which translates into distance.

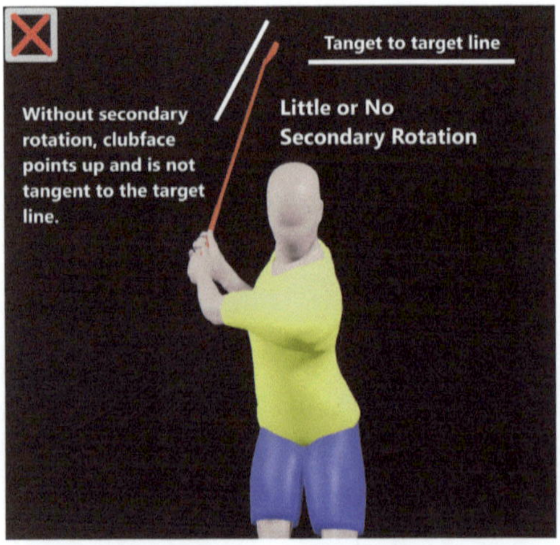

Figure 202: Limited Secondary Rotation

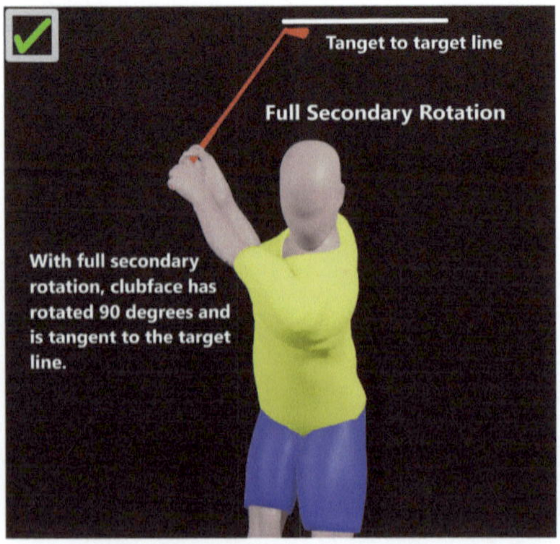

Figure 203: Full Secondary Rotation

Good rotation means a full 90 degree clockwise rotation of the straight left arm during the takeaway and full 180 degree rotation during the downswing and through the release. That means 90 degree counterclockwise secondary rotation into impact and 90 degree counterclockwise secondary rotation during follow-through after impact.

Suggestion: Consistent practice of the exercises in Chapter 9 will go a long way toward establishing both the motions necessary for good secondary rotation as well as the tempo (timing) required.

8. Tempo—Starting the Downswing with the Arms Instead of the Shoulders

Starting the downswing with the arms instead of the shoulders is another common issue. Remember the example of the wagon from Chapter 7. If you've ever pulled a child in a wagon, you know it's much easier to pull the wagon along a path with the wagon handle than it is to push the wagon along the same path with the handle. That's not to say that it's impossible to push the wagon along that path, but it requires a lot of extra steering to accomplish the task. If you pull the wagon, it will easily follow a natural path.

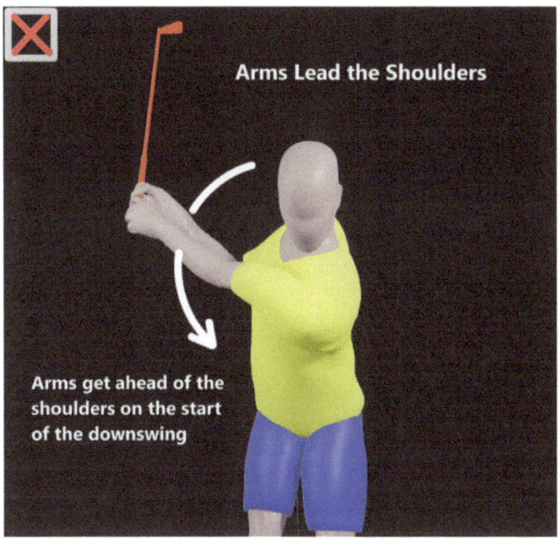

Figure 205: Arms Ahead of Shoulders

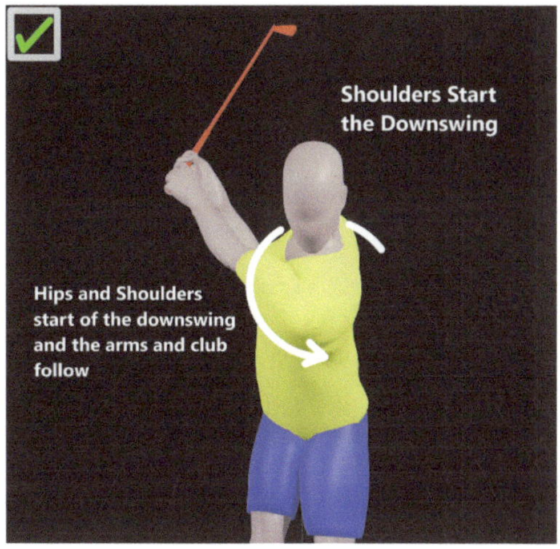

Figure 204: Shoulders Lead Arms

At the top of the backswing, you need to give the arms and golf club a chance to slow down and stop before you reverse the direction of the shoulders and begin the downswing. As the arms and club stop, you need to reverse their direction by pulling the left arm with the left shoulder. When done properly, the left shoulder pulls the left arm, which, in turn, pulls the club back along the natural swing path if you maintained good geometry during the backswing and kept the clubhead in the swing plane.

Suggestion: The one-handed release (OHR) exercises in Chapters 9 and 10 are an excellent way of developing the proper timing for the start of the downswing.

9. Tempo—Releasing Secondary Rotation Too Soon

If you find that you're not getting distance even when pulling the club with your shoulders and a flat left wrist, it's likely due to releasing the club (secondary rotation) too soon. Remember that from the address, you initially rotate the club back with the shoulders (initial takeaway) and then proceed into the takeaway, which is the full 90 degree rotation of the straight left arm. The full secondary rotation should be complete before the shoulders (primary rotation) have completed 45 degrees. It is then all primary rotation to the top of the swing.

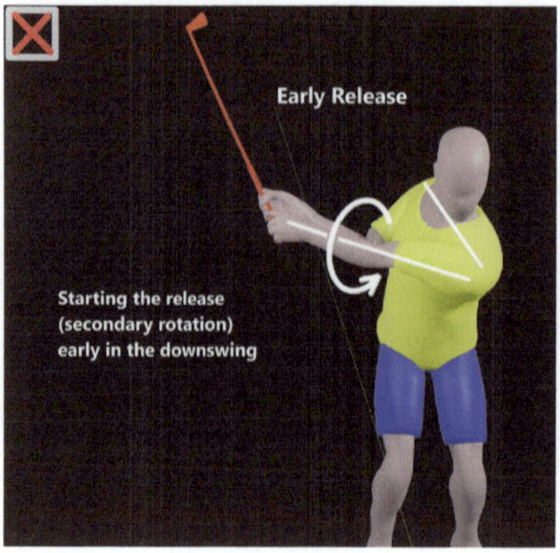

Figure 206: Early Release

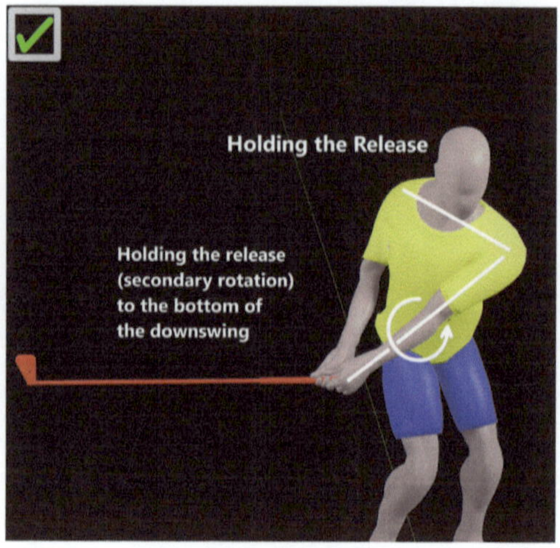

Figure 207: Holding Release

After a pause, you start the downswing by pulling the club into the slot with the left shoulder using primary rotation only. You need to keep the right elbow tight against the side (no secondary rotation) until the shoulders have rotated at least 45 degrees counterclockwise before allowing the right elbow and arm to straighten (the release). If you start the release at the top of the swing, you lose all the potential acceleration and speed associated with holding the release on the downswing.

You don't gain speed (or distance) by rotating faster; you gain speed (and distance) by holding the release as long as possible. If you hold the release too long, you could end up slicing the ball, meaning the clubface does not have sufficient time to rotate to the neutral position before impact and will be open on contact with the ball.

Again, there are no shortcuts for developing this motion. It's a combination of understanding and practice. You must time the release of the secondary rotation with the primary rotation so that the clubface is in the neutral position for both primary and secondary on impact (more about this in the next chapter).

Suggestion: Experiment with holding the release of the secondary rotation using some of the exercises in Chapter 10. Find the correct tempo for each club and then repeat, repeat, repeat.

10. Tempo—Follow-Through and Finish

The backswing and the downswing are all about staying centered. You build up energy on the backswing and you release that energy during the downswing and into impact. After impact during the follow through, you need to now shift your center of gravity forward as you finish the swing.

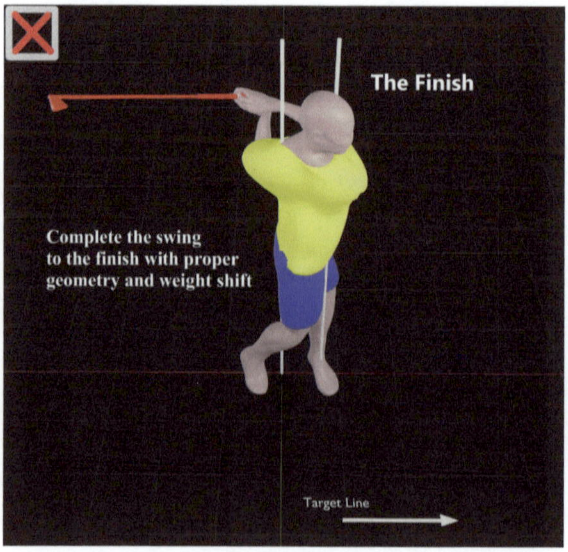

Figure 208: Complete the Swing

Remember the example of the race car? You don't want to let up on the gas until you cross the finish line, and then you coast to a stop. Likewise, you need to have the maximum rotational velocity at impact to get maximum distance, which means you can't relax your swing until impact.

But just like the race-car analogy, you must let your body "coast" to a stop after impact, which is the purpose of a good finish.

Suggestion: Complete the swing to the finish with proper geometry and weight shift. Practice the exercises in Chapter 12 until the motions feel smooth and natural.

* * *

The ten flaws (golf demons) listed above by no means represent a full list. There are many more, but these ten are among the most common. Just being aware of their existence goes a long way to controlling them.

And one of the biggest sins in golf is to try to correct a golf flaw (a demon) by introducing another demon. I've seen many examples of this at the range. For example, to get more distance, an instructor might have the student use a stronger grip. However, the stronger grip might then cause a wicked hook, which is, in turn, corrected by changing the address to a more open stance. All of this may work temporarily at the range but will not work consistently on the course and will have many other unintended consequences.

And again, there are some demons that can and are used by professionals to their advantage. But unless you have numerous hours a day to practice and/or have supreme athleticism to boot, I'd suggest you stick to the basics.

For the average golfer, good fundamentals would dictate good kinematics (i.e., good geometry and an overall awareness of the demons).

Takeaways:

So what did we learn in Chapter 13?

1. Understanding the golf swing goes a long way toward both recognizing golf flaws as well as correcting them.
2. Many golf flaws fall into three categories:
    a. Improper grip or setup
    b. Geometry issues
    c. Timing or tempo issues
3. Trying to fix a flaw by introducing another flaw is a flawed approach.

CHAPTER 15

Advanced Concepts: Shaping Shots

Curiouser and curiouser!

—Lewis Carroll, Alice in Wonderland

If you've come this far, it's now time to go a bit further. Chapters 1 through 8 present the model and fundamentals of the swing. Chapters 9 through 13 provide step-by-step exercises that help develop the neuromuscular connections in the brain (i.e., hand-eye coordination) needed to put that knowledge to use.

This chapter presents some concepts that will be useful for shaping shots. At this point in the journey, we now speak a common language. I call it the

PST approach to golf—simply put, the understanding of primary and secondary rotation and the tertiary motion that ties them together.

Shaping a shot is the ability to strike the ball in such a way as to influence the path it takes to go from you to the target. There are many factors that affect ball path, including ball type, lie (e.g., fluffy or hard), slope, and, of course, clubhead orientation. We will limit this discussion to orientation of the clubface as it impacts the golf ball and specifically some of the variables that are associated with kinematics and dynamics. These include:

1. Clubface Loft: Loft is the angle between the clubface and the ground. That angle is measured in degrees of loft.
2. Clubface Angle Relative to Target Line: Either open, straight, or closed.
3. Clubface Angle Relative to Clubhead Path: Either open, straight, or closed.
4. Clubface Path: Path In-to-In, In-to-Out, or Out-to-In.
5. Clubhead Speed: the speed of a golf club head when it reaches the ball.

First, let's look at some of the basic paths the golf ball can take to the target. They are summarized in the illustration below. The shots we will focus on are the straight shot, the draw, and the fade.

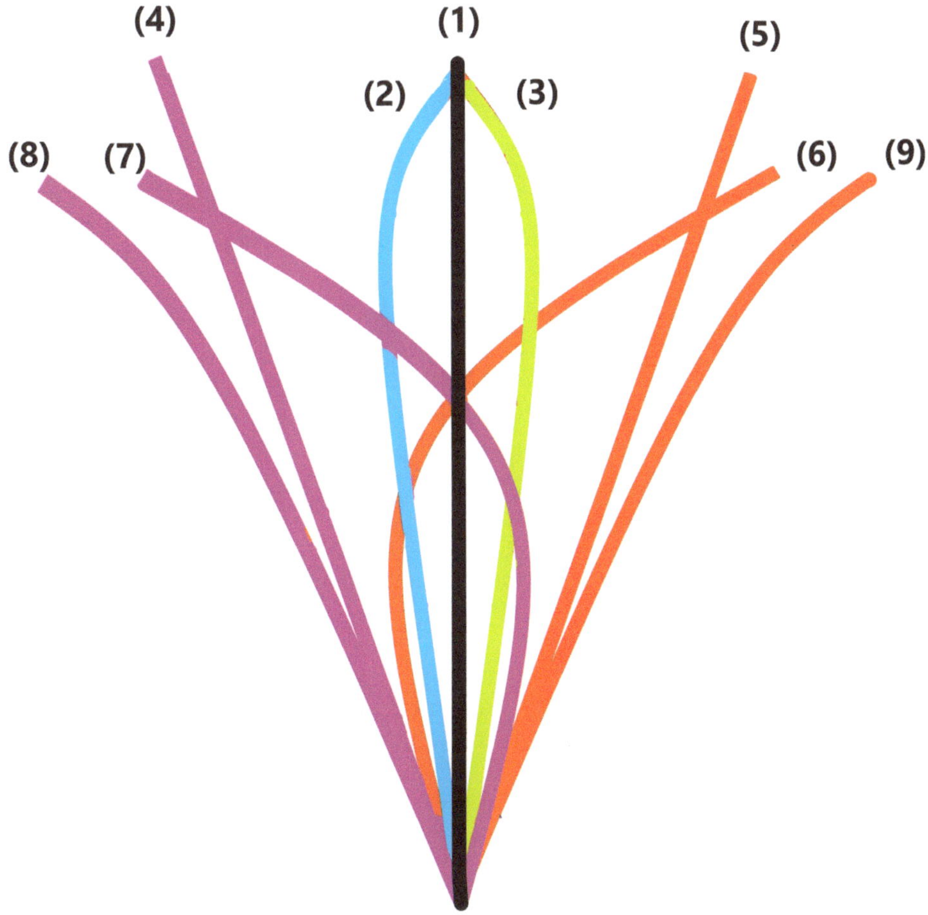

Figure 209: The Nine Ball Flights

1.	Straight	Ball flight is on the target line from beginning to end.
2.	Fade	Ball flight starts left of target line, but clockwise spin causes ball to return to target line.
3.	Draw	Ball flight starts right of target line, but counterclockwise spin causes ball to return to target line.
4.	Pull	Ball flight starts left of target line and continues left of the target line because there is no sidespin.
5.	Push	Ball flight starts right of target line and continues right of the target line because there is no sidespin.
6.	Slice	Ball flight starts left of target line, but excessive clockwise spin causes ball to veer right.
7.	Hook	Ball flight starts along target line, but excessive counter-clockwise spin causes ball to veer left.
8.	Pull Hook	Ball flight starts left of target line, and counterclockwise spin causes the ball to continue left.
9.	Push Slice	Ball flight starts right of target line, and clockwise spin causes the ball to continue right.

Item	Shot Type	Starting Ball Flight	Ball Spin	Club Path	Clubface Relative to Target Line	Clubface Relative to Club Path
1	Straight	straight	0	In-to-In	perpendicular	perpendicular
2	Fade	left	CW	Out-to-In	closed	open
3	Draw	right	CCW	In-to-Out	open	closed
4	Pull	left	0	Out-to-In	closed	perpendicular
5	Push	right	0	In-to-Out	open	perpendicular
6	Slice	starts left but spins right	excessive CW	Out-to-In	closed	excessive open
7	Hook	starts right but spins left	excessive CCW	In-to-Out	open	excessive closed
8	Pull Hook	left	CCW	Out-to-In	closed	closed
9	Push Slice	right	CW	In-to-Out	open	open

Of the nine shot types listed above, generally three types are by design and the other seven types are usually considered mishits. The chart and table contain a lot of information, so let's start by discussing what causes the three desirable shot types: the straight shot, the fade shot, and the draw shot.

- o Straight Shot: The ball goes straight with little or no sidespin.
- o Fade Shot: The ball starts left of the azimuth (line to the target), but due to the right amount of clockwise sidespin, it fades back to the target line.
- o Draw Shot: The ball starts right of the azimuth (line to the target), but due to the right amount of counterclockwise sidespin, it draws back to the target line.

Before we discuss the straight, draw, and fade shots, let's review some important definitions.

- Target Line: A straight line from the ball to the target
- Clubhead Path: The path that the clubhead follows during the swing
- Clubface Angle: Orientation of the clubface with respect to the target line or clubhead path
- Ball Path: Path that the ball follows after impact

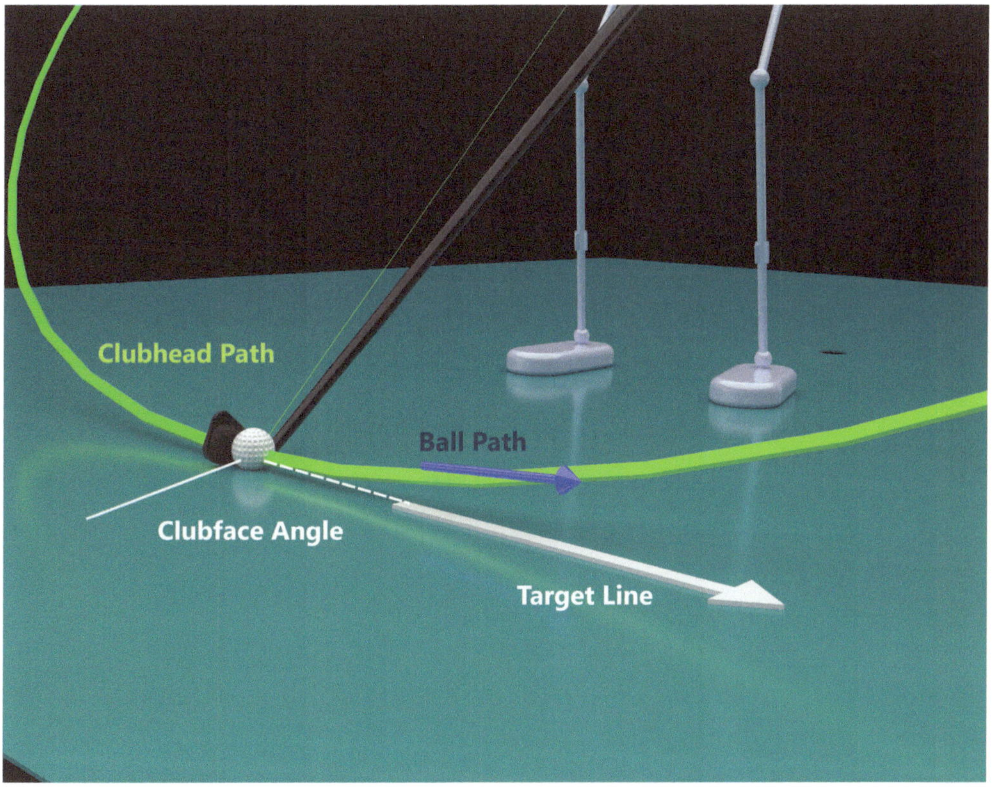

Figure 210: Golf Path/Ball Path/Target Line

The two main factors affecting ball flight are **clubface angle at impact** and **sidespin**.

Clubface Angle

Clubface angle is the orientation of the clubface with respect to the target line. The clubface angle at the point of impact is by far the biggest and most important influence on the ball's starting direction and accounts for about 85 percent of the initial shot direction. There are three possible clubface angles relative to the target line or clubhead path for a particular swing: open, perpendicular, and closed.

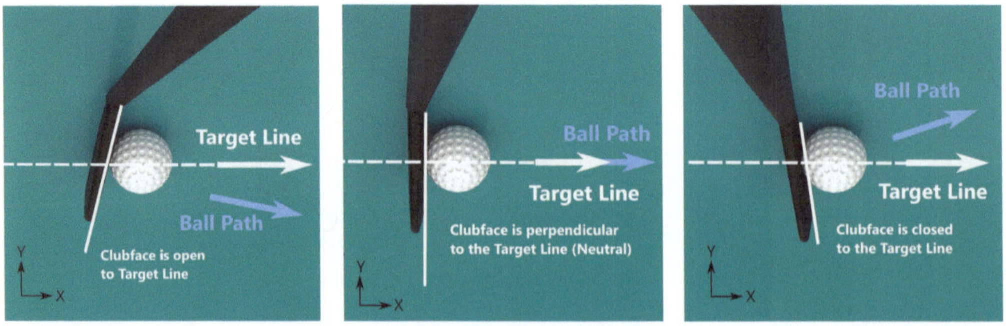

Figure 211: Clubface Angle

Sidespin

Ball spin is the rotation of the ball around the spin axis. The spin axis is the combination of the horizontal axis (backspin) and the vertical axis (sidespin). Total spin is generally viewed as a combination of two types of spin in golf: backspin and sidespin. Each of these spins is suitable for different situations and is used with different intentions. We will focus on sidespin, how to create sidespin, and how it affects ball flight. There are three categories of sidespin: clockwise spin, no sidespin, and counterclockwise spin.

To create sidespin, the clubface must provide a shear force (side-to-side force) at impact. There will be no shear force and therefore no sidespin if the clubface contacts the ball perpendicular to the clubhead path at impact.

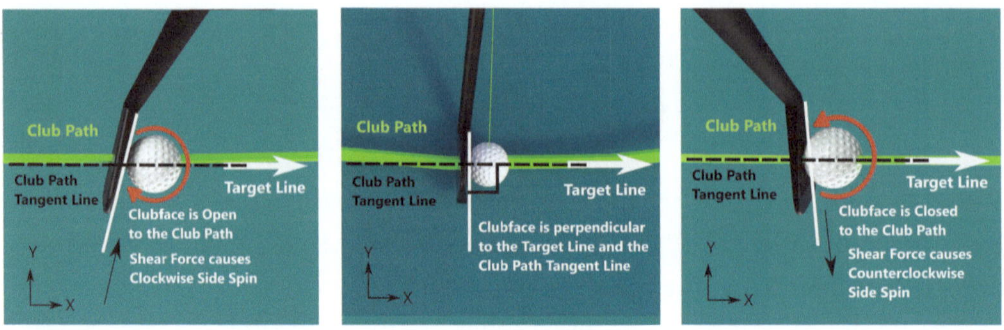

Figure 212: Side Spin

Club Path

This is a good time to review the three types of club paths from Chapter 6. The three club paths are as follows:

- The In-to-In club path is on the swing plane and has a clubhead path line that is tangent and parallel to the target line at impact point.
- The In-to-Out club path is below the swing plane on the downswing and above the swing plane after impact. The clubhead path goes from inside the target line to outside the target line at the impact point.
- The Out-to-In club path is above the swing plane on the downswing and below the swing plane after impact. The clubhead path goes from outside the target line to inside the target line at the impact point.

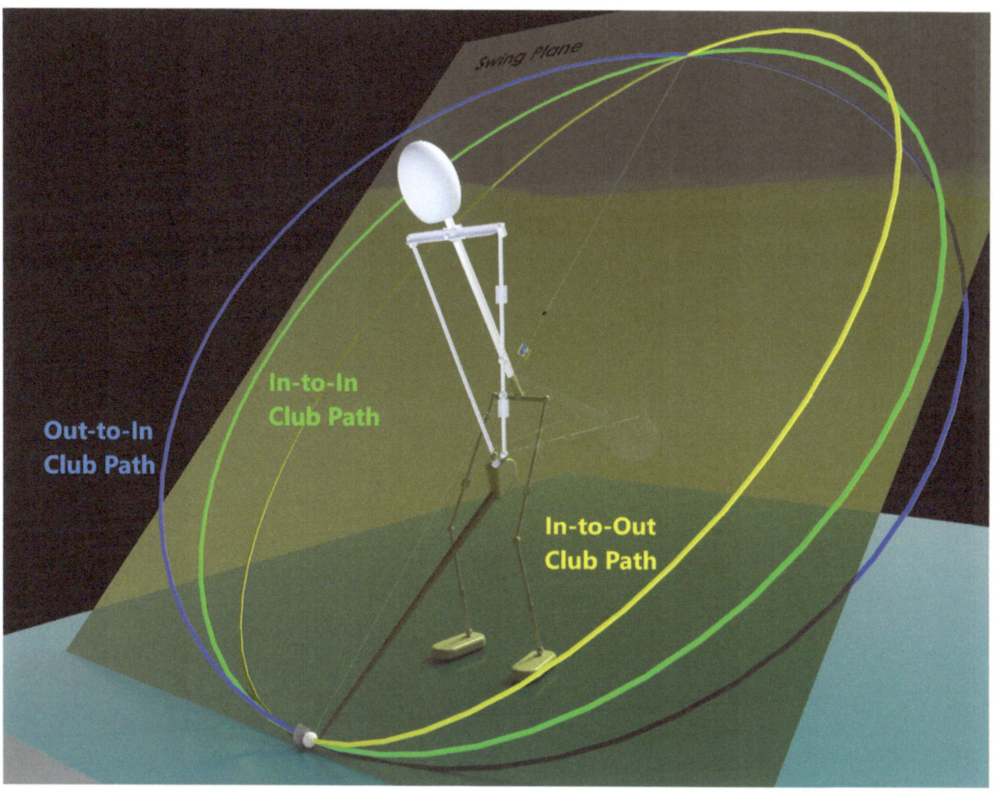

Figure 213: Club Path

Remember that the full swing club path is a combination of the primary rotation and the secondary rotation tied together using tertiary motion. Tertiary motion determines whether the path is In-to-In, In-to-Out, or Out-to-In.

- If primary and secondary rotation are synchronized, the club path is In-to-In.
- If secondary rotation *lags* primary rotation, the club path is In-to-Out.
- If secondary rotation *leads* primary rotation, the club path is Out-to-In.

Let's see what happens when you use different combinations of club path, clubface angle, and sidespin.

The Straight Shot—Clubface Perpendicular/ No Spin

The shot will be straight if the clubface is *perpendicular* to the club path and the target line. This results in a ball flight *along* the target line with no sidespin. Note that the club path is parallel with respect to the target line at impact.

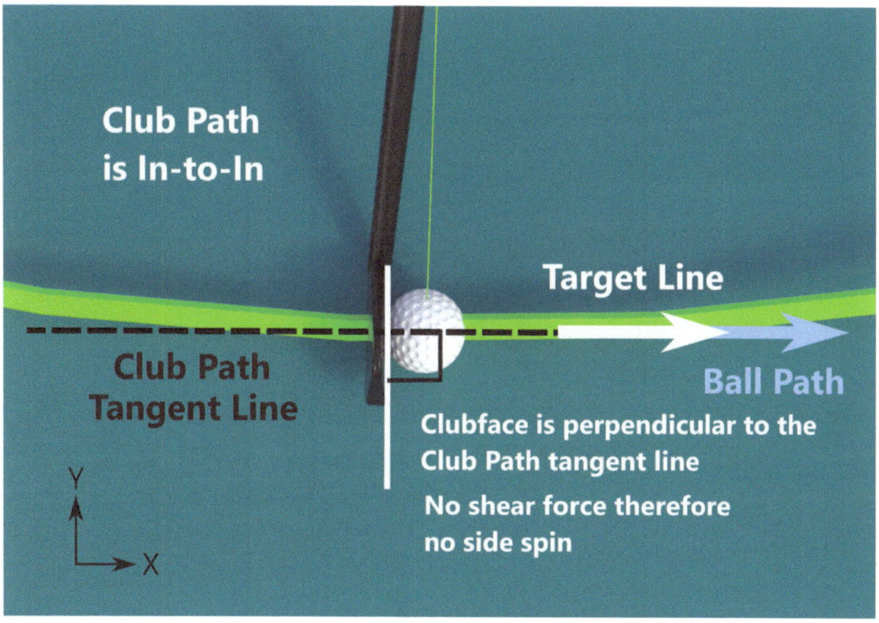

Figure 214: The Straight Shot

The ball will start out straight along the target line and continue in that direction until it stops.

Key Points of the Straight Shot

- The ball path starts straight and remains straight.
- The clubhead path is In-to-In.
- There is no sidespin.

Fade—Clubface Closed/Clockwise Spin

There are times when a fade shot is more desirable than a straight shot or a draw shot.

1. You may want to hit a fade when the fairway doglegs to the right for RH golfers or to the left for LH golfers. Since a fade's shape mirrors the curve of the course, there's a better chance to land on the fairway.
2. Draws typically travel further due to topspin, while fades stop more quickly because of backspin. Fades are often considered more accurate and easier to control than draws, as the backspin helps to minimize the effect of wind on the ball flight.
3. You may want to hit a fade to avoid an object that is in between you and the target, such as a tree branch.

If we want to hit a fade shot, the clubface must be pointed left of the target line at impact but must have the right amount of clockwise sidespin on the ball so that it returns to the target line. To accomplish this, the club path will be Out-to-In, and the clubface will be closed with respect to the target.

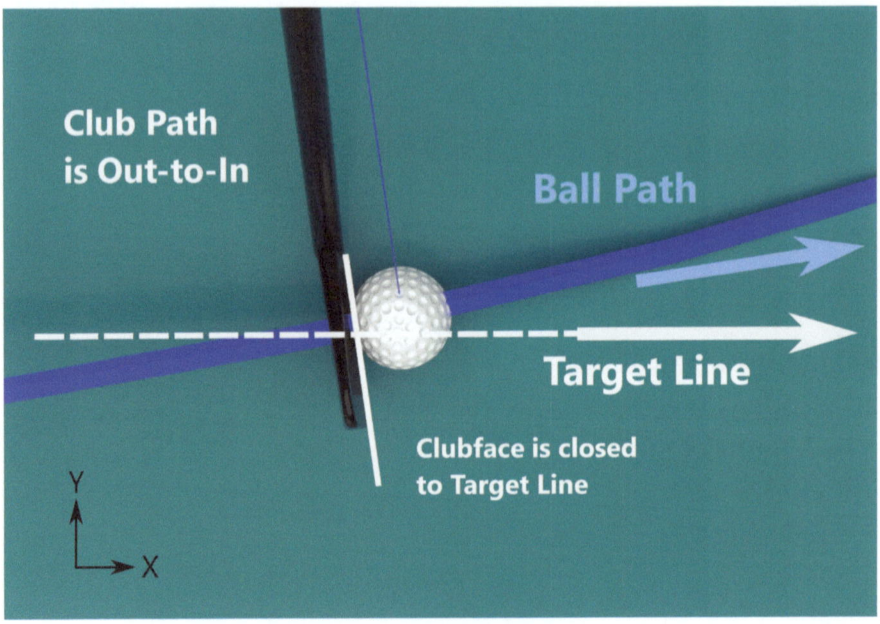

Figure 215: The Fade Direction

To create side-to-side forces for clockwise rotation, the clubface must be moving from outside the target line to inside the target line during impact. The clubface must be open with respect to the club path to create clockwise spin. This is done by *leading* the secondary rotation ahead of the primary rotation (i.e., releasing early).

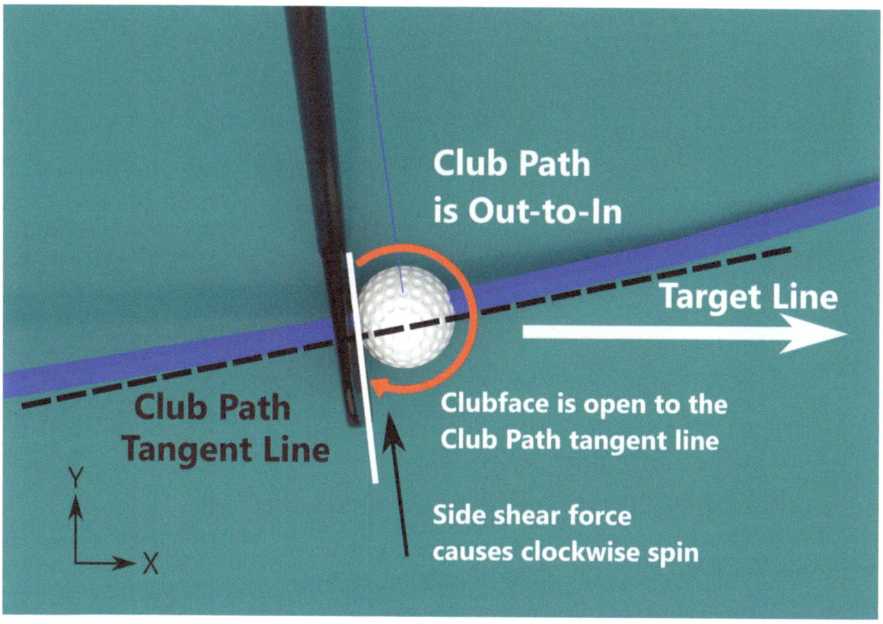

Figure 216: The Fade Side Spin

The ball will start left of the target line because the clubface is closed with respect to the target line. The ball will veer to the right due to the clockwise spin of the ball because the clubface is open with respect to the club path.

Key Points of the Fade

- The ball path starts left of the target line but veers right.
- The clubhead path is Out-to-In.
- The rotation is clockwise.

Draw—Clubface Open/Counterclockwise Spin

Just like with the fade, there are times when a draw shot is more desirable than a straight or fade shot.

1. You may want to hit a fade when the fairway doglegs to the left for RH golfers or to the right for LH golfers. Since a draw's shape more closely mirrors the curve of the course, there's a better chance to land on the fairway.
2. The biggest plus to playing a draw is extra roll on tee shots. Draws tend to roll more than fades, because draws have less backspin. For much the same reason, a drawing shot usually flies lower and penetrates the wind better than a fade.
3. You may want to hit a draw to avoid an object that is in between you and the target, such as a tree branch.

If we want to hit a draw shot, the clubface must be pointed right of the target line at impact but must have the right amount of counterclockwise sidespin on the ball so that it returns to the target line.

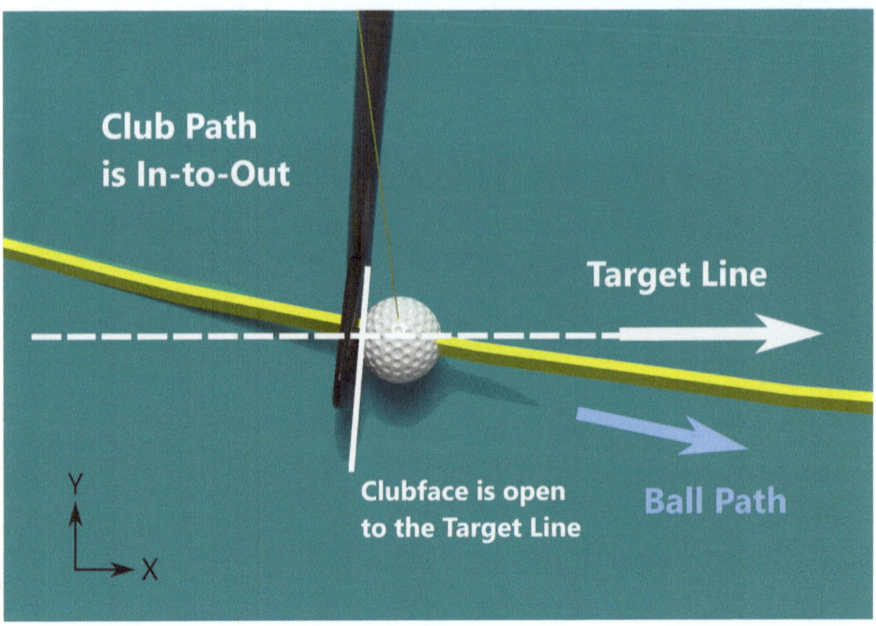

Figure 217: The Draw Direction

To accomplish this, the club path will be In-to-Out, and the clubface will be open with respect to the target. To create side-to-side forces for counterclockwise rotation, the clubface must be moving from inside the target line to outside the target line during impact. The clubface must be closed with respect to the club path to create counterclockwise spin. This is done by *lagging* the secondary rotation behind the primary rotation (i.e., holding the release).

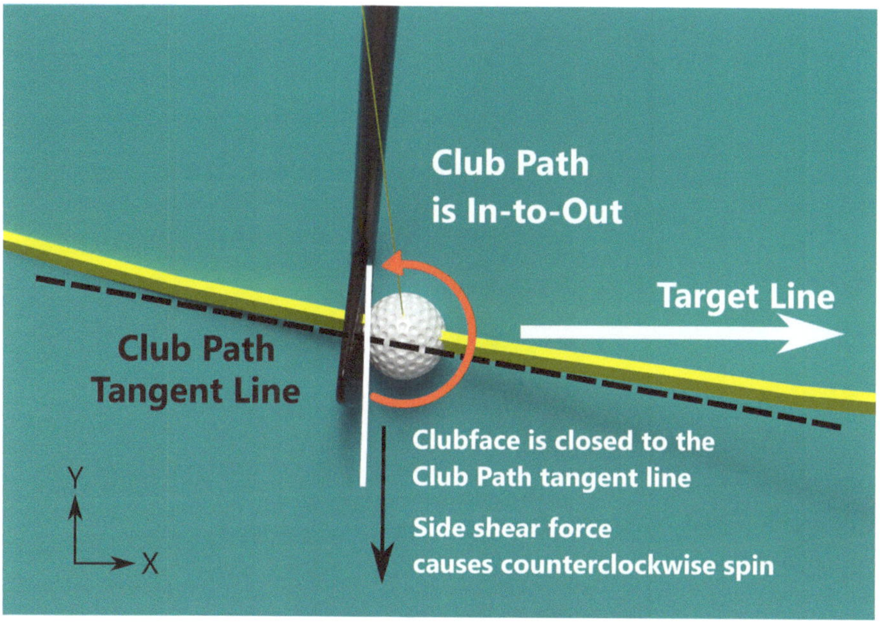

Figure 218: The Draw Side Spin

The ball will start right of the target line because the clubface is open with respect to the target line. The ball will veer to the right due to the counterclockwise rotation of the ball, because the clubface is closed with respect to the club path.

Key Points of the Draw

- The ball path starts right of the target line, but veers left.
- The clubhead path is In-to-Out.
- The rotation is counterclockwise.

The Pull—Clubface Closed/No Spin

The pull shot is *usually* an unintentional shot and the result of a mishit. The shot is considered a pull if the ball starts out to the left of the target line and continues straight in that direction until it stops.

This occurs when the club path is Out-to-In and the clubface is perpendicular to the club path and *closed* with respect to the target line. This can result in a ball path to the *left* of the target line with no sidespin.

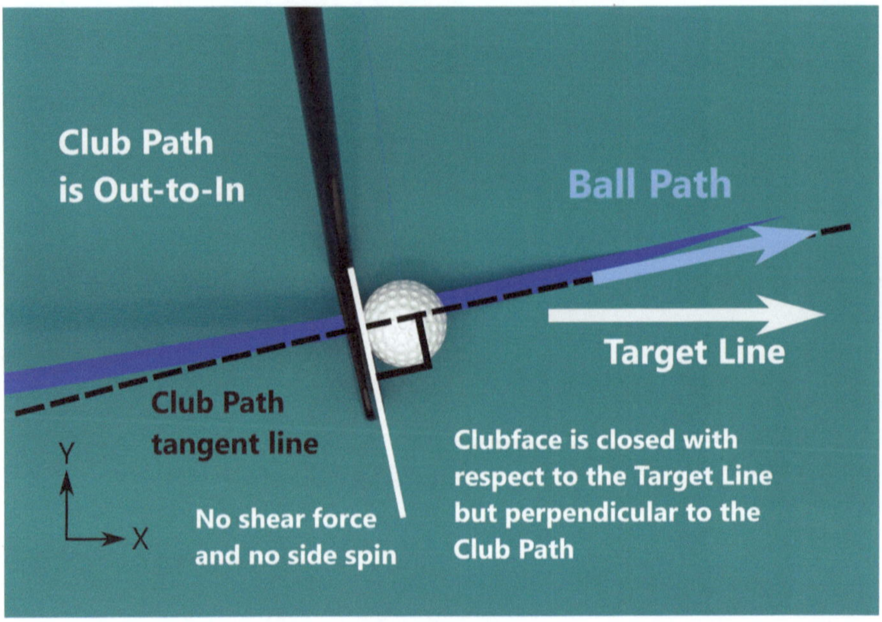

Figure 219: The Pull

The Push—Clubface Open/No Spin

The push shot is *usually* an unintentional shot and the result of a mishit. The shot is considered a push if the ball starts out to the right of the target line and continues straight in that direction until it stops.

This occurs when the club path is In-to-Out and the clubface is perpendicular to the club path and *open* with respect to the target line. This can result in a ball path to the *right* of the target line with no sidespin.

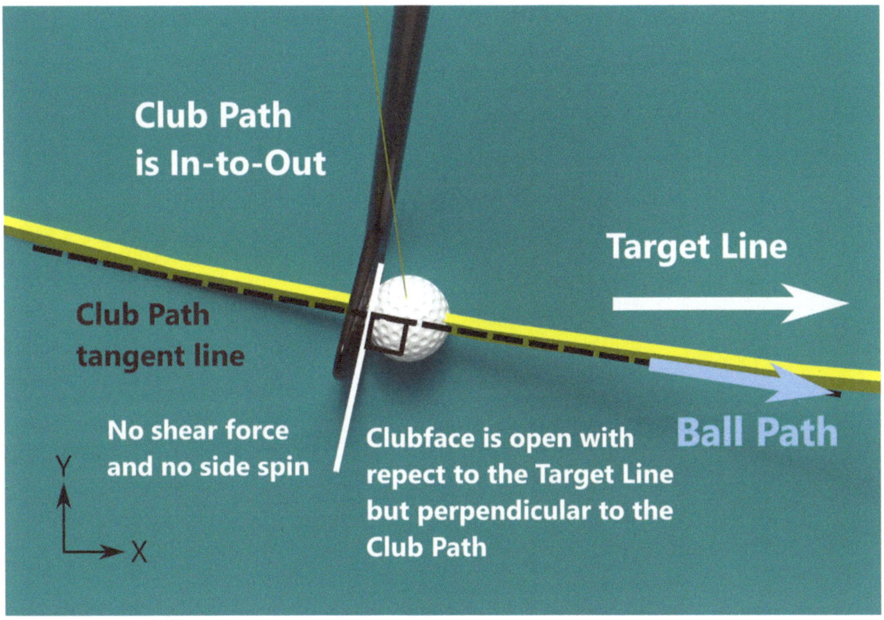

Figure 220: The Push

The Slice—Clubface Closed/Excessive Clockwise Spin

A dreaded slice occurs if the clubface is pointed left of the target line at impact but there is too much clockwise sidespin on the ball. The ball will start left of the target line but veer to the right of the target line due to the excessive clockwise rotation of the ball.

If the club path is Out-to-In and the clubface is closed with respect to the target line, the ball will start to the left of the target line, similar to a fade.

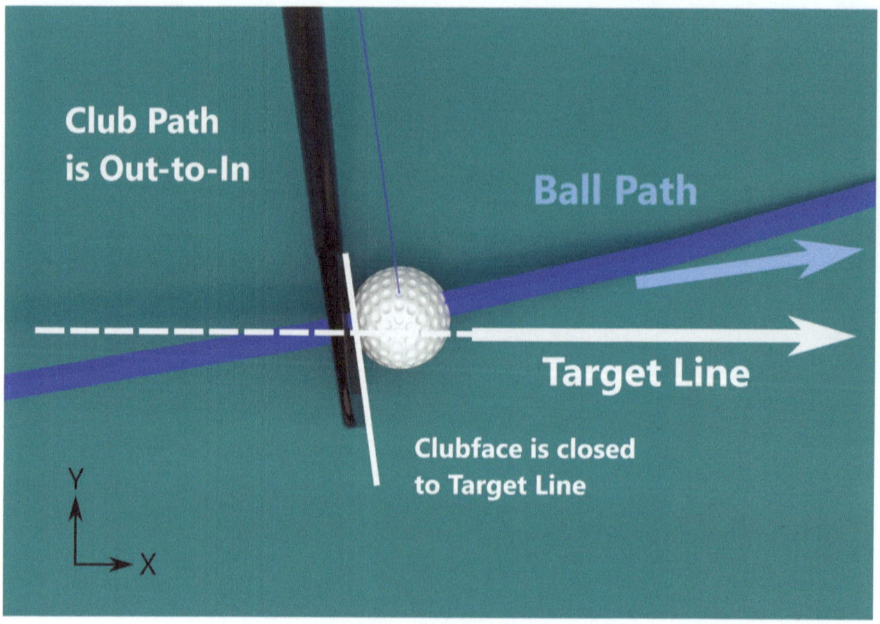

Figure 221: The Slice Direction

If the clubface is open too much with respect to the club path, there will be high shear forces, which create excessive clockwise spin. The ball will start to the left of the target line, but the excessive clockwise spin will cause the ball to veer to the right and across the target line.

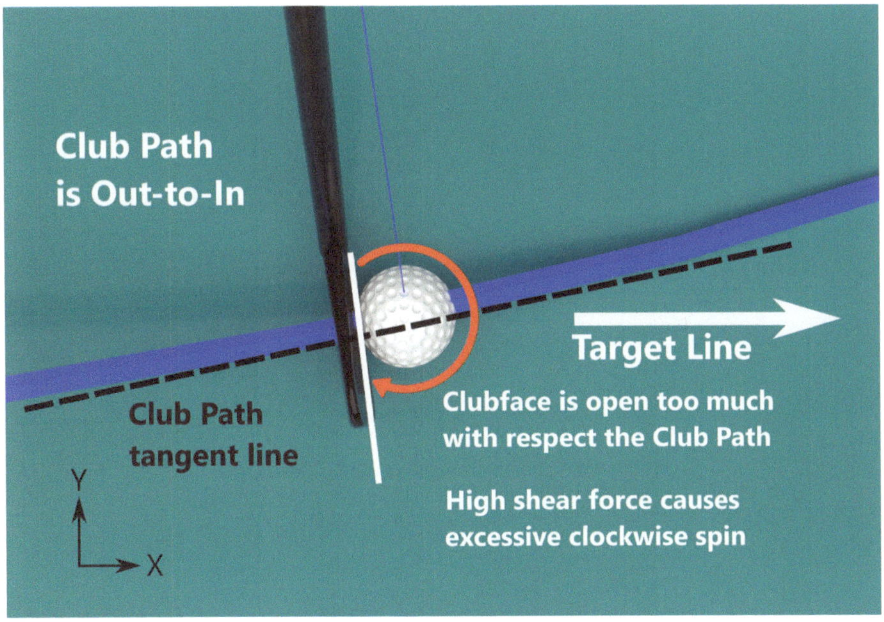

Figure 222: The Slice Side Spin

The Hook—Clubface Open/Excessive Counterclockwise Spin

The unfortunate hook occurs if the clubface is pointed right of the target line at impact but creates excessive counterclockwise sidespin on the ball. The ball will start right of the target line but veer to the left of the target line due to the excessive counterclockwise rotation of the ball.

If the club path is In-to-Out and the clubface is open with respect to the target line, the ball will start to the right of the target line, similar to a draw.

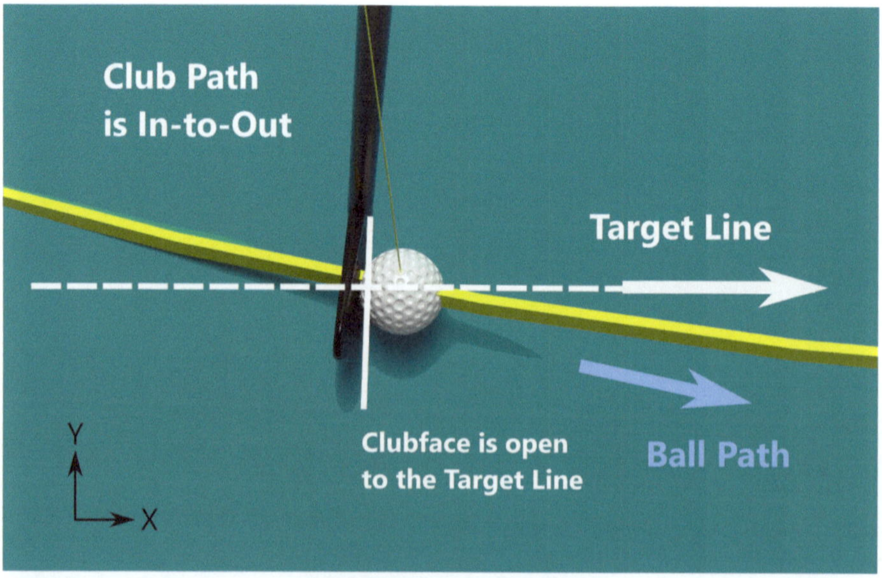

Figure 223: The Hook Direction

If the clubface is closed too much with respect to the club path, there will be high shear forces, which create excessive counterclockwise spin. The ball will start to the right of the target line, but the excessive counterclockwise spin will cause the ball to veer to the left and across the target line.

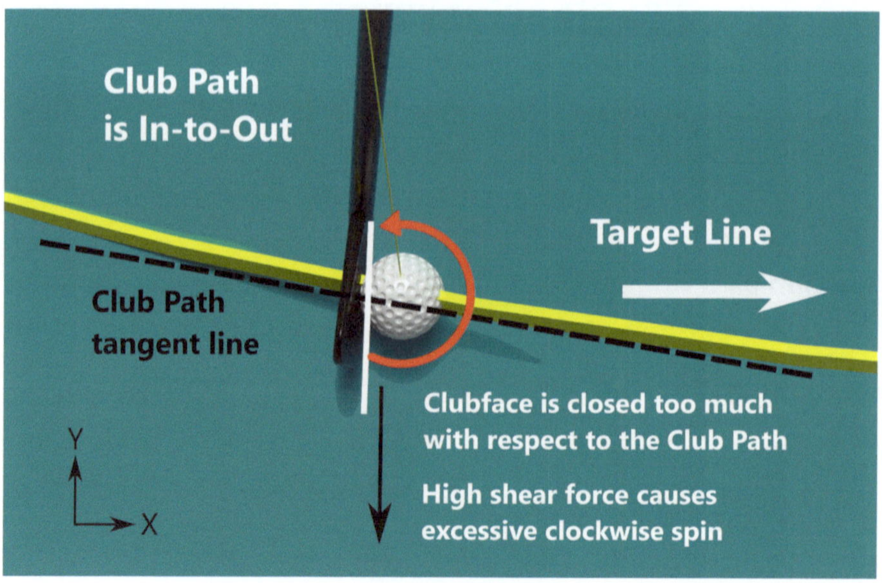

Figure 224: The Hook Side Spin

Of all of the shot types listed above, the first three types are by design: the straight shot, the fade shot, and the draw shot. The fade and the draw shot are a bit more interesting. These shots can be done by one of two ways:

1. Altering Geometry—adjusting the kinematics (geometry) of the shot
2. Altering Timing—changing the timing between primary rotation and secondary rotation

Altering Geometry

Much of the discussion in this book has centered around the geometry required to hit a good straight ball shot. The straight shot comes with neutral geometry, which include shoulders, hips, and feet parallel to the target line, a good neutral grip, and good timing of primary rotation and secondary rotation. The club path is parallel to the target line at impact. If all of these are done properly, the clubface will be perpendicular to the target line at impact. The resulting shot will be up the middle with little or no sidespin.

Remember, the two main factors affecting ball flight are *clubface angle at impact* and *sidespin*. A change to one or both will alter the ball path. You can alter clubface angle and/or sidespin by changing the setup geometry.

Clubface Angle:

The common ways of altering geometry include the following:

1) Setup Stance:
- Stance—The hips, shoulders, and feet are pointed to the right of the target line.
- Neutral Stance—The hips, shoulders, and feet are parallel to the target line. This sets the clubface perpendicular to the target line.
- Closed Stance—The hips, shoulders, and feet are pointed to the left of the target line.

2) Grip:
- Wrist Hinge In (Flexion)—This is called a weak grip, which results in an open clubface with respect to the target line.
- No Wrist Hinge (Neutral)—This is called a neutral grip, which results in a perpendicular clubface with respect to the target line.
- Wrist Hinge Out (Extension)—This is called a strong grip, which results in a closed clubface with respect to the target line.

3) Address Ball Position:
- Forward—At address, the ball is placed in front of the strike plane.
- Neutral—At address, the ball is placed on the strike plane.
- Back—At address the ball is placed behind the strike plane.

At setup, a weak grip would result in an open clubface with respect to the target line, but we naturally rotate the arm counterclockwise to square the clubface up to the ball. Likewise, a strong grip would result in a closed clubface with respect to the target line, but we naturally rotate the arm clockwise to square the clubface up to the ball.

I personally do not like the terminology "weak" and "strong" grip, because it denotes physical strength rather than geometry. However, both are commonly used in the golf world and ingrained in golf speak.

Sidespin

Sidespin requires that the clubface be either open or closed at impact with respect to the club path. Don't confuse that with clubface angle with respect to the target line.

There are two common ways of altering sidespin using geometry:

1. Hold the clubface open.
2. Hold the clubface closed.

If you hold the clubface open with respect to the club path, you will get clockwise spin. Likewise, if you hold the clubface closed with respect to the club path, you will get counterclockwise spin.

These geometry changes certainly do affect the clubface angle and sidespin and can be used individually or in combination to affect the ball path. I intentionally don't use the word "desired" in regard to club path. There are a limitless number of combinations or geometry changes that can affect the geometry of the swing, and there are usually limitless outcomes.

Professional golfers will sometimes do this to gain extra yardage or shape a shot, but they have a good understanding of the consequences of altering geometry of the setup. They also hit hundreds of balls a day for practice, which allows them to do things with a golf club that we mere mortals can only dream of.

Altering geometry can have a lot of unintended consequences, especially for the amateur golfer. There is an easier way, and it doesn't require changes to the geometry of the setup.

Altering Timing

If you watch the pros, their setup at address is textbook: back straight; shoulders, hips, and feet parallel to the target line; good grip; arms straight; and so on. They may make some geometry changes for short shots or to get out of trouble in abnormal situations, but for the most part, they maintain good geometry both at address and during the swing.

What you don't see is the slight changes that they make in timing between their shoulder rotation and the release of the leading arm during the swing. They use this relationship between primary rotation relative to secondary rotation to affect the shape of a shot.

Please indulge me once more for a short example that may help with your understanding of timing.

Cars that have engines use gasoline for power. The gasoline is injected into the engine's cylinders. Spark plugs fire at the precise moment to release the energy of the fuel, which provides power to move the car. The spark plug must fire at exactly the right moment to get the most power out of the fuel. Depending on the timing, the spark is either advanced or retarded so that it fires at the optimum moment. A car that is well tuned and has the right timing runs smoothly and with lots of power. Conversely, if the timing is off, the car spits and sputters and may not run at all.

What does that have to do with the golf swing? To get the desired result from a golf swing, we need to time the primary rotation of the shoulders perfectly with the secondary rotation of the leading arm. Depending on the swing type, we may need to advance (lead) or retard (lag) the release of secondary rotation to get the desired swing type. If a golfer understands and practices the right movements and learns to time these properly, the swing will be smooth with lots of power. Conversely, if the timing is off, the swing is awkward, the ball flight will not be as intended, and the ball may not fly at all.

If you have come this far in the journey, you now have a sense of good geometry for addressing the ball during setup. You also understand motions involved in a full swing: primary rotation, secondary rotation, and tertiary motion, which synchronizes these two rotations.

The exercises in Chapters 9 through 12 will help you to develop the neuromuscular connections to execute these motions perfectly to hit the ball with power up the middle. You can use all that training now to also affect the shape of the shot by learning to adjust the timing between primary and secondary rotation.

Revelation #22

Understanding the geometry of the golf swing as well as the timing relationship between primary and secondary rotation goes a long way toward learning to shape shots as well as avoiding hitting bad shots.

All you need to understand is the following:

- If primary and secondary rotation are synchronized perfectly together, the club path is In-to-In.
- If secondary rotation *lags* primary rotation, the club path is In-to-Out.
- If secondary rotation *leads* primary rotation, the club path is Out-to-In.

Timing can be used to hit good straight shots or to shape good shots. Just as importantly, we can use that knowledge to understand and avoid some of the less desirable shots in the chart, including a push, a slice, and a push/slice or a pull, a hook, or a pull hook.

Understanding the PST model allows you to uncover many of the secrets of the golf swing that previously were a bit of a mystery. And with that understanding comes the ability to practice effectively and to continually improve your swing.

Takeaways:

So what did we learn in Chapter 14?

1. You can shape a shot by changing the geometry of the shot or by changing the timing between primary and secondary rotation.
2. You adjust the timing between primary rotation and secondary rotation by changing the timing of the release. Slight changes in this timing determine the clubface orientation and the sidespin at impact and therefore the shape of the shot.
3. You can use your knowledge of the PST model to learn to shape desirable shots, the draw, the fade, and the straight shot. You can also use this knowledge to undesirable shots, the slice, and the hook.

CHAPTER 16
Takeaways

Find the journey's end in every step.

—Ralph Waldo Emerson

In the beginning of this book, I made the disclaimer that I am neither a professional writer nor a professional golfer. This book was written through the eyes of an engineer, and as an engineer, I felt the need to know both the *what* and the *why* of the golf swing, the yin and the yang. My journey started nearly three years ago when I was not able to get satisfactory answers to some very simple questions. That led me to starting all over from scratch and studying the golf swing in a way that I was trained to do.

I started looking at the pure kinematics of the golf swing, and I realized that the geometry and the physics of hitting a golf ball properly requires a precise, defined combination of movements that rely on the rotation of the club. That single realization is the cornerstone behind understanding that the golf swing is not actually a swing. Remember the first revelation in Chapter 1:

Revelation #1

The golf swing is not a swing but rather a rotation, and to be more precise, it's the combination of two rotations—the primary rotation and the secondary rotation—which are tied together using tertiary motion.

I also realized that the physics (dynamic forces) of the swing are important, but unless you get the geometry of the swing correct, the physics of the motion don't work.

Revelation #2

If you don't get the kinematics of the golf swing right, the physics of the golf swing don't really matter.

This led to creating a new model of the golf swing. The PST model is a three-dimensional representation of the golf swing and breaks the swing into three distinct motions: primary rotation, secondary rotation, and tertiary motion. With this three-dimensional model, the golf swing can be accurately represented and understood.

The model is a simple and yet groundbreaking way to understand and learn about the golf swing without a lot of complicated mechanics or physics.

This last chapter contains a list of the major points that I hope you will take away with you. These are centered on the revelations I experienced during my quest for answers and have shared with you throughout the book. These revelations are rooted in Revelation #1: You do not *swing* a golf club; you *rotate* it.

The Model

The first few revelations in Chapters 4, 5, and 6 provide a model for understanding the golf swing. Each revelation is a step in the journey to understanding both the what and the why of the golf swing.

Remember that the PST model is a three-dimensional model that represents the golf swing as three distinct motions: primary rotation, secondary rotation, and tertiary motion. The acronym **PST** refers to the primary rotation, secondary rotation, and tertiary motion that are the basis for the model.

Revelation #3

Primary rotation is the rotation of the upper body, shoulders, and club around the centerline of the body, the primary axis.

Revelation #4

Primary rotation provides *power* and *control.*

Revelation #5

Secondary rotation is the rotation of the leading arm (SLA) and club around the secondary axis that runs through the left arm. The clubface is perpendicular to the secondary club path, which is at the base of the cone created by rotating the club with the left arm.

Revelation #6

Secondary rotation provides speed and therefore distance.

Revelation #7

Tertiary Motion provides coordination between primary rotation and secondary rotation. This is done by shortening the distance between the wrists and the trailing shoulder, by bending the trailing elbow against the torso during the backswing.

Revelation #8

Tertiary motion connects primary rotation and secondary rotation together into the coordinated motion necessary to *lift* the clubhead into the swing plane and *rotate* the clubface into the proper orientation on the club path.

The *lift* is accomplished by shortening the distance between the hands and the trailing shoulder (right shoulder for right-handed golfers).

The *rotation* of the leading arm is determined by the amount of the right wrist hinge (extension) to maintain a flat left wrist (FLW) on the leading arm (for RH golfers).

Revelation #9

In the golf swing, the takeaway involves the rotation of the leading arm (straight left arm for RH golfers) 90 degrees clockwise while bending the right elbow into your side and while turning your shoulders clockwise during the initial backswing.

Revelation #10

The full swing is a combination of the primary rotation and the secondary rotation tied together using tertiary motion. The resulting club path is on the swing plane. The clubface is perpendicular to the swing path at the neutral position (address and impact positions) and tangent to the swing path at the top of the backswing and at the finish.

Revelation #11

The two main factors that affect ball flight are *clubface angle at impact* and *sidespin*. The clubface angle and side-spin are determined by the club path. The club path is the result of primary rotation and secondary rotation tied together using tertiary motion.

The three club paths are as follows:

- The In-to-In club path has a line that is tangent to the target line at impact point and produces no ball spin, which results when primary rotation is perfectly synchronized with secondary rotation.

- The In-to-Out club path has a line that goes from inside the target line to outside the target line at the impact point, which produces counterclockwise ball spin as a result of when secondary rotation lags primary rotation.
- The Out-to-In club path has a line that goes from outside the target line to inside the target line at the impact point, which produces clockwise ball spin as a result of when secondary rotation leads primary rotation.

The Physics

Revelation #12

There are three forces that affect the golf swing: *applied* force, *centripetal* force, and *gravity*. Applied force is supplied by the golfer when they apply torque using the upper body (primary torque) and leading arm (secondary torque). Centripetal force is a radial force resulting from rotation. Gravity is a force that attracts a body toward the center of the earth.

Revelation #13

When you rotate a mass around an axis, there is an optimum path, the natural path, which is on the swing plane. In the case of the golf swing, the mass is the golf club, and the path is the combination of the combined primary rotation and the secondary rotation.

Putting It All Together

Revelation #14

The full swing is a combination of 90 degree rotations:

- Backswing is 90 degrees clockwise rotation of the primary rotation (shoulders) and 90 degrees clockwise rotation of the secondary rotation (straight leading arm) to the top of swing.
- Downswing is 90 degrees counterclockwise rotation of the primary rotation (shoulders) and 90 degrees counterclockwise rotation of the secondary rotation (straight left arm) to impact (the inflection point).
- Follow-through is 90 degrees counterclockwise rotation of the primary rotation (shoulders) and 90 degrees counterclockwise rotation of the secondary rotation (straight left arm) to the finish.

Revelation #15

One element of tempo is the pause at the top of the backswing that allows the club to slow down and change direction. This creates the proper lag between the leading forearm and the club shaft as the momentum of the backswing rotates the arms and club clockwise while the shoulders stop and reverse direction.

Revelation #16

Another element of tempo is the timing of the release so that the clubface angle of the secondary rotation coincides with the clubface angle of primary rotation to yield the desired combined clubface angle.

The release involves the straightening of the trailing elbow and wrist, which allows the secondary rotation to occur. Timing of the release during the downswing determines speed of the secondary rotation and therefore distance.

Revelation #17

A good swing needs a good follow-through and a good finish with the proper weight shift.

Practice with a Purpose

Revelation #18

To be able to strike a ball properly, you need to develop the required neuromuscular connections for all the motions involved. This comes in part by practice and repetition of the *correct* motions.

Revelation #19

Taking a stepwise approach to learning the swing involves training individual motions and muscle groups through repetition and exercise. Once these individual skills are mastered, they can be combined into an effective full swing.

Putting, Chipping, Pitching, and the Full Swing

Revelation #20

There are five specific club types: the putter, the wedges, the irons, the fairway woods, and of course, the driver. Each of these club types uses primary rotation and may use some degree of secondary rotation.

Swing Flaws

Revelation #21

Understanding the geometry of the golf swing goes a long way toward both recognizing swing flaws as well as correcting them.

Shaping Shots

Revelation #22

Understanding the geometry of the golf swing as well as the timing relationship between primary and secondary rotation goes a long way toward learning to shape shots as well as avoiding hitting bad shots.

Shaping Shots

Revelation #22

Understanding the geometry of the golf swing as well as the timing relationship between primary and secondary rotation goes a long way toward learning to shape shots as well as avoiding hitting bad shots.

Indulge me for one last story. When I first got into golf, I took lessons, read books and magazines, watched tons of instructional videos on the internet, and talked with other more experienced golfers. I would go to the range to practice often and would usually leave the range with a sense that I had not really accomplished very much, other than emptying another bucket of balls.

Now when I go to the range, I see a lot of golfers following that same path. Like me, they have learned *what* without really understanding *why*. I sense the same frustrations that I had before taking my journey. I often want to speak up, but I don't know how to. I want to tell them that they will continue to be frustrated until they are ready to take a different path, perhaps a path less traveled. That path requires a willingness to understand why. And that can make all the difference.

That is what inspired me to write this book. I wanted to share what I have learned about the kinematics of the golf swing along with some of the physics. That knowledge is empowering and has allowed me to understand, improve, and more fully enjoy the game.

Now I practice with a purpose, and every practice has meaning. I see the golf swing through an entirely different paradigm. Hopefully you have found this book and the journey worthwhile.

It's no use going back to yesterday, because I was a different person then.

—Lewis Carroll

Table of Figures

About the Author

Gregory M. Skovira, a mechanical engineer with degrees from Lehigh and Villanova University, is the retired founder and CEO of software integration company, EZSoft Inc. Despite not being a professional golfer or writer, Greg's passion for golf, which he picked up later in life, led him to analyze the game from a unique perspective. After years of lessons, practice, and research, he found traditional methods yielded diminishing results. This realization motivated him to explore the golf swing from a fresh angle. His book, *The Paradigm of Golf*, is a testament to his analytical approach to the game.

Milton Keynes UK
Ingram Content Group UK Ltd.
UKHW050258231124
451399UK00010B/170
9798822951419